HOME IN AMERICA

Home in America

On Loss and Retrieval

THOMAS DUMM

THE BELKNAP PRESS OF
HARVARD UNIVERSITY PRESS

Cambridge, Massachusetts
London, England
2019

First printing

Library of Congress Cataloging-in-Publication Data

Names: Dumm, Thomas L., author.
Title: Home in America : on loss and retrieval / Thomas Dumm.
Description: Cambridge, Massachusetts : The Belknap Press of Harvard University Press, 2019.
Identifiers: LCCN 2019017829 | ISBN 9780674057715 (hardcover)
Subjects: LCSH: Home—United States—History. | Home in popular culture—United
States—History. | Home in literature. | United States—Race relations—History.
Classification: LCC HQ535 .D76 2019 | DDC 306.850973—dc23
LC record available at https://lccn.loc.gov/2019017829

For Judy

Contents

Preface

I am haunted by home.

I am guessing that you are, too. Because home is where the ghosts are, that place full of the familiars of our common and separate pasts, the site of our deepest desires and fears. I have written *Home in America* in the vain hope of exorcising some of the ghosts that have haunted me over the years. Vain hope, indeed, because I realize in advance that there is no possible exorcism, only a chance that I might placate some of them.

I think of home as an always fraught domestic space, a place of privacy and privation, of refuge and imprisonment, of quests never quite completed and questions never fully answered. Home, however we hold it in our hearts and minds, is a place where there are concrete realizations not only of our dreams but also of our nightmares. Home is an imagined and realized place that provides us with elusive metaphors for other elements of our lives while remaining an elusive metaphor for itself.

Home is not only a place of ghosts. All of the homes I explore in *Home in America* are real places, in the sense that they stand for themselves, not as metaphors for homelands or countries, or even for Earth itself, although, as it happens, they also operate as such metaphors and are in other ways deeply connected to homeland, country, and Earth. My effort in these essays is to try to explore the uncanniness, the *unhomeliness,* of home in such a way as to follow on the desire for home as a place of rest and homemaking, understanding the fulfillment of that desire to be the impossible requisite for that rest. I take some famous American homes and their homemakers as my primary exemplars, thinking about them and their inhabitants, owners and owned, colonizers and subalterns, majors and minors, to explore how different Americans have thought about and acted on what it means to be at home. I have done this not as an end in itself but because the perilous period through which we humans are passing is making the very possibility of being at home a more dangerous matter than it has been for a very long time. Because of our precarious condition, I am interested in questions that concern *being* itself, how we come to feel at home in a world that seems increasingly to be denying us the security we want from home. Such questions revert to something that we might call *economy,* though I will be exploring economy in a way that is somewhat different from how most of our modern practitioners of the dismal science do so.

What you have before you, then, are a series of meditations, essays about different people who explicitly set out to create and sustain homes, who met with various levels of success and failure, and who have left us with a variety of often contradictory ways of thinking about what it means to be at home. Most of these people are famous, even if some of the stories I tell about them address less celebrated, or even less noticed, elements of their lives as they worked in their homes. That is the way it sometimes is—all homes hold secrets, some willingly, some unwillingly.

In telling these stories about homes, I also try to remember elements of my own childhood. My personal stories are not intended to compete with, but instead to complement and provide contrast with, the stories these other home dwellers have left for us to contemplate. In truth, as should become clear early in the Prologue, I first thought about what it may mean to say one is "home" over the course of making a series of journeys from Amherst, Massachusetts, to visit my aged father, who was living alone during his final years in central Pennsylvania. If it is the case that I have continued to pursue a path first taken in a book I wrote about loneliness, a sort of prequel to this one—a path inordinately *personal* for someone who as a trained social scientist is supposed to strive toward objectivity—I hope there are enough of you who have tolerated my past transgressions in this regard and are willing to join me again on this always strange but, for me at least, surprisingly rewarding path.

HOME IN AMERICA

Dad

It is no longer night, but it is not yet day. Into the car, packed bags jigsawed into the trunk, house locked up, dog cared for, everyone buckled into their seat. From Lincoln Avenue, we head west through Amherst center down the hill on Route 9. Many years ago, Route 9 was the central artery of cross-state traffic. Now it isn't. We cut through the ugliness of the shopping malls and big-box stores that line both sides of the road in Hadley—Target anchors one mall, Walmart the other—catching glimpses of the rich river bottom hidden behind the clusters of hotels, garden stores, used car lots and garages, and a scattering of run-down houses (houses that were caught too close to the main drag when it became the main drag). We cross the Connecticut River at the Calvin Coolidge Bridge, touch the edge of Northampton, and then turn onto Interstate 91 South. We'll be on one or another limited-access highway all day. This segment, I-91, is the shortest one of our interstate sojourn, our most familiar path, and we head on it straight south with the sun almost ready to rise over the Holyoke Range. Just north of Springfield, I-91 connects us to I-90—the Massachusetts Turnpike made famous by "Sweet Baby James," James Taylor's song of himself, in which he describes those western mountains beloved by romantics from Hawthorne to the present: "The Berkshires looked dream-like on account of that frosting/with ten miles behind me and ten thousand more to go." The morning sun behind us, we head west. When we pass through the tollbooth dividing the Mass Pike from the New York State Thruway, the landscape shifts, subtly, but clearly enough— we're not in New England anymore. The freshly painted barns and groomed fields give way to barns and fields less cared for, the hills become less Berkshire mountainous and more Sleepy Hollow–ominous, buildings slightly more dilapidated, but fields still fecund, still bucolic. We leave the thruway after only a few miles, turning south onto the Taconic Parkway. Feeling the blessed absence of trucks, we drive through a region not simply rural but forested, the Catskills occasionally visible from the west window, the passenger side, scenic overviews all looking toward the mighty Hudson River, itself obscured from this road, invisibly flowing parallel to it. We pass old diners past their prime, neon signs that can be seen from a distance at night, and shabby country stores, one paint job behind, that offer up groceries but also sell gas, propane, and alcohol. While the primary danger on the Taconic has always been wandering deer, especially during hunting season, wild turkeys are a greater road hazard nowadays than when we made this trip in years long past, and buzzards are more common as well. Someone reliable has said that global warming is changing habitats for those birds as well as for other flora and fauna, though one would think that roadkill tastes the same regardless of latitude. Off the Taconic, again turning right, now onto the normal ugly of Interstate 84—our zigzag path, south then west, south then west, not unlike the tacking of an imaginary sailboat making forward progress indirectly, moving in a pattern similar to what Ralph Waldo Emerson once suggested is how we ought to be living our lives. No foolish consistency, no straight lines, will ever get *us* where we are going. We cross lower upstate New York and head toward Pennsylvania. Now we are in the heart of hard-core interstate highway land—McDonald's, Burger King, Denny's, Taco Bell, ExxonMobil, second-tier convenience stores, 7-Elevens, rinse and repeat—nothing here escapes the lower reaches of the American corporate net as it gathers dribbles of income from potato chips, soda, stale coffee, overpriced gasoline, and other consumables that only ever seem to be for sale at roadside stops and "convenience" stores. Tractor trailers, zoom, zoom, noise and fume. Our marker of progress during this leg of the journey is the glimpse we get of the supermax units of Downstate Correctional Facility near Fishkill, squat cubes, concrete, bunker-like, behind two fences, both shiny with concertina wire and razors, signs along the road warning us not to pick up hitchhikers—as if we would even have room for another passenger—bright lights reflecting off those prison walls 24-7. For all the trips we've made, we've yet to see a living soul outside a vehicle on this stretch of highway. And yet we know there are living souls inside those buildings we have passed from afar. (Maybe there is someone behind those walls who has been in there for as long as we have been making this trip—a terrible thought, but likely true.) Crossing the Hudson, we mark the miles to the Pennsylvania line. Onward we go, across the border from New York and into the Keystone State, from the Delaware Water Gap through Port Jervis toward the Pocono Mountains, but not really, because we bypass the heart of that region, its honeymoon hotels with their heart-shaped Jacuzzis and champagne-glass-shaped bathtubs, the ghosts of old comedians haunting tacky resort lounges, resorts trying to resurrect themselves by becoming casinos, now licensed for gambling and still sordid, a minor league Borscht Belt. Rather than detour, we stay on the main line and help form an informal procession, motorists, truck drivers, passengers, all of us preparing to leap across the amazing interchange where I-84 turns into I-81 (via I-380). Interstate 81 seems to be a permanent highway construction site, stretching from the northeastern edge of Scranton to the hills above southwest Wilkes-Barre. The geography at this point is like that of central Pennsylvania, even this far to the east. The brief passage from Scranton to Wilkes-Barre feels like the most perilous leg of this journey, big rigs everywhere, maneuvering around each other at sixty miles per hour at least (though we are warned not to speed above fifty in this construction zone), narrow lanes, strange left turnoffs, flashing lights funneling traffic into one-lane jams, local experts mingling with foreign amateurs like me who are merely passing through, white-knuckle grip on the steering wheel for a few miles. But we're past that clogged artery soon enough. Enervated, this is where we usually stop for lunch, as much out of habit as fatigue, at the same Friendly's restaurant right off the first exit past Wilkes-Barre proper. We do not linger (it isn't really a place for lingering anyway): this pause is as much a refueling stop and bathroom break as anything else. We climb back into our car and catch a whiff of the perfume formed by a combination of the detritus of snack food wrappers, stale coffee in the bottom of paper cups, and slightly sweaty bodies, that off-odor needing more than open windows to disperse. We sigh and settle in for the remainder of the ride. Back on I-81, south of Wilkes-Barre, there are climbing lanes for the heavy sixteen-wheelers and careful-slow geriatric drivers. Only halfway there, it feels as though we are much closer to our destination. To the west we can see the Susquehanna Valley spread before us, where in the summer of 1972 a stalled hurricane named Agnes dumped so much water so suddenly upon the valley and surrounding region that the river flooded its banks more spectacularly than ever before or since, a cataclysm, one of the worst events being not the death of the living, though many died—death is almost always the worst—but a second death for the dead, the washing away of an entire cemetery, so that volunteers were needed to search for the disinterred so they could be put back in their graves, some lost for good, others reburied though forever disturbed. After reaching the top of that great hill, we coast down the other side, past the surprisingly named Nuangola, Pennsylvania, and then we are even closer, turning west onto I-80, the greatest artery of the entire interstate system (I-90 is admittedly the longer road, but I-80 carries more traffic), bisecting the continent from east to west, across the middle of the Lower 48 like a belt, from Teaneck, New Jersey, to San Francisco, California, constructed over the path of the first motor vehicle highway to traverse the North American continent, the fabled and then forgotten Lincoln Highway. It is the sleepy part of the drive, midafternoon, kids plugged into their iPods as I search the radio dial for anything other than fundamentalist Christian religious stations or Rush Limbaugh and his wannabes. (In recent years—too late to help us on our periodic pilgrimages that are now but a memory— satellite radio has narrowed my tolerance for Rush and his ilk by expanding my listening choices.) We ride I-80 until we are almost to our destination. This is the landscape I have known from child- hood, the Allegheny Mountains, a formation of the Appalachians that, I learned in a required elective Penn State earth science course in 1974, was once so elevated that some geologists con- jecture that it had been almost twice as high as the Himalayas, jutting into the lower reaches of outer space proper, meteors smashing into its high points as though the range was designed to gather those strange, pyrite-laden rocks on its slopes like a proverbial star catcher. Now—if you think of "now" in terms of the most recent several million years—the range is so worn down as to barely justify calling these hills mountains, although they presented a formidable enough barrier to earlier Anglo-European pioneers trying to cross into the Ohio territories, just high enough, rugged enough, and wild enough to isolate many of the rural set- tlers in the early years of white settlement and conquest over the natives. Some linguists claim that the cadences of the further reaches of western Pennsylvania and West Virginia still echo the accents of Elizabethan England. Farms here, save those reclaimed by Amish folk, are often messy wrecks—rusty machinery of use unknown to the living sprawled across what ought to be front yards, uncertain crops growing unevenly on exhausted hillsides, usually just out of sight of the droning of the highway, from where we once in a while imagine how their occupants are living their seemingly diminished lives. Sometimes their houses appear in the distance, worse than we thought, but not as bad as we dreaded. Automobile graveyards peek through as well, a larger scale of ruin, occasionally from behind old collapsing fences, as though the owners are vaguely ashamed to have scarred their fields with scrap metal. We are sojourning in the region where people cling to their guns and their religion and their hatred of the unfamiliar—in other words, Trump country. Here progress has taken the form of the last completed section of the current interstate highway system, I-99, the Bud Shuster Highway, named after a cheerfully corrupt local congressman who for a time, after the Republican ascendancy of 1994, chaired the House Transportation Committee and forced through Congress billions of dollars of financing for his pet road's construction. (These were the pre–Tea Party days of Republican fiscal hypocrisy. In that older tradition, sons succeeded their fathers into office, and sure enough, Bud was replaced when he grew too old by Bud Jr., who currently represents my old hometown.) Completed around 2004, it is the final link connecting I-80 to I-70. (I-70, also known as the Pennsylvania Turnpike, is the first limited-access highway constructed in the United States, a highway that was built along the surveyed path of a railroad proposed by Andrew Carnegie in the late nineteenth century when he was at war with the Pennsylvania Railroad over the rates it charged to ship iron ore and coal to his steel mills. The railroad eventually relented—they knew who they were dealing with—and Carnegie abandoned the

project as soon as he secured his new deal.) We are almost at
the end of our drive, because, while I-99 is an ecological disaster,
it sure is convenient. These days we are able to bypass the ter-
rors of the old US Route 220, which until 2005 was the only way
to get from here to there, a road we would approach with trepi-
dation. This three-lane, alternative-passing-lane, blacktop nightmare was long known for its many casualties, said victims composed of drunken teenagers, salesmen in a hurry, all sorts of
motorists fleeing central Pennsylvania as if the region itself
somehow intended to be an impediment to better travel experiences, the more anxious ones passing where they had no business passing, crashing headlong into oncoming vehicles, death
by impatience. Instead of Route 220, we pass another old land-
mark that is newly visible from the new highway, Beaver Stadium,
home of the Penn State Nittany Lions (site of the criminal acts of
assistant football coach Jerry Sandusky and the subsequent dis-
grace of his boss, Joe Paterno, and the university, a tale of hubris that lacks tragic dimensions—even though some try to make
it so—because of its general sordidness and a lack of heroes actually facing their fates). After State College we bypass Port
Matilda, a town so named by real estate speculators who reasonably concluded that if people thought there was land available
in a place located near a port, it would be worth something. (Of
course, there is no port in Port Matilda, just as there isn't a shore
in Jersey Shore, another cleverly named town in central Pennsylvania.) The highway hugs the mountainside as we zip past the
dead paper mill town of Tyrone. Then the road descends and we
cross the city limits into the place of my birth and upbringing,
Altoona. We glide down the mountainside, exit the interstate onto
Frankstown Road, and head toward Pleasant Valley Boulevard,
with its concentration of shopping centers, chain restaurants—
Denny's, Taco Bell, Applebee's, McDonald's, Burger King, Red
Lobster, TGI Fridays, Olive Garden, Hooters, and perhaps a
dozen more, with the beginning of a southern tone in franchise

ambience, Cracker Barrel, Jethro's, Sheetz convenience stores and gas stations (the very first Sheetz store is in Altoona, and its corporate headquarters is now located there)—and at least as many discount outlets, dollar stores, and their ilk, the ones that feed below the waterline of the more famous discount giants, places displaying surplus goods, abandoned pallets of generic whatever, primordial commodities, what future archaeologists will study for signs of life as we knew it. Usually we head toward the local Hampton Inn, where our reserved rooms await us. But today we don't stop there first. Instead we drive past the hotel, into the older neighborhoods of the city, cruising numbered streets and named avenues—Union, Broad, Maple, Oak, West Chestnut, Beale—to my father's most recent abode, an apartment off of Seventh Avenue near the Broad Avenue Extension, one with a view across the valley facing Brush Mountain, in a neighborhood no more run-down than most in this old railroad town and less run-down than many. A sign of the times—after I-99 was finished, Altoona became a minor crossroads in the methamphetamine trade of West Virginia and western Pennsylvania, one more hidden gear in the local economies of our Rust Belt cities and dying rural villages, chemical laboratories of contemporary neoliberalism. I think of this development as a special, ironic benefit that the Bud Shuster Highway has provided the town by finally linking it to the larger world. (Now, opioids prevail as the illicit drug of sorrow. Time passes . . .) Altoona peaked in population and prosperity long before the Second World War, operating as a sort of O'Hare Airport in the age of railroads, home of the "World Famous Horseshoe Curve," though the curve isn't nearly as world famous now as it was back then. (As late as my adolescence there was a brewery in Altoona that produced "Curve" beer. As I write, the Altoona Curve is a double-A minor-league baseball team for the once champion and always striving Pittsburgh Pirates.) This was still the era of vaudeville, and most of its stars would come through, performing at the

Mishler Theatre downtown. (The late comedian George Burns, a veteran of that stage, entitled one of his various memoirs *They Still Love Me in Altoona,* and long after the decline of vaudeville, in 1966, I got to see Ethel Merman perform as the title character in a national tour version of *Annie Get Your Gun* on its stage. She was fifty-eight years old at the time, playing an ingenue, belting out "There's No Business Like Show Business" at the finale!) After the war, as the rest of the United States embraced automobiles with a vengeance, the political leaders of central Pennsylvania—never a very forward-looking bunch—didn't know what hit them. When Eisenhower signed the Federal-Aid Highway Act in 1956, creating the interstate system, one of Shuster's predecessors, Republican congressman James Van Zandt, voted against it, contributing in his own small way to the isolation and further decline of the town as the rest of the country was knitted together, for better or worse, by concrete slabs instead of steel rails. The new Interstate 99 has performed as expected—Altoona has revived, sort of, and is now a version of much of the rest of the country, haunted by the same consumer desires as everybody else. (On second thought, it may well be that the rest of the country has become more like Altoona in the recent years following the financial collapse of 2008 rather than the other way around.) We pull into my father's parking lot and, having been repeatedly warned by Dad not to take up a space belonging to any of the elderly residents of the complex, park in an appropriately distant spot. We get out of the car, stretch, smell the fresh air, and begin to shake off the lethargy of travel. We gather at the front door of the apartment building. I push the buzzer to announce our arrival. The outside door clicks open. Dad stands in the hallway by the door to his apartment, big hugs for everyone, ushers us in, and offers us drinks and snacks. I smile. I feel the twinge of guilt that comes from experiencing that old generation gap, the fighting that seemed so meaningful at the time, now so much a part of the distant past. Altoona is so small now, so much where I came from, and so much not where I am going. But Dad is still here. It is now a time to protect him. From what, I cannot yet say. As if I ever could protect him, even if I knew what the what was. "Welcome home!" he exclaims.

My Father's Houses

This is a book about being at home. The stories I tell in this book describe and comment upon a variety of ways people have imagined and inhabited places that they either already understood to be or came to understand to be their homes. Depending on who it is, there are varying degrees to which home is a theme in these persons' lives. But for each of these individuals, the home they made or attempted to make presents an aspect of being at home that varies from the others.

This is also a book about what is commonly called America. I fully recognize the chauvinism of the metonymic gesture—I am rendering the nation-state of the United States of America into the strange, pseudobiographical name of a man named Vespucci, a name shared by two continents in the same hemisphere—but that is partly my point. I wish to make explicit what is still too often assumed by most of us, for better or worse, to be the unconscious heritage of an exceptional state, an exceptional culture. Ways of being at home in America present us with a multitude of con-fusions, paradoxes, and contradictions, some parochial in character, to be sure, but others of world-historical significance. As I hope will become more apparent, being at home (in America), as a place and an experience, is of critical import for whatever we may understand about the politics of being human more generally.

Finally, this is also a book about the impossibility of being at home, and about the impossibility of America. By this I do not mean that there is no such thing as home, or no such thing as America, if only as what Benedict Anderson once brilliantly described as being an imagined community, but instead that the quest to make a home and the quest to create a nation are affectively connected in such ways as to defy any certain realization.[1] The fact is that we are always longing to be at home, even when safely there. This unhomeliness, this uncanniness, forms much of the affective substance of home itself. It is the purpose of this book to explain why this is so.

I argue that home is the primary place through which we humans live our finitude. All of the places where we experience the emotional and temporal limits of ourselves, our various senses of our personal mortality, all of them lead us back to home. Hence, whatever privations we may experience, whatever precarities we live through, are echoes of a larger finitude. The loss of others with whom we have shared intimacies, the various deprivations of freedom we may have been through, the state of being owned by others, the ghostliness of being deprived of recognition and of life itself—all of these lead us back to this familiar but strange place we call home. Another way of saying this is that home is the place where we seek comfort in the face of our awareness of our eventual death. And our awareness of that eventuality is schooled by our experiences of the loss of kindred souls to death as well. As a student of finitude once wrote, "There is no finitude in or of itself. Finitude can only make itself known through the other's mortality."[2]

But it is also true that most of us do not want to die. Most of us fear death for most of our lives. Hence to be human is also to resist finitude. Whether expressed through desires for historical or personal immortality, for escape into the pleasures of Eros, whether sublimated or not, for an infinite expansion of consumption that is the hallmark of late capitalism, or even for a quest for absolute knowledge, we struggle against finitude as we move through our lives. Much of that struggle infiltrates our homes in various ways and with different degrees of effect.

So, what might Dad have meant when he welcomed us home? This question doesn't have a simple answer, even though simplicity may be what we think we most desire when we imagine what home ought to be. Dad's simple greeting has an ancient and fraught history. Welcoming, hospitality, has long been at odds with the close and protected sense of being at home, even as it helps shape its meaning. (We are welcomed home, but our welcoming party is also relieved when we depart.) This four-letter word is one of the most complicated words that humans have invented. Dad was not one to reflect on that complexity, but he bore the history of our species in the language he spoke, the postures he held, the gestures he used, the emotions he expressed. He may have read Ralph Waldo Emerson as a child (Emerson once was in the common curriculum of primary and high school education in this country), but, on second thought, as a product of an American parochial school education, perhaps he never did, Emerson being the heretic that he was. Still, I wonder if he ever read this sentence from "Experience": "We lie in the lap of an immense intelligence." Stanley Cavell, one of the most profound interpreters of Emerson I have encountered, took this sentence to express Emerson's sense of a human dependence not on God but on language, a phenomenon that we collectively create and which in turn creates us.[3] Languages are very much a way that we are able to experience home, even as they are apart from home itself.

Embedded in every word is a deep past, available to us through etymological excavation. What of this word, *home?* It expresses an amazing range of experiences, even as it is tied to very specific real and imagined spaces. Across Indo-European languages a strange consistency inheres within its meaning, despite the vast variety of references toward which different languages incline it. In English, the word *home* is derived most clearly from the northern reaches: Norse runes emphasizing the guttural, the soft consonants of *h* and *m* easy on the throat. One might say that *home* is comfortable in the mouth. Yet the word is as elusive as it is expressive, ever ramifying in meaning. A home can be an abode, a castle and its surrounds, a village, a city, a country, a planet, a local galaxy, a feeling, a direction, a destination, an end, a beginning, a memory palace of various eternities, a grave for mortals known in some cultures as "the long home." *Home* exists as a resting place for something we know deep in our bones. If there is such a thing as a universal human experience, that experience is the one of home. A site of longing when missed, it is parochial, provincial, suffocating when its hold on our self seems irrevocable and our imagination of alternatives fails us.

Home is a time and space of human being. We live from the past and into the future. We also do so while resting and moving within the spaces of the world. Yet time and space are not neutral, empty backdrops for the drama of human being. The world is a space composed of spaces, and many of the spaces of the world are places. When does a space become a place? This is one of the questions concerning home. Time is composed of narratives of past and imagined futures, what we call the stories of our lives. Home, for each one of us, is a particular story and particular place. When do we move from act to the story of the act? This is another question concerning home, an element of what we might call a genealogy of home. How we place ourselves in time and think of time outside of place may give us a better sense of the worlds we inhabit and the ways that home is at war and at peace with those worlds.

At the center of this book is a series of stories about homes, of their origins, trajectories, and architectures. These most broadly may be thought of as architectures of the human, understood in terms of some of the many ways we humans try to relate to our existence as finite beings. None of these stories are right or wrong, but depending on how anyone may want to think about what it may mean to be at home, they present alternative, sometimes complementary and sometimes contradictory ways of thinking about how we have arrived at the point in time and space where we are, and where we may be going when we say we are on our way home.

Did my father mean anything like what I have just written when he said, "Welcome home"? Obviously, Dad's vocabulary was not that of the trained academic I eventually became. But he was, as most of us are, someone who thought carefully about the circumstances that shaped his life and what he believed to be the true meaning of that life. His ongoing care and devotion to his wife and children, and his children's children, made him a sage of sorts. And toward the end of his life, as he anticipated and welcomed his own dying, he came closer to reconciling his life with his impending death. So, there is much to be learned by thinking about his life and his experience of living it even if he no longer is able to think with us. In that sense, Dad was a representative man, in the best sense of the term.

I have never thought of Dad's apartment as my home, nor, during the years I would visit him and Mom, did I think of Altoona as my home once I had moved away, and certainly not since I had settled in Amherst with a wife and eventually with children. But there is no need for confusion here: we all know what Dad meant. It was *his* home, and because it was his home, it had to be ours as well. But one of our problems is that there is so much more to being at home than where your parents have lived and died.

Or is there? Consider this account of where my father lived and traveled throughout his life.

Dad was born in a two-room house with no running water in the village of Newry, Pennsylvania, in April 1918. Newry is about eight miles from Altoona. When Dad was thirteen, his family lost their home, primarily due to his father's unemployment from the Pennsylvania Railroad—Grandpa (Leo) Dumm had suffered a shoulder injury on the job, but there was no union at the PRR and no mandatory workers' compensation in those days. The family moved into a rental house in Altoona. With no one else to take on the responsibility, Dad had to go to work to support his family, which consisted of not only his parents but also four younger brothers. Lucky and persistent, he pieced together different jobs through the worst years of the Great Depression. Thanks to the generous and discreet aid of his parish priest and the local diocese, he was also able to graduate with his class from the local Catholic high school in 1936.

With the coming of World War II Dad was drafted into the army. He was twenty-four years old at the time. Through testing, the army learned that James Eugene Dumm excelled at certain skills, among them mathematics, and after his first year of service as a noncommissioned officer (he had risen to the rank of corporal), he applied for and was accepted into the Army Air Corps to be trained as a bombardier. He eventually learned to use the complex Norden bombsight, a mechanical analog computer that required quickness of calculation and calmness of mind on the part of its operator to predict accurately the trajectory of bombs to target. Dad was spared from being deployed to the European front, where, given the specific hazards B-17 bomber crews faced from the flak of Nazi antiaircraft guns, he would have had a great chance of dying (a plot point in the novel by Joseph Heller, *Catch-22*). What saved him was that he suffered severely from airsickness, brought on by an inner-ear malformation. So instead of bombing, he taught others how to bomb. During this period of the war, he was assigned to different bases in Lake Charles, Louisiana; Pensacola, Florida; and Roswell, New Mexico.

In May 1944, while on leave, Dad married Mom. After the war, he came home to Altoona having been honorably discharged as a second lieutenant. First finding work as a painter and wallpaper hanger, on a tip from another veteran Dad learned of an open position to become a salesman/agent for the Metropolitan Life Insurance Company. He applied and was hired. Dad and Mom's first house together, purchased in 1946, was a modest three-bedroom, three-story wood-frame building on West Chestnut Avenue, two blocks from where Mom's parents lived. After six years there, during which the family had grown to five children, they moved into a second, much larger brick house, four blocks from their first house but on the same avenue and in the same parish, Our Lady of Lourdes. Eventually, my parents and, for a time, all nine of their children resided here. Eighteen years later, with the steady trickle away from home and into the world of my older siblings, the family moved again, into a slightly smaller house in a more upscale neighborhood and in a new parish, Saint John's of Lakemont. Mom and Dad lived in this house on Shawnee Avenue with the five youngest children, then four, then three, and finally two, from the autumn of 1970 to the spring of 1976.

Following his retirement from Met Life, Dad accepted a position as special assistant to the insurance commissioner for the Commonwealth of Pennsylvania. This meant moving to Harrisburg, the state capital, with only one remaining child in tow, my brother Denis. There they bought a newly built house in a suburban development east of downtown, where they stayed for six years. In 1982, Dad retired permanently, and Mom and he (finally empty nesters) returned to Altoona, where they purchased a condominium on the second floor of a building in a quiet complex on the outskirts of town. They moved once more as a couple, to the ground floor of the same building, in the mid-1990s, when Mom's health began to fail and staircases became a problem.

Mom died early on January 1, 2001, making it to the first day of the new millennium. Shortly after her death, Dad moved once more, into an apartment closer to the center of Altoona. This was our destination on our trip from Amherst. (Briefly, prior to this move, at the invitation of my older sister Katie, Dad moved to Lenox, Massachusetts, an experiment that failed miserably: the core of the problem was that he was simply homesick. He returned to Altoona after a few months.) Living independently for more than a decade, gradually becoming frail, and realizing that with his failing eyesight he should no longer drive a car, Dad voluntarily moved into assisted living for his final years. He resided in a Catholic-run home for the elderly, Garvey Manor and Our Lady of the Alleghenies, just outside of Altoona, in Hollidaysburg, not far at all from the village of Newry where he was born. During the first half decade I spent thinking about and beginning to write this book, his body gradually wore out. He patiently waited for death with the quiet stoicism and humor with which he had lived in the late years of his long life. He died on November 20, 2013, and is now buried beside Mom in Calvary Cemetery, across the road from the farm Mom grew up on as one of the ten children of Denis O'Leary and Catherine Duffy O'Leary. (Closing a circle, they are buried on land that Grandpa O'Leary long ago had donated to the Catholic diocese for the establishment of this cemetery, a pasture that had been a part of his farm.)

In his ninety-five years, not counting his years of military service, my father lived in eleven places he could reasonably call his home.

His grave may be considered his final home, his long home, which would make the total twelve. In this, he is in step with most of the other members of his generation, those who lived through the Great Depression and the establishment of America's welfare state, the worldwide upheaval of the Second World War and the aftermath of that catastrophe, including the triumph of global capitalism at the end of the second millennium, the still incomplete overturning of American apartheid and other injustices through civil rights movements in the United States, the Cold War, the displacement of many millions of people through the demise of colonialism, the recrudescence of fundamentalisms both religious and political throughout the world, as well as the great reaction against the welfare state by the forces of neoliberalism, and the rise of new nationalist powers out of the ruins of Soviet communism. In short, my father was a representative man, a human whose traces contain many elements of the long twentieth century he passed through.

These various buildings are united mainly by the fact that my parents and siblings, and eventually my father himself alone, lived in them. So, is home simply where those who nourish children have lived? That is, can we attach our sense of home to the fact of parenthood, to the persons who have stood for us, cared for us, and loved us? To suggest that home is embodied in or is synonymous with the fact of parenthood doesn't seem to make sense. What happens when parents die? Are we homeless children, as adults, providing the next generation only a fleeting sense of where they may return someday? We resist this sense every time we ourselves become parents. But what of those who choose not to be, or cannot be, parents? And what of those among us who choose to live alone, or by dint of circumstance find themselves living alone? It may be that for them as well, a sense of generational continuity applies to this idea of being at home.

But perhaps not, perhaps instead they have a sense of home that may be more expansive, more sensitive to time's passage, and more nuanced about the affective connections that can be made among people we know and love than is provided in a more simple or conventional sense of family or the familiar. Such a sensibility might allow more of us to imagine that we may be grounded in a past that we hold in common with others. But it may also be that not even this sensibility informs their understanding of home. In the extraordinary ordinary that is the life experience of most of us, signs of home constantly infiltrate our consciousness (and our unconscious). Yet as specific and particular as the home life of each of us may be, nonetheless we make generalizations that may help us better understand what is at stake in thinking about home.

This sense of home as being an intimate space of the *family*— understood in a conventional mid-twentieth-century America of the stereotypical, white, patriarchal, nuclear family, so well rendered in television situation comedies of the time—is, from a broader perspective, but one way people have addressed the fact of finitude. That are many others. In fact, I am tempted to pun that there are a potentially infinite number of ways in which to live out one's finitude. In the chapters that follow I focus on a much smaller number of arrangements, some proceeding in major keys of life, others in minor.

Home and Homeless

In many ways, my father's experience is typical of the times in which he lived. To the extent that he was able to think that his home was not simply where he was housed, but where he felt as though he had some sense of permanence, some sense of continuity, a place to rest from which he could venture into another place we could call the world, it would suggest that home is not simply a place but is indeed where the heart is. Dad's dwelling was his home, his family was his home, but then again, so were his neighborhood and his town and his country. His always welcoming gesture when his children and their families came to visit him, his assumption that he was at home there and hence so were we, might allow me to say, yes, this is what we mean when we say we are home, there is no need to go further, and this is the end of my inquiry.

I could then move on to reflect on the car journey we made to Altoona, to note the propulsive force of this American network of limited-access highways, to reflect further on the emptiness of the landscape, the deep history underneath the detritus-strewn surface, the formerly popular power of the automobile now receding in the rearview mirror of the American imagination, a sign of a certain exhaustion of this culture and perhaps of the emergence of something new. Again, a narrative familiar to us, this would be a tale of decline and displacement, a story of the old and familiar overwhelmed by the new and strange, what cheerleaders for capitalism, for some strange reason, have long approvingly called "creative destruction."

This relatively brief highway trip may illuminate for us something more than a narrative of decline and regeneration if we care to look more closely. We might begin to see the landscape of the United States as it is haunted by potent ghosts, buried bodies (and un-buried) whose presence / absence marks every place of human habitation in this country.[4] The impact those souls have made is a haunting that extends from the eastern to the western lands and back, from the north to the south and back, a southwestern bias in the direction of its wildness. Attending to these stories, we may also be able to understand better the abodes we ourselves have built on those lands and the power that the shaping of the land itself has imposed upon our abodes.

But what are these stories? How do they come into play for us? That is, how do they get our attention? Emerson once observed, "The soul is no traveler; the wise man stays at home, and when his necessities, his duties, on any occasion call him from his house, or into foreign lands, he is at home still, and shall make men sensible by the expression of his countenance, that he goes the missionary of wisdom and virtue, and visits cities and men like a sovereign, and not like an interloper or a valet."[5] Friedrich Nietzsche, who counted Emerson as one of his most important companions in thought, may have been thinking of that passage from "Self-Reliance" when he in turn wrote,

> We children of the future, how *could* we be at home today? We feel disfavor for all ideals that might lead one to feel at home even in this fragile, broken time of transition; as for its "realities," we do not believe that they will *last.* The ice that still supports people today has become very thin; the wind that brings the thaw is blowing; we ourselves who are homeless constitute a force that breaks open ice and other all too thin "realities."[6]

If Nietzsche's aphorism serves as a response to Emerson, it would seem that he was convinced that the wisdom of the soul who stays at home has been lost to us. In that case, we denizens of the present are the homeless, living in the very future he prophesied. He would have us believe that we cannot stay at home with honor because honest souls currently do not have a home to stay in even when they seek one.

What for Nietzsche is a certainty, however, I take to be an open question—whether we are at home, or homeless. That is, what is the future that he predicted? What is our present? Are we, following one direction of his thought, working to become a force that breaks open the ice of our realities, and / or, following another path, do we seek the companions on the road who may sympathize with us in our longing, who will also be wanting to be on the way home in an honest and honorable sense? Perhaps the two desires are not so distant from each other as they may seem. Emerson described the condition of one who travels to lose one's sadness: "My giant goes with me wherever I go."[7] There is, in other words, no escape from ourselves, no way to burrow away from what cannot be forgotten, and yet no way to do anything other than live with this thought.

The first time I saw Nietzsche's aphorism used as an epigraph was in a book about travel of sorts, Paul Gilroy's *The Black Atlantic*.[8] Gilroy's remarkable study was a largely successful attempt to describe the circulation of Afro-European-American moderns: he told stories of those who have experienced a specifically African form of exile from and inclusion within modernity. I flatter myself by imagining that Gilroy may be thought of as a predecessor, or belated companion, to the thoughts that inform this book, in that the way toward home I seek to chart seems to require learning to think through the double consciousness of modern subjects. That consciousness has so far been primarily the unbidden gift of those thinkers whose harsh experiences have combined with their genius: a W. E. B. DuBois, or a Ralph Ellison, or a Toni Morrison, or a Duke Ellington, or a Billie Holiday, or a Charles Mingus, or a James Baldwin, or a Michael Jackson, or a Pauli Murray, or an Aretha Franklin, or an Octavia Butler, or a Cornel West, exemplars all. These African American thinkers / artists, and many more, have themselves restlessly sought ways home, while realizing, each in his or her own way, how the stubborn facts of life spur us on our travels and prevent us from finding a resting place.

I try to keep in mind this circulation of Afro-American modernity, a leavening of the loaf of the American ordinary that may, when set in contact with our superaltern norms—in contact with our Thomas Jeffersons, for instance—allow more of us to gain a perspective on what it may mean to be on the way home in this new millennium. How traveling may be productive of a place of rest, how the sojourns of repressed minorities and majorities may map paths for those of us who have existed too comfortably within the postcolonialist powers, giving us new paths to pursue as we repudiate or otherwise lose our racial, gender, economic, and other forms of privilege, as we lose our homes—what we sometimes call justice—is an unabashed hope of this book. For this form of political theory, the end is simple enough, a vision and a path toward what justice might be: but the path, as always seems to be the case, is never well mapped in advance of our explorations of it.

It is also the case that there are injustices that can never be righted, that there are ghosts who cannot be mollified, that an uncanny haunts the landscape of any home we may want to provide. The American uncanny presents this tragic possibility, and it may well be that we must learn to live with a tragic sensibility that we have long tried to repress. Native American graveyards have been plowed under, sacred mountains have been defiled, the bodies of untold millions have disappeared from the face of the Earth. What are we to do with these invisible presences?[9]

If the circulation of persecuted, repressed and exploited bodies underpinned the rise of American modernity, our modern homelessness, then we are faced now with another circumstance affecting our sense of home, the outlines of which are only beginning to come into focus. Let me put it as a question: Thirty years from now, will it be possible to imagine going on a journey home such as the one I made to my father's house in Altoona, time after time over decades, driving on highways, drinking gasoline by the hundreds of gallons, or otherwise using such extravagant amounts of energy in ways both direct and indirect? Or will such a trip by then be seen as obscenely expensive, or even impossible? The imagined journey home that far into in the geological era of the Anthropocene will not, I suspect, allow for such extravagances.

The Anthropocene looms large in this book—much larger than I would have imagined when I began to focus attention on this subject. Retrospectively, it makes sense that the topic would be unavoidable. The idea that humankind has so influenced the Earth as to have marked it on the scale of the permanence of millions of years, and in such a way as to risk the extinction of *Homo sapiens,* and hence of humanity's home in one of the largest possible senses, introduces yet another level of complexity to this experience and place.

Perhaps one lesson to be learned as we enter the Anthropocene is that we may be focusing on the wrong extravagances. It seems clear that we humans need to rethink our luxurious way of being, not so much to deny ourselves a luxurious existence as to allow ourselves new luxuries while giving up on old ones. That is to say, it may be essential to the ongoing discovery of who we are and who we will become to explore a different kind of extravagance, an extravagance that Thoreau explored, the vagrancy of the hobo, not simply of thought, but of life itself. This experience of extravagance has been an American contribution to the quasi-universal experience of being at home. But even at its best, American comfort has

depended not so much on stillness as on the restless quest to <u>find</u> that still place, that quiet corner from where we can further launch ourselves, becoming more than we were, but less than we will be. Perhaps it is time to consider another way.

It is crucial to keep constantly in mind that American comfort has also depended on the slave labor of abducted Africans, the seizure of lands of aboriginal tribes, the sexual exploitation of women, the permanent project of empire, and the ongoing degradation of those who would oppose majoritarian cultural norms, all to the benefit of a privileged minority. This is a large part of the backdrop that makes the use of the word *we* so tricky, especially when your narrator is hardly one who has not enjoyed the fruits of this system of inequality. All that I can do is plead my self-awareness of the partiality of my understanding, note my flaws, try to appreciate my incomplete constitution, and do my best to be clear about what it is that I may be offering.

What must we do to preserve a sense of becoming in a future that may not allow us the experiences that were fundamental to its creation? One of the questions informing this book is exactly this: How can we find a way home when we have so spoiled its very possibility? What if we are condemned to be outcasts in place, needing to go but with nowhere to go? What if the future is a revisiting of the internal exile, an exponentially magnified repetition of the climatic refugee crisis that occurred during the Great Depression, a Steinbeckian nightmare of homelessness and starvation of spirit, with all of us forced onto the road, latter-day Joads with no sense of redemption?

Questions concerning home and homelessness are political not only because the homeless have become so numerous but because they are now the children of our future. The face and effacement of the refugee has become the most important political subject of our time, as both an object of concern and a subject of power. The refugee camp, meant to be not a home but a space of transition, is the exemplary symptom of our deepest fears about homelessness. How does one live in a refugee camp? How does one live without a home? We know that the answer to such a question is that one cannot live without a home. But that answer is not so much a comfort as a warning.

A sense of place, of stillness, what the philosopher Gaston Bachelard once described as the space of intimacy that allows us to day-
dream, is as close to a universal experience as we humans share.[10]
The comedy and tragedy of home are contained within our contradictory longing to be properly where we are, located, while we continue to feel that we are not and never will be where we ought to be.
Put bluntly, home is so important to us that we risk the world in
order to obtain it. Yet once obtained it sours on us: the housekeeping,
the repetition, the boredom so crushing that we run away from it.

I find myself lost. Yet I also realize that my sense of the stubborn-
ness of the object I seek to know, my frustration at its slipperiness,
is a mood I must confront and come to understand if I am to study
such a subject. The anxiety, the sorrow, the giant—they are all there,
all gathered under one roof, so to speak. Perhaps I am only following
a *whim*, akin to the whim Emerson embraced as a motivating power
for his thought and action. In the end, I hope it is more than that.
Emulating Emerson, I want, instead of following the sublime and
the beautiful, to explore and poeticize the low and the common in
the name of transmuting facts into truths. It is an old tradition, this
poetics. Almost as old is the tradition of condemning poetry, for poetry is indeed a dangerous way of finding truth. It remains to be
seen whether this particular exploration of the ordinary is safely immune from the more grandiose ambitions of some of those who
would claim the only map, the only way home. For the way home is
never one particular way, but a multiplicity of ways.

In the chapters that follow, I try to conjure some fairly specific
ghosts, both historic and fictive. Whether Thomas Jefferson, Henry
David Thoreau, Laura Ingalls Wilder, Emily Dickinson, Herman
Wallace (most of them familiar names, others perhaps not so
much)—or any of an indefinite number of other seekers and de-
stroyers who make cameo appearances, fleshy apparitions of the

American past and present—I want to listen to their voices, to ventriloquize their stories. In conjuring them I want to ask them how they have tried to find ways of being at home in this world, as they have variously succeeded and failed.

In a broad sense, they are on the same highway traveled by Dad, and this book itself is, among other things, my belated attempt to better know the man my father was, to learn from his now permanent silence, to embrace the metempsychosis of his soul to mine, to acknowledge what he did in living a life that has so contributed to the constitution of mine, and to that of all of his children. Why I have chosen these specific stories of home and homelessness as my representatives requires more explanation than I can provide here, perhaps even more than I can ever fully comprehend. I do know that there are more secrets buried in the wilderness of this country and in our common prose than it is possible to count. I also know I have my own secrets, even if most of them are unwillingly held. And so, of course, do you. Perhaps this book is in the end only a detailing of some of the secrets we cannot otherwise share.

Habitations of the Human

Who was the first human being to look out a window?
—ROBERTO BOLAÑO

Linear Time, or Managing the Infinite

In Copenhagen's city hall, off of the vestibule for the main entrance, there is a glass-enclosed room. Within this room stands a mechanical clock.[1] It is a very large clock. Visitors are able to examine it closely because it is mounted within a transparent case that shows its face from the front but also, when one walks around it to its rear, some of its internal works. It is named the Jens Olsen's World Clock after the man who designed and helped to build it. Some thirty years were devoted to the calculations necessary for its design and another twelve to its construction. Powered by gravity, it was set in motion in 1955, or, to be more precise, at 1500 hours on December 15, 1955. (The king of Denmark and Olsen's granddaughter jointly started the clock's mechanism.) The clock has eleven separate works. For those who can read its many faces, the clock tells the local time of day as

well as the local solar time (solar time defined as the result of the
calculation of the local meridian in relation to the sun), the time at
every designated time zone in the world, the time of sunrise and
sunset, the length of day and night. A perpetual calendar marks the
year, the day of the week, the date of the month, and the month itself. This particular piece of the clockwork is reset once a year and
is automatic in its calculations for 2,500 years. That is, it requires
no intervention for that long a period. The clock also has a work that
is unduplicated by any other clock in the world, one that measures
the precession of the Earth's axis, the slow wobbling of the Earth's
axis as marked by the shifting position of its poles, an event that
unfolds once over the course of every 25,753 years. The gear that
marks this movement is the slowest clockwork gear ever made; actually, it is only one-quarter of a complete gear, the makers perhaps
fearing that the clock might not last long enough for it to complete a
full rotation over such a long, long period of time.

I visited this clock on a dark December afternoon in 2013, stumbling upon it serendipitously while in Copenhagen for other reasons.
Perhaps because I was previously unaware of its existence, perhaps
because I was already slightly obsessed with such matters, when I
found myself in the presence of this extraordinary mechanism, time
itself seemed to slow. A rotation that occurs once every 25,753 years
is such that no one human with the opportunity to observe the gear
over the course of an ordinary lifetime would be able to discern any
change in the gear's position by use of the naked eye alone. It felt to
me as though the timepiece maker was attempting to mark the infinite, to inflect the emptiness of duration, to imagine a constancy of
measure far beyond the history of the human so far, deep into the
future, yet on a tangible, if invisible, scale.

I am still puzzled by my odd perception that time was slowing when
I was in the presence of this clock. One may imagine that observing

the clock would provoke the opposite response: as one sees the scale of time expand, one's fleeting moment of life might seem to move more quickly in comparison to the immensity of the time being marked, and one might feel more profoundly the transience of one's own period of being alive. But what is required of us to appreciate this clock is the ability to imagine a future in which existence continues, without the presence of any humans now alive. Perhaps this feeling, my imagining that time is passing in my absence, accounts for my sense of slowness. The feeling is similar to the way I begin to feel when I am forced to think about the size of the known universe, the sense of incredible smallness in the face of an incomprehensible immensity—smallness and slowness in the face of immensity and speed.

In one way, this clock is like any other clock. It is a truism, though perhaps not so obvious, that all clocks are time machines. But this particular clock is of such a scale that it made palpable something that was always theoretically clear but never so concretely apparent to me before—how telling time itself is an element of the human attempt to manage the infinite. Jens Olsen's World Clock is designed to demonstrate a temporal continuity that transcends the finitude of any individual human being's life. It moves in the direction of geologic time, a time we have always assumed, until the advent of the Anthropocene, to be beyond the human, and even potentially beyond animal life itself. We gaze upon the slowest gear and see nothing moving at all, even as we know that movement of some sort, far below the register of our perception, is occurring. Our knowledge of this imperceptible movement raises questions. What else can we not see, what else moves forward, what is the history of technology itself if not the deployment of an invisible control over our perception of time through the movement of mechanical devices? From our earliest observations of growth in plants and animals, from our notice of processes of decay, from our discovery of rapid movements—movements occurring too fast to be seen—from telescope, photograph, atomic clock, on and on, we humans have tried to survey the domain of the infinite in order to manage it.

The desire to manage the infinite is in some ways the very definition of the human. We don't tend to think of the idea of extending ourselves forward in time as having to do with infinitude so much as with our facing an indeterminate, yet comprehensible and hopefully somewhat predictable future. Yet we have not managed to control the future, to in any way contain the infinite within the scope of our schemes. That we have even tried is a sign of our Icarus-like hubris. But the persistence of that very unpredictability is also, surprisingly, a potential sign of hope.

To be human is to be both in and out of time. The future constantly exceeds our grasp, even as we struggle to be present in the present. Every moment that we live is at the end of the world. (There can be dark humor in this sensibility, this acute awareness of time's passage. As Don DeLillo once wrote, "There are more dead people now than at any other time in human history.")[2] In the epoch some of us call late modernity, it seems we humans have made our predicament even more fraught because we have come to associate being at home with living in or for the future, imagining our freedom to lie somewhere beyond our present, even as we remain homeless in the present. This unsettling sense of time and our untimely presence within some space of time in late modernity are closely related to what Sigmund Freud, himself a great reader of Nietzsche, identified as the sense of the *uncanny*.[3] Indeed the very term for the uncanny in German, *unheimlich,* can be translated into English clumsily, if literally, as "un-homely," somehow evoking the feeling of not being at home, perhaps the feeling associated with being homeless.

So that if our point of return is to a past not realized, then we are always moving through a time that is out of joint.

The spreading sense of homelessness might be misunderstood as an ironic fable of this epoch, a period in which we humans have so spread ourselves across the face of Earth that we might be able to identify any given place—at least on the land—as a possible human habitat, a possible home, a possible *sedes,* or seat. As the far reaches of the globe have been mapped and photographed, as our technologies of transportation and architecture have rendered so much of the Earth potential habitat, as the networks of electric pulses and light have made instantaneous communication to every piece of ground on the planet possible, all places on the Earth have become potential homes for human beings. As a species we are, it seems, in an increasingly expansive sense, always already at home. This most recent age of global capital is one in which humans can seemingly be at home anywhere and everywhere. To the extent that this is true, questions of departure and return should fade away as we all come to embrace a cosmopolitan sense of being at home.

But this sense of cosmopolitan possibility is not readily available to all. The constitution of "we" is always a political question, tied to gross issues of economic, racial, and gendered inequalities, imperium, capital, resentments of those in power toward those without, the ongoing problem of the withdrawal of consent from above by those who benefit most from the status quo that is a hallmark of the epoch of global neoliberalism.[4] And it is further marked by the unequal geographic distribution of pain associated with the Anthropocene. All of these questions concerning justice and power play directly into what we may think of as being at home. All of them provide partial responses to this quasi-universal experience of home.

How could this be? Perhaps the spreading sense of homelessness only means that the world itself has become uncanny. To be perfectly at home may now be imagined as the same as being perfectly homeless. To be found may now be understood as another way of being lost.[5] Distinctions between inside and outside, between private and public, and lost and found are coming to be more difficult to sustain the further we are able to map the world. It is as though the more fervent the claim we make to be at home in this world, the more fraught our position becomes. Yet while to say that the world is our home is true and crucially important to remember, it still is true only in the most general sense. Within that larger home, the planet itself, we make our homes, and the problem of homecoming is never resolved. It only shifts in focus. Perhaps there is something in the very idea of home that prevents us from being there. We are always on the way: we never arrive.

This observation may strike some as, well, obvious, and for those familiar with her work, a simplistic derivation of a more complex set of distinctions that Hannah Arendt once made between Earth and world.[6] Arendt argued that our human *world* is composed of what we make, how we condition ourselves, how we develop the technologies and the artifacts that make possible our existence. Unlike Earth, the world is ours. Unlike Earth, *we* have fabricated the world; we have *made* it. And as we have made it, we possess it, we have mastered it. For her, our desires to depart, to explore, to begin anew are but varied expressions of essentially the same impulse, a common desire to go beyond the planet we inhabit, but to take our world with us as we leave or, paraphrasing her language, to exchange the free gift of life that comes from nowhere (secularly speaking) with something we have made for ourselves.[7] She went so far as to suggest, in the late 1950s, that the launching of Sputnik was "an event, second in importance to no other," a telling demonstration of the deep desire humans have to escape Earth, made possible not by religious belief but by the event of modern science that culminated in the launch of that satellite.[8]

Arendt did not celebrate or condemn this development so much as she took it as a given, that is, understood it as the emergent ground on which our common capacity to make decisions in concert with each other is to be (re)built. One of her concerns was that the technological advances enabled by modern science put that capacity for action, as she termed it, at risk of diminishment, perhaps even erasure. Political problems become transmuted into technical ones, and in that transmutation, something essential about the human is misplaced, because our capacity to act in concert is central to our human condition. Hence we have in front of us a core paradox of modern life. The human ability to act politically is threatened by the knowledge that increasingly determines the fate of humanity. Politics comes to be reduced to power, and knowledge becomes no more or less than the primary instrument of power. Politics as people acting in concert threatens to disappear.

Arendt's observation is akin to what Michel Foucault once identified as a core problem of the power / knowledge nexus, though he did not think that a revived or reimagined version of the *polis* would provide a solution to the problem of the eclipse of the political. He didn't think it possible or even desirable. What Arendt understood to be the overcoming of power as acting in concert with knowledge in the form of science, Foucault understood to be a complex interweaving of the two. Unlike Arendt, Foucault did not posit power / knowledge as a problem that would result in the disappearance of freedom, so much as a predicament which demands that we think more imaginatively about how we are to be free, what ways may be available to us to exercise our freedom.[9] In this sense, Foucault's understanding of the domain of the human and its limitations presses hard against the more sovereign sense of the political to which Arendt seemed so attached.

But both Arendt and Foucault were sensitive to the presence of the past in our attempts to move through time. This is the paradox presented to us by the existence of linear time. We move forward, and there is an irrevocable quality to that movement. There is no return to a past, but the ongoing accumulation and expansion of our knowledge of the historical grounds undergirding the conditions of existence. Destruction is understood as regression, or at least the primary cost of progress. Where else can we go, once the Earth is full of us and our progress, other than outward, forward, ever marching onward into an unknown future?

However critical she was of the alienating effects of modern science, like many other American intellectuals of the postwar era, Arendt engaged in a romance with the technological advances that science enabled during this period. And as did many others, she overestimated the extent to which the more specific emergent technologies of space exploration would actually develop materially. (She was, perhaps, more prescient concerning advances in the biological sciences, but here too she presented a picture of those advances that misread where and how the dangers of genetic manipulation would manifest themselves.)

Despite such visions, we need to remember something very basic about the limits of such speculation concerning Earth, our place on Earth, and any possible departure from Earth. With certain minor exceptions, which allow for a select few of us to attain the reaches of outer space, for several centuries to come it is extremely unlikely that human beings will be able in meaningful numbers to travel much farther into outer space than the middle reaches of the solar system, to other local earths, such as Mars, or the moons of Jupiter, places more hostile to our animal being than Earth itself, even as the era of the Anthropocene further unfolds. (And that is an extremely optimistic forecast in and of itself.) And despite the extraordinary advances in the biological sciences and accompanying technologies that have occurred since Arendt wrote, which are still occurring, and which will continue to occur, whatever cybernetic mutations of our bodies come about in the foreseeable future, we will still be creatures of Earth, sharing our animal being with its other inhabitants. In regard to the fossil past and the clarity it sheds concerning our place in the cosmos, the sublime terror that such a casting back may enable does little to allow us to think through how we are to be able to bear the weight of our own present and immediate future.[10]

Even if Arendt were to modify her assumptions, to begin thinking of our departure from Earth in virtual terms, we would still be left with questions she seems not to want to ask. Were we to create avatars that are somehow impervious to the vagaries of time and space, and that would enable us, to use the terms employed so glibly by the inventor and futurist Ray Kurzweil, to overcome our biological limits by reaching the moment of "singularity," we would still be faced with the question, What would we be leaving when we make such a departure into the virtual and away from Earth? In the Kurzweilian scenario, rather than locate our continued progress outward through space, we move ever farther inward, reaching yet another threshold of the human, seeking to expand our knowledge so far as to overcome our bodily limitations by becoming virtual. This digital expansion of information suggests for him that we can remain human in the face of the loss of our biological existence. But there is much to suggest that, were we able to do so, we would become something other than human and lose whatever sense of home we might still have.[11]

We may note that, in either of these scenarios, the vast majority of human beings are left out of the equation, that is, we are simply to be left behind, the world diminished by the depredations of environmental damage and the departure of the privileged. This is the dystopian assumption—levels of political, economic, and social inequality unmatched across the entirety of human history—that those investing in such projects do not mention in public, but which inform their willingness to abandon the rest of us. It is here that the struggle between finitude and the infinite manifests itself most extremely. In the contemporary world, the struggle to be(come) human seems to entail a balancing act between the wish to achieve a virtual immortality through strategies of disembodiment, such as advanced by people such as Kurtzweil, and the recognition that the abandonment of embodiment results in the devastation of those who do not meet the standards, economic and political, that would otherwise allow them the ordinary comforts of life.

Despite the failure of political imagination underlying these technological solutions to the problem of our Earth as home, such speculations concerning the temporal and spatial limits of the human are based, I think reasonably, on an understanding that a desire for home is a sort of empirical human universal, that is, a phenomenon that unites all human beings in a practical sense, as a way of being in the world we have made on Earth. They enable questions such as this: Why would we want to return to a home that is of this Earth? Or, better, what desire compels some of us to return to our perceived place of origin, and what makes those of us who see ourselves as being homeless, unable or unwilling to return to such a place, feel as though we are somehow excluded from something that is of the essence of being human?

This vacillation between home and homelessness is at the heart of the puzzle over what, for lack of a better phrase, we might still call the fate of humanity. To be at home in the Anthropocene may mean to live through a period when that movement reaches such a height as to cause a crisis, both material and conceptual, in regard to home itself. But even as we explore this movement, we need to keep in mind something else: that whatever we may think about the possible end of home, it continues to exist even as it seems to become impossible to persist in our lives and imaginations. I think this is so in part because we have no viable alternatives to being at home in our human world.

Sometimes desperate measures are taken. In the spring of 1997, a group of people living in common in a mansion in the suburbs of San Diego, California, under the leadership of a person named Marshall Applegate, but who called himself "Do," appeared to have committed mass suicide. Yet in recorded interviews they left behind, the members of this cult that called itself Heaven's Gate insisted that they were not killing themselves but leaving the Earth, departing their "vessels" in order to transfer their true selves to a spaceship that was trailing the Hale-Bopp comet, hiding within or behind its tail. (Hale-Bopp was during this period visible to the naked eye from Earth. I remember pointing it out to my then young children in the night sky while on a family camping trip along the California coast that spring.) All of the male members of Heaven's Gate had been castrated in the months prior to their death—a desire to end desire seemed to be at least a part of their solution to the sense of despair felt by the members of the group. While most of these travelers seemed to harbor no doubts concerning their transport to outer space, in one of the many video recordings found in the mansion, left behind as farewell messages by individual members, one who did have doubts also noted, "Maybe they're crazy for all I know. But I don't have any choice but to go for it, because I've been on this planet 31 years and there's nothing for me here."[12]

I have long been haunted by this story, and especially by the plaint of this person, who could not find anything here for herself. For there to be nothing "here" for anyone of us is as radical a critique of the human as we might imagine. It encourages solipsism as a way of life, life so attenuated as to teeter on the edge of nonexistence. It radically deepens the sense of Earth alienation evoked by Arendt. It moves us from the desire to explore more deeply our residence on the face of Earth to a desire to leave Earth altogether, an active desire to give up on life on Earth, to become, in a very exacting but extremely peculiar sense, posthuman. It is an impulse to surrender to death without ever having lived, as though in the contest of Eros and Thanatos, Eros never showed up.[13]

Even those like Kurzweil, who think about the possibility of there being some sort of synthetic immortality, seem to imagine that immortality in terms of a loneliness that any of us might recognize as no more than a horrifyingly Gothic materialization of Descartes's most abstract imaginings, the dismal thought that our bodies are but vessels, or machines, that mind is all, and that, paradoxically, mindlessness is as easily, if not more easily, within our grasp because of the minds we have made of ourselves. For Kurzweil and his devotees, in the end mind itself becomes machine.

I think of the story of Heaven's Gate as a secular parable about the problem of being at home, an attempt to return to a place that may no longer exist, if ever it did. It is a frightening tale not simply because of the tremendous sadness of so many deaths but because of what it suggests about those of us who remain behind. It is almost as if the devotees of Heaven's Gate peered into a Kurzweilian future and found to live in it to be impossible. If indeed there is nothing for us here anymore, then the answer to the question of what a home is will inevitably be rooted in final resting places far away from where we are, places we have been running away from for most of our collective existence. Our oldest myths concerning paradise and hell are formed by these flights. That is yet another reason why the question of what it means to be at home is both so important and yet so dangerous.

This secularization of the appeal to heaven in the wake of the decline of religious belief, while claiming to be based on a lived reality that is very distant from unbidden faith in a God, echoes the millennialism of some evangelical Christians. Some of these Christians have imagined a near future when the Rapture will occur, lifting those who are faithful off of the Earth and into heaven, leaving behind those who are not worthy to face the Tribulations. In that sense, the parable of Heaven's Gate is also a sign of the ultimate hollowness of such appeals, the despair that entices people to imagine their exclusivity in negative terms, the surrender to hatred of others more immediately at hand than is the Devil himself.

The Heaven's Gate cult was a marginal and strange phenomenon. But it has a current, more optimistic, and widely hailed counterpart in the Mars One project, proposed by a group from the Netherlands that has come up with a new idea: that the exploration of Mars would be more feasible if those who volunteered to go on the mission would also accept that they would never return to Earth. While this idea may seem radical, in a sense these volunteers would be following an old example. As the project's website indicates, "Not unlike the ancient Chinese, Micronesians, and untold Africans, the Vikings and famed explorers of Old World Europe, who left everything behind to spend the majority of their lives at sea, a one-way mission to Mars is about exploring a new world and the opportunity to conduct the most revolutionary research ever conceived, to build a new home for humans on another planet."[14] But underlying this optimistic vision is the same doubt that informed the members of Heaven's Gate, that the future of humankind is not to be found here on Earth. This desire to leave Earth, to seek a home elsewhere—could there be a clearer symptom of the homesickness Nietzsche noted?

When fantasies of escape from Earth transmute into events of history, we become witnesses to a secular transformation of the religious quest to overcome the finitude of death. Such a transformation is made more possible when we ignore other dimensions of living, other scales of time. In our attempts to manage the infinite, we humans have suppressed our knowledge of the *kinds* of time that we could also associate with being at home, intensities of erotic attractions broadly understood that may otherwise punctuate our perceptions of life, durations of waiting, sensibilities of presence that are suppressed by the ticking of the clock, humming its tunes of boredom and terror. It seems as though we have turned our homes inside out, made them a part of the universal clock. And we keep bumping up against the limits imposed on us by the infinite as we continue to try to manage it.

Naming the Human, or Animals of Earth

Assessing the importance of our understandings of time for being at home is one of our problems. Another problem has to do with our understanding of the human as animal, and how our understanding bears upon our relationships with other animals. Our homes both exclude and include other animals. The terms by which we include and exclude these and other beings thus contribute to how we shape our sense of being at home.

At least since Descartes wrote of the cogito—actually, since the obscure origins of our recognition of ourselves as thinking creatures—claims concerning the human and our distinctiveness in comparison to other animals have been largely derived from assumptions concerning the supposed richness of the thinking human world we have made versus the unthinking worlds that other species of animals supposedly have only inhabited.[15] But the supposed uniqueness of the human animal is so filled with exceptions to the rule as to have put into question and, in a peculiar way, endangered our understanding of the human itself. *Subhuman* and *superhuman* are the terms used to suggest that there are categories of biological being that are arranged hierarchically as either below the human or above the human, and the terms are considered by so many to be so pejorative as to render incoherent claims by philosophers who both embrace human uniqueness and claim to want an ethical relationship to other animals.[16]

In asking about the relationships human beings have with other animals, I am not trying to make a strong claim regarding the terrifically difficult problem of the human use and abuse of other animals. That is a crucial and important study, but one that cannot be the primary focus of what I am trying to undertake here. Nonetheless, the question of the human in relationship to others pervades whatever sense of being at home we may try to reach. Aspirational fables of home are associated with a striving to become human under conditions of animality, but achieving the human, so to speak, is exceedingly difficult. This is one of the points of such striving: it is a part of the form of moral perfectionism associated with the work of Stanley Cavell, a kind of perfectionism which insists that it is the effort, not the end, that matters. As a part of that striving, then, the relationship of human beings to other animals remains a profound and basic element of how we humans both *make* our home and *are* at home.

Other animals—indeed, a plethora of other nonhuman agents—have directly and indirectly shaped the worlds we humans have supposedly made by ourselves, by our own labors. Why and how we came to enslave so many of these other animals is a part of what we are, as is our illusion that we are indeed able to master so many of them.[17] This will to mastery is increasingly problematic as the epoch of the Anthropocene unfolds. The Anthropocene casts a strange light on the problem of home, as it shows how the human conquest of the Earth has created the conditions that threaten to destroy the Earth as home not only for us but also for these other animals. This material crisis of the ecological conditions underpinning animal and other living beings is mirrored in the conceptual crisis of the idea of home itself. And a large part of that conceptual crisis goes back to how we have thought about our bodies and souls.

This predicament was anticipated by both Arendt and Foucault. In the late 1950s, Arendt wrote, "Although Christians have spoken of the earth as a vale of tears and philosophers have looked upon their body as a prison of mind or soul, nobody in the history of mankind has ever conceived of the earth as a prison for men's bodies or shown such eagerness to go literally from here to the moon." She goes on to note the many scientific endeavors that have been undertaken "toward making life also 'artificial,' toward cutting the last tie through which man even belongs among the children of nature."[18] She points in a particular direction, understanding the human animal to be running away from its animality, imagining the human in terms of the body being the prison of the soul.

For Foucault, it is not Earth that imprisons but the creation of a set of conditions that confines the body, the apparatuses of disciplinary society. Through his studies of governmentality, presented as lectures at the College de France in the 1970s and 1980s, some of which found their way into his book *The History of Sexuality,* Foucault investigates the more general alienation of the human animal from the Earth and underlines the terrible political risk humankind was taking in the name of security. Like Arendt, he notes the potential outcome of the destruction of all animal life on Earth as a consequence of nuclear war.[19]

Arendt may have felt that the abandonment of our bodies was more of a possibility than did Foucault. And Foucault may have seen a way to new practices of freedom that would reconcile our bodies and souls. But neither of them directly anticipated the entry of humankind into the Anthropocene. In their anticipation of nuclear devastation both of them adhered to a particular timeline that posed humankind as on the brink of destruction. But the timeline of the Anthropocene is more complex than that. Several time scales are entailed and entangled; durations are composed of both short-term catastrophe and long-term disaster.[20] We experience periods of sabbatical and event, depth and shallowness, connection and dissociation across hours and lifetimes.

The human sharing of existence on Earth with other living beings is inescapably a part of these experiences not only because we share Earth with other animals but also because we are animals that share. Animality is intrinsic to human being, just as it is to wolves and whales, bees and birds. Ironically, our insistence on human uniqueness may be the only thing that actually makes human beings unique as a species. But, pace Wittgenstein, that we talk is not something that elevates us above other animals; instead, it is the kind of language we use (and what we choose to talk about), what Walter Benjamin once called the language of man, a *naming* language.[21] And it is not clear that such a naming language is an elevating language at all.

Here is one such name. The word *human* is etymologically connected to *humus,* to decay, to the *Earth*, not to the world. (This is why I have been capitalizing the word, in recognition of this existential connection.) To be human is not simply to be the animal *Homo sapiens.* It is to belong to this Earth. In that sense, our animal sense, we humans are grounded by our placement as animals of the ground. Robert Pogue Harrison puts it this way: "Humanity is not a species; it is a connection with the humus. . . . If one day we colonize other worlds, then we might be able to say, empirically and definitely, that 'man' was not 'determined' to be upon this earth after all. But such a 'man,' when and if he comes to exist, will no longer be human, at least not in the sense in which Vico talked of *homo humandi*."[22] Harrison notes that it is not necessary to leave Earth to dehumanize our nature, to uproot us. He suggests that if it is the case that this uprooting is under way, that we are, for instance, becoming so forgetful of our earthly existence as to develop pretenses toward departure and then act on them, that to think of our species being as human being will be a "retrospective probing of the obsolete ground of an obsolete human nature." But if it is not the case, that is, if contemporary talk of the posthuman is an anxious and inadequate response to human modernity, then "we are faced with the task of reclaiming the claims that the earth and our dead make on that nature—and what a genuinely modern response to those claims would consist in. Meanwhile we find ourselves in a situation where each of us must choose an allegiance—either to the post-human, the virtual and the synthetic, or to the earth, the real and the dead in their humic densities."[23]

When Harrison speculates about what it would mean for us to cease to be human, arguing that if we were to leave Earth we would become something other than human even as we might continue to exhibit the worldly qualities of "man," he could just as well be challenging Arendt's claim that even if we were to leave Earth we would remain human because we are conditioned beings who make our world. Harrison's intervention is to suggest that the loss of a connection to Earth, regardless of the qualities that might then make us into something wondrous and beautiful, or terrific and grotesque, would nonetheless make us something other than human. What that might be is not clear. But if such a something is attainable, and may be thought of as a gain over what we now are, it is also true that with that gain there would be a profound loss. (Of course, even to speak of such changes in terms of gain and loss may in fact be a sign of our own poverty of language.)

I have already discussed the import of speculations about leaving Earth, whether made as mind experiments, as predictions concerning the future, or as expressions of a desire to somehow become something other than ourselves while preserving ourselves as separate from the Earth, understanding them to represent an extreme limit on the attempt to manage the infinite by extending ourselves both forward in time and outward from place. But another extreme limit, rather than looking so radically forward, looks radically backward, making the question of origins the tipping point between our human distinctiveness from other species. Perhaps it was the invention of cooking, perhaps the grasping of a tool, perhaps the mythical appearance of a black monolith in central Africa tens of thousands of years ago, perhaps the partial extinction of the Neanderthal that gave *Homo sapiens* the living space to grow. Perhaps it was all of these and more, the imperative for survival that made us begin to walk upright, fatefully changing the scope of our vision and the extent of our ambit. Here the horizon of the precise measurement of fossil remains, or the question of the scientifically certain knowledge of the creation of the Earth itself some 4.5 billion years ago, provides the most absolute measure against which we are to reckon ourselves as beings.[24] This is what might be called the danger of thinking in geologic time when it is not modified by other scales of time.

Or, is it simply a matter of *saying* that we are human that makes it so? If such were the case, if (because humans are those whose language is a *naming* language, to return to Benjamin's argument)[25] it were to follow that naming is making it so, then we would find ourselves as we name ourselves. Such a thought is not as strange as it may seem. Indeed, it is one of the functions of modern analytical philosophy to aid in the naming process, even as its own blinders to the rest of what we do prevent it from having a more meaningful role in thinking through the *consequences* of naming than it does.[26] Benjamin's point, I think, was not to take up an argument concerning names but to consider more carefully what it means to think about the task God gave to Adam and rethink it in terms of the human itself. Benjamin suggests a more modest path for us, one by which we can live with ourselves, perhaps melancholically, but with the recognition that our human language is not the only one or the only kind. In this, he signals an alternative way to think about home as a site where we name ourselves. Is it the case, he wants to ask, that we are human to the extent that we name ourselves as such?

It is worth noting here that the Hebrew word for Earth is *adamah*. When God named Adam, the Earth had already been formed. The name Adam is thus a metonym; Adam is the one who is made from the Earth, and who comes to stand for the Earth. As a common word and not a name, *adam* means "human." God's naming of Adam, then, may not have been a naming at all but an iteration of an existing name for Earth, and its subsequent reiteration into humanity.[27] Such a closeness—asserting the origins of Earth and the origins of humanity as being the consequence of the same act—has enormous implications for thinking about the fate of the human as the Anthropocene era begins, suggesting that human being has, in turning away from the Earth in order to make a world, worked toward destroying its home even as it has tried to build it.

The power of naming comes from the fact that it is one way of performing our humanness. But we do not perform our humanness only by asserting that we are human. While speaking is so often involved, other sorts of actions we take are as important. We might even find ourselves allegorizing and becoming the subjects of allegory. Our doors will shut, we will raise families like fields of beans, decorate our lives with memories and pictures; our doors will open once again to the worlds we have made, and then we will leave those worlds of our own making and return to the Earth. Henry David Thoreau called this *economy*. And his economy was both a philosophy of life and a political theory. The politics of finding a way home are thus entwined with the incidents and accidents that occur along the way of ordinary life as enacted in its various sites. It may be that we need to focus on what we can know about what we humans are, not in distinction from other animals but in terms of our aspirations to find a way home for ourselves, just the same as other animals do, only differently.

Dwelling, or Catastrophe

When did we begin to imagine that we might become human beings? Upon reflection, the very existence of each of us as a human being is always in question to one extent or another. It is as though we are constantly at risk of losing something that we will only miss upon realizing its absence. Trying to find an answer to the question of the threshold of the human may lead us nowhere, but we must nonetheless pursue it because the question itself is intimately, if obscurely, tied to how we tend to think about finding a way home, where and when we may find it and lose it.

Asking the question by looking into the origins of language and culture leads us directly to Martin Heidegger's reflections on human existence, especially his essay "Building, Dwelling, Thinking."[28] The form this question takes for him presumes that it is human language itself that separates us from and connects us to other beings, that language is the primary foundation of our world. Here our question would be, if we look back into the origins of language, what can we say constitutes the order of existence that could lead us on the way home? Heidegger also tells us that we face a great danger, that we may now be so far from home that we are essentially homeless. In that, he amplifies Nietzsche's understanding of modernity as being shaped by our condition of homelessness. This dangerous understanding of our homelessness is an element of the precarious circumstances of our dwelling.

The relationship between philosophy and home for Heidegger concerns more than simply the facts of his biography. Nonetheless, it is worth noting that it was immediately after his disastrous political engagement with Nazism that he retreated to his hut in the mountain forests of Bavaria to think.[29] I believe it would be a mistake to underestimate the importance of this retreat as an element of his thought. But through all his misadventures, Heidegger always wanted to encourage a particular kind of thinking that he thought may lead to a closer relationship to truth. This thinking had been sorely tried when he joined it to the racist nationalism of Hitler. So his testing in "Building, Dwelling, Thinking" could be thought of as representing his struggle to find a way through the aftermath of a catastrophe.

Heidegger notes that not all kinds of thinking get us as close to the essence of truth as do others. The correspondence of one thing with another, for instance, is one particular kind of truth, as is common sense. But in a typical turn in his thought, Heidegger suggests that truths such as these fail to lead us further into the meaning of truth. Paradoxically, it is only by seeing how they fail in their truthfulness, in their errancy, how they fall short, so to speak, that we can begin to understand how their very limitations lead us closer to truth.[30]

For Heidegger, truth has a deep relationship to dwelling, which he considers to be a way of thinking, or at least a way *toward* thinking. Heidegger is at great pains to distinguish between building and dwelling, in both senses, as nouns and activities. As activities, we build in order to dwell. Dwelling is the purpose of building, understood as a way of living that gives us access to truth. But as structures, he notes, not all buildings are "dwelling places." Nonetheless, because he is so profoundly interested in the problem of what he thinks of as the underlying coherence all things have with each other, especially how Truth inheres in Being as a revealing, he still asserts, "Even so, these buildings are in the domain of our dwelling" (347). He insists on the relevance of buildings that are not dwellings being in the domain of dwelling for much the same reason that he insists that correspondence and common sense are, even in their superficiality and errancy, nonetheless elements of truth. For him there are many kinds of housing that do not fulfill the end of dwelling itself. But even though he knows there are many buildings that are not designed to be dwellings, that are buildings of other sorts—office buildings, concert halls, and bridges, for example— their explicit, utilitarian purpose is less important to notice than their existence within the domain of dwelling. Moreover, while building is in one sense the *means* toward the end of dwelling, in a deeper sense to build is already to dwell. And, of crucial importance for us, Heidegger insists that to dwell is *how* we are human. He writes, "The way in which you and I *are* on the earth is *buan,* dwelling. To be a human being means to be on the earth as a mortal. It means to dwell" (349).

Dwelling is served by building in two distinct but deeply related ways. There is building as erecting edifices, which is what is commonly thought of as building. But there is also building as cultivation. In cultivating, we cherish and protect growing things. Both of these ways of building belong to dwelling, Heidegger argues, and yet in our habits, our in*habit*ing of the world, dwelling itself falls into oblivion, hidden behind the more specific characters of cultivation and construction. Our sense of dwelling recedes from us, and we find ourselves somehow without a sense of home or, perhaps more specifically, unaware that the home we have failed to inhabit *is* a dwelling.

In the face of this unawareness, Heidegger presents us with his idea of thinking. He writes:

> The proper dwelling plight lies in this, that mortals ever search anew for the essence of dwelling, that they *must ever learn to dwell.* What if man's homelessness consisted in this, that man still does not even think of the *proper* plight of dwelling as *the* plight? Yet as soon as man *gives thought* to his homelessness, it is a misery no longer. Rightly considered and kept well in mind, it is the sole summons that *calls* mortals into their dwelling. (363)

For him, we build out of dwelling, and think for the sake of dwelling. To think about dwelling is to think about our state of homelessness, and hence to no longer feel it as a misery but as the first thinking that will lead us to dwell. We will understand that as mortals our dwelling is *there,* in the very learning of mortality. This way of thinking, this handicraft as he calls it elsewhere, is deliberate and simplifying, though it is often imagined to be obscure and unavailable to us. Indeed, in Heidegger's hands the thinking of truth sometimes seems almost impossible, as though he is trying to keep thoughts away from most of us even as he urges us on to think. For him to suggest that our movement from homelessness to dwelling is to be accomplished always in the first instance by thinking would also suggest that our failure to recognize our condition of homelessness means that we have not yet begun to think. His lesson seems to be that even if the task of thinking is available to us all, thinking is the most difficult thing we can do. Perhaps it is.

This difficulty *does* seem to be intractable at times. It becomes almost impossible to imagine the level of receptivity that would be required of us to meet Heidegger's demand for thinking. It is more than our need to awaken from dogmatic slumbers that is at stake here. In his search for the beginning of the way to language it is almost as though, in a parody of Einstein, Heidegger is suggesting that by peering far enough into the past of language we will eventually be able to see the backs of our own heads. Put more starkly, his search for a unity in human existence risks unraveling the more intently he *thinks* it. His attempt to embrace a radical receptivity comes undone because of this search, a search that endorses a radical *passivity,* in that it is thinking that triumphs over action or, more accurately, thinking that becomes something other than acting. Receptivity is one element of dwelling, but it is not the only element of dwelling, and this seems to be what Heidegger, who tells us that we have forgotten, seems himself to forget.

We also might note that for Heidegger the homelessness that leads to dwelling is a homelessness that longs for home. What of those wanderers who are not inclined to such a longing, who are homeless in a cosmopolitan sense, who embrace any form of nomadism? Trouble arises from the very longing for home when Heidegger makes such an exclusion. The dog whistle of philosophical racism—*cosmopolitan* as the code word for Jew, *nomadic* as that for the Gypsies, and so on—can have, and has had, devastating consequences for those who have been among the homeless, those perceived by Heidegger as not properly longing for home.

Heidegger's sense of time—perhaps we could call it his own attempt to manage the infinite—stands behind the thinking of other

linear time thinkers, perhaps, most important, Hannah Arendt herself. Such thinking, which was designed to liberate humankind
from an earlier tyranny of time, has brushed up against its own
limitations. We are now in a human predicament in which the ha-
bitual failure to think in ways that enable us to recognize how we
dwell contributes to a great forgetfulness. This forgetfulness is what
might be called the disaster. It is something deeply related to what
we ordinarily would call the catastrophic, an event that profoundly
disrupts the grounds of the ordinary. A catastrophe has a scale of
harm that can only be measured against the rhythms and forms of
ordinary life. We feel the catastrophic as a disorientation of self, the
loss of the ground beneath our feet, the wiping away of those rhythms
and forms.

That these thinkers are so deeply attuned to the problem posed
by our forgetting of finitude makes their reliance on a sense of time
that underestimates or even abandons considerations of the cyclical
character, the diurnal rhythms, and the gradual decline of life toward
death puzzling. Their insights into the catastrophic are less con-
vincing than they otherwise might be. Alternatively, Maurice Blanchot has taught that the catastrophe is the event of the disaster and
the destruction of meaning that we can only comprehend as destruction and only feel as loss.[31] It becomes the event of the disaster
when we are unable to do anything other than live it and its varia-
tions, its own patterns of meaninglessness. The disaster is when catastrophe becomes ordinary. That is, the disorientation, the wiping
away of the rhythm and form of the event of the catastrophe, is what
we may perceive as the eventfulness of modern life.

Heidegger put it this way: "Having become God-less and world-
less, the modern human is home-less."[32] As it is for Nietzsche, for
Heidegger homelessness is an ontological condition, a state of being.
To be homeless no longer is to be of the humus, of the ground, but

to be swept away. To live at home is now to live in (bad?) faith, to know that it is not possible to be at home in a home at all, but to pretend otherwise. It is the wiping away of the rhythms of life that is so crucial here.

When a hurricane destroys a city, when a flood erases a town, when an earthquake reduces a country to rubble, leaving the human-built edifices in ruins, we are realizing only that which we already somehow have realized, that we are without a home. And yet we live, in the rubble, in the ruins, still human. How much longer can we still live on in the ruins?

The terrible reality we face as we enter the Anthropocene is not composed simply of extinction events and strange weather, destructive fires and rising seas, the elimination of buildings we call our homes. It is also, and more important, the ongoing upbuilding of our world civilization from the very toxins that fuel these and other like phenomena. Our homes in this situation are sites of denial, sustained by debts that will never be repaid, nourished by wastes that no longer can be removed. Whatever rhythms we try to sustain are overturned in the chaos of the immediate. Our homes render us homeless. If we are to face up to the disaster that is now our catastrophic condition, we must confront this essential truth of homelessness.

What of those who once felt they had homes, those who have been forced to leave the homes they once thought they had? The ever-increasing, ever-intensifying ranks of the refugees throughout the world: Are they really homeless because they have not yet properly dwelled? One is tempted to dismiss the musings of Heidegger because they seem to offer nothing to those who suffer in this way. But we must remember that Heidegger, along with so many other Germans of his generation who survived World War II, also had the experience of living in ruins. Those whom they killed and burned to ash haunt those ruins. We may imagine that he learned something from that experience. Even if he didn't, it still would be too hasty to dismiss him, if only because what he may have missed could be as important as what he comprehended.

What are we to make of this sense of loss that accompanies Heidegger's thinking of home and homelessness? Is it too large a jump to move from our state of homelessness to the idea that such a state means that we are called to recognize that to be on the way home is to be on the way to our death? Heidegger's death-bound ontology is rejected by so many precisely because it seems to leave us bereft, grieving our lives before we have even lived them. But his own resignation to the fate of the human, as expressed in "Only a God Can Save Us Now," a posthumously published interview, need not lead us to the same conclusions regarding our own futurity, our own existential struggles with the fate of our thinking, our dwelling, not simply in our fronting or facing death, but in our living with our dead.

Cyclical Time, or Forests

When did we become human? In Giambattista Vico's *New Science,* we might turn to a speculative but also, in its own paradoxical way, a more grounded understanding of the origins of home than we find in Heidegger's philosophy, one that may displace the insights of his ontology in a useful way.[33] Vico, rather than focusing only on the etymological roots of language—though he worked intensely as a philologist—read the history of the *gentes,* as he called the ancient civilizations that he studied (aside from the Hebrews, God's chosen people) through the ways they came to establish what he called their "primary institutions" of religion, marriage, and burial.

While commenting on Vico's *New Science,* Harrison notes the findings of contemporary cultural anthropologists and their essential agreement with the studies of ancient societies by classicists, who suggest that our first homes were homes for our dead, that when our distant ancestors lingered with the dead, when they first buried them and then stayed nearby to worship them, *Homo sapiens* became something more than a smart primate with opposable thumbs; *Homo sapiens* became human. We made our first connection of the past to the present, and the present to the future, when we realized that we must look back to our deceased forebears if we are to project a future for our descendants.

For Vico, to be human is to be of this earth. In this understanding, he anticipates Heidegger. To be mortal is to be rooted to the Earth, which for Heidegger is the great achievement of the human, our ability to die. "To die," Heidegger writes in "Building, Dwelling, Thinking," "means to be capable of death *as* death. Only man dies, and indeed continually, as long as he remains on the earth, under the sky, before the divinities" (352). Heidegger suggests that to the extent that mortals dwell, we are in the fourfold that is one, composed of earth, sky, divinities, and mortals. In fact, etymologically *home* and *haunt* share the same root. This haunting of the living by the dead is the way in which we humans first developed this difficult thing that is not a thing, the conscience. And without a conscience, can we be said to be human?

Vico's central thought is that the rise of human civilization followed a long trajectory through several stages, achieving in the end a specifically historical realization of a universal human nature. But he recognized that the realization of this universal human nature is a precarious achievement that unfolds in such a way as to lead us to cataclysmic decline, to an atavistic cycling into barbarism. This decline is not so much an historical inevitability as it is a tendency, a fall to be resisted in the ongoing attempt to retain our humanity. In other words, historical time is cyclical, composed of an ongoing struggle by humans to overcome our inarticulate ignorance, an ignorance that is always threatening to return. (It is as though Plato's cycle of governance described in *The Republic* were grafted onto a discourse on language.)

On the basis of his etymological and historical studies, Vico concluded that the rise of human nature follows a common pattern, based on similar migratory movements from forest to open land undergone by separate human tribes or nations. Only after similar though mutually isolated struggles of all the gentile nations to reach the point of the emergence of vulgate languages, after lengthy eras in which humans struggled to articulate meaning through the use of base symbols and then poetic expressions, could the outline of this common nature be seen by the scholar of the human. This is a fabricated humanity, a common nature built painstakingly, though not by foreknowledge, institution by institution, a made world, a made language.

Vico's fabulous history of the rise of the human is a story of inarticulate giants living in a post-Flood world, scattered through the forests of Earth, various groups of not-yet-humans, randomly copulating, brutal beasts who have no higher law than their own instinctual desires. The question becomes: How do such beings emerge from such a state of an absolute poverty of language and learn to speak?[34] Harrison gives us a rendering of the key passages of *The New Science* that bear upon this becoming.[35] For Vico, after the giants were scattered into the forests, a few of the most robust were in the higher mountains when, some centuries after the Flood, the Earth dried up enough to send liquid matter into the air, causing lightning to flash and thunder to burst for the first time since the Flood. The appearance of lightning and the sound of thunder caused

these giants to look up and become aware of the sky. Harrison cites
this passage:

> And because in such a case the nature of the human mind leads
> it to attribute its own nature to the effect, and because in that
> state their nature was that of men all robust bodily strength, who
> expressed their very violent passions by shouting and grum-
> bling, they pictured the sky to themselves as a great animated
> body, which in that aspect they called Jove, the first god of the
> so-called greater gentes, who meant to tell them something by
> the hiss of his bolts and clap of his thunder. (*New Science,* § 377)

Harrison explains:

> But what did the giants see when they raised their eyes? What
> does one see vertically or laterally in a dense forest? The mute
> closure of foliage. The boundless oblivion of the dormant
> mind. What, then, did the giants see when they raised their
> eyes? They saw nothing: a sudden illumination of nothing-
> ness. They heard the "hiss of his bolts of lightning and clap
> of his thunder," but precisely because they saw nothing, or at
> least nothing definite, they had to "picture the sky to them-
> selves" in the aspect of a huge animated body: a body not seen
> but imagined as there beyond the treetops. (*Forests,* 4)

For Vico this act marks the first humanizing event in prehistory, the
picturing of an image, the first human idea. As Harrison notes, "All
of nature turned uncanny for the giants, for they now believed 'that
Jove commanded by signs, that such signs were real words, and that
nature was the language of Jove' (*New Science,* §379). . . . The world
suddenly became meaningful. It became phenomenal. It became,
precisely, a world—and no longer a mere habitat" (*Forests,* 5). The
new importance of the sky rendered the forests an abomination to

these early humans, since their canopies obscured a view of the sky. Harrison tells us, "We find here in Vico's text a fabulous insight, for the abomination of forests in Western history derives above all from the fact that, since Greek and Roman times at least, we have been a civilization of sky-worshippers, children of a celestial father" (*Forests*, 6). The appeal to heaven, the desire to leave the earth so poignantly described by Arendt, so fervently hoped for by the members of Heaven's Gate and Mars One, for Vico has its precursor in the moment those giants looked to the sky for signs of Jove.

As with religion, so too with matrimony and burial. The first marriage, Vico speculated, must have occurred when thunder clapped in the moment when some of the giants were in the act of copulation, and they took it as a sign of Jove's command to eternalize that union. Such a permanence of union could not occur in the forest, which would disorient and lead back to random promiscuity, so clearing the forest and settling under the open sky became necessary. Burial followed. As Harrison explains, "Burial guaranteed the full appropriation of ground and its ultimate sacralization. Through burial of the dead the family defined the boundary of its place of belonging, rooting itself quite literally in the *humus*, where ancestral fathers lived underground" (*Forests*, 7).

For Vico, burial is so closely connected to the origins of language as to be interwoven with it. He writes:

LVIII

Mutes utter formless sounds by singing, and stammerers by singing teach their tongues to pronounce.

LIX

Men vent great passions by breaking into song, as we observe in the most grief-stricken and the most joyful.

> From Axioms LVIII–LIX it follows that the founders of the
> gentile nations, having wandered about in the wild state of
> dumb beasts and being therefore sluggish, were inexpressive
> save under the impulse of violent passions, and formed their
> first languages by singing. (*New Science,* ¶¶ 228–230)

In this speculative anthropology of language, our wordless ancestors, faced with the death of those they loved, would cry out, their
inarticulate howls and keening filling all with dread and sorrow. To
transduce the glossary of full-throated yelps and cries to the coherence of song, and then from song to sign, and *then* from sign to word,
marks the gradual transformation of giants into heroes, and heroes
into *gentes,* or gentiles. The time of the heroes is a time of the pri-
macy of myth, when the gods and heroes mingled.[36] Language thus
originates in the grief we feel for our dead and transforms grief into
remembrance through the worship of ancestors, the first religion
being a religion of the household.

Vico stands in strong contrast to Heidegger when it comes to assessing the human ability to understand the experience of death,
and what that understanding implies about our very humanity.
Perhaps the most serious difference between them concerns the
meaning of death: how we are to discern it, and what we are to learn
from it. For Heidegger our human condition is fundamentally premised on our self-consciousness concerning the singular character
of our individual prospective deaths. Death shapes the limits of the
human, makes the experience of our world that of a constant falling.
(Emerson once put it this way: "It is very unhappy, but too late to
be helped, the discovery we have made, that we exist. That discovery is called the Fall of Man.")[37] But for Vico, that we know we
will die is not the most important element of our self-knowledge.
How we relate to those who have died before us *is.* We constantly

need to acknowledge the ongoing presence of the dead among us, the living. We try to establish our institutions (religion, burial, marriage) in relation to the dead in such ways as to enable us to develop a memory, a record, a memorial—characters of language that speak for us, that become our human nature. Becoming human for Vico is the great accomplishment of the gentile nations and is embedded in all the civilizations of which he was aware.[38] Simply put, humans are the ones who learned to bury humans, and in mourning we continually establish our humanity.

In *The Ancient City*, Denis Foustel de Coulages painstakingly recreates that architecture in both ancient Greek and Roman households. He shows how the patterns of marriage and ancestor worship were intimately connected to the rituals of households, prayers, and burnt offerings of meals for the dead who were, in fact, contained in mausoleums within the house. The mausoleums recreated the rooms of the home, with special cooking facilities to prepare meals for the departed ancestors. If a family were to end the rituals of respect for their dead, they would, in a sense, be casting their dead out of their houses, forcing them to wander through the netherworld with no one to succor their hunger or slake their thirst. But they would be doing so at great risk to themselves, for two related reasons. First, those dead in their unhappy state of exile would curse the living. Second, when it came time for the new generation to die, they would have no one to accompany them in the land of the dead. They would, even if the chain of worship were restored for them, be alone in their wanderings in the afterlife.

These old ways are obscure to us in the modern age. They are not so much hidden from us as they are ignored. Not only our hearths, but our halls, and not only our halls, but our bedrooms, and parlors, and baths, our windows and doors, our garages even, contain secrets of our pasts, secrets readily given up to us if we were only to pay attention in the proper way, prepared to mourn, to pray. All of these rooms have evolved over centuries, and each culture has its own collection of spaces that more specifically tell those who live in them secret things about themselves, and their own ways of mourning and remembering.

Would it be an exaggeration to claim that every house is haunted? We might even say that there can be no home without the buried dead, a human in the humus, known to be there in the Earth, always remembered incompletely, but remembered nonetheless. All burials are incomplete, all memories flawed, and hence we are haunted.

Harrison suggests that the question, "What is a house?" may in fact be the most important philosophical question of our time. In *Dominion of the Dead,* he writes, in criticizing Heidegger, "It is not by thinking the essence of being more appropriately that we will come to know what a house is; if anything, it is by thinking the essence of a house that we will come to know what being is."[39] While he insists on the idea that we think (at least) about what a house is so that we may better understand how we are human, from the vantage of working through the ordinary ways we go about thinking about our houses as homes, I want to consider home in such a way that we may be able to carefully evaluate the ways of life that encourage or discourage us in becoming human. Another way of putting this is to ask two questions: not only What is a house? but also What makes a house a home? or When and where are we at home?

It may be that we have made such a mess of things that our houses are not our homes, that we are in fact, homeless within our houses, and that this hidden homelessness is at the root of much that is destructive of our humanity. The contemporary housing crisis in the United States would then be seen as an exemplar of the crisis of home as well, and we would need to inform our contemporary economists of the home economy they have neglected. Similarly, the contemporary refugee situation would be seen as a sign of our retreat away from being human.

There are dangers that lurk within the Vicean definition of the human, dangers Harrison sometimes tacitly, sometimes explicitly, acknowledges. The most prominent one is that, despite some caveats he makes regarding the alternative practices of others, he sets such a great store on the intimate connection between burial and home that, in a strange parallel to Heidegger, he may risk excluding from the human the nomadic, those peoples who do not bury their dead, who may not even linger over the remains of their dead, who may, in fact, abandon their dead most directly to the forces of nature and remember them in ways that are not nearly as grounded as he would want. If to be *Homo sapiens* is not yet to be human, if to be human is presented as an achievement, what of those of us who cannot yet or do not ever want to achieve this particular state of being human, according to Vico, according to Harrison, indeed, according to any one of us? The use of any or all of our intellectual criteria to determine who may or may not be human, without accounting for other elements of how we receive experience, especially if not exclusively, accounting for the powers of mutual recognition, the affective states that enable us to love and hate, to be delighted and disgusted, to feel the animal that we also are, and to feel other animals as well, may be a way of being human, but it is a dubious humanity that is achieved by exclusion.

In a sense we are constantly becoming human, doing so in response to other humans, the world we have built with each other, and the Earth we inhabit together. While there is a sorrow concerning the incompleteness of our humanity, there also is a comfort in understanding this fact—comfort, because it suggests that there may be another way open to us, an ongoing possibility of more to do. We who are homeless are always, it seems, seeking a way home, even as we have become more acutely aware than ever before of the futility of the search.

It would be good for humans to consider more thoughtfully our dead and their presence in our lives, to begin again to build our homes with their presence in mind and in this way to emphasize the ever-incomplete character of our humanity, for while there is a sorrow concerning the incompleteness of our humanity, there also is a comfort in our understanding this fact of life. There is comfort because the fact of our dead, their presence in our lives, suggests that there is always another way open, a return to the Earth that does not depend upon a departure.

Alternatively, or perhaps even complementarily, as we enter the era of the Anthropocene we may think of ourselves as returning to the Vicean forest. A new great barbarism may be unfolding that, as a part of its destructive force, could wipe out our memories of this latest cycle of human being, a (hopefully incomplete) forgetting of the empty time of the infinite. This would be a ruinous shift, but a shift that might enable other ways of scaling time to emerge, allow for a relaxation of the death grip that our fabricated human nature has had upon us, a disabling that is an enabling, as we slowly enter the shade of new trees, reimagined, in Deleuzian terms, not as the arboreal domination of the rhizome but as a shelter protecting us from the empty sky with its empty time.

Coda: Deserving Home

So where do we find ourselves? What may we learn from the ways that death infuses our experiences of home? What might we learn from how the mute presence of the dead shapes the future of our homes? From whom and from what can we learn? The materials are strewn on the ground, so to speak, in the common culture we keep, in those artifacts that constitute the popular distillation of some of our most profound and banal thoughts. As a preface, of sorts, to the stories of home contained in the following chapters, I want to explore two exemplary artifacts, two texts that may allow us to begin to meditate on death and its difficult relationship to home, to metaphorically, at least, bring us to the American experiences I wish to explore. Both of my examples are, (not) surprisingly, culled from American sources. (I say surprisingly because the common canard, one I have often shared, is that most Americans refuse to think about death if they can, that they try to avoid grieving when they can.[40] Of course, this is ironic, hence the use of a parenthetical "not," given the American proclivity to celebrate violent death in our popular culture.) These examples are taken from Robert Frost's poem "The Death of the Hired Hand" and Clint Eastwood's film *Unforgiven*.

Perhaps the least we can say is that home is a place we rest secure, where we know we will be able to rest. Even in this most restless epoch in human history, we need to rest (and eventually every one of us will, whether we want to or not).[41] To be able to rest we must find a resting place, whether it is final or not. In Frost's poem, the hired hand intuitively understands that "Home is the place where, when you have to go there, / They have to take you in."[42] The speaker of that sentence, the husband Warren, is said by Frost, the narrator of the poem, to be mocking gently. But perhaps that is because the effect of his mockery is modified by the rebuking response of his wife, Mary, that follows on the next lines: "I should have called it / Something you somehow haven't to deserve." These enigmatic lines seem to confirm the idea that home is a deathly abode. The idea that home is a place where you *have* to go, that is, that by necessity you *must* go, suggests that it is an inevitable ending place, a final place of being, the place of death itself.

For Warren, that they *have* to take you in suggests the same basic idea, the necessity of death being something we do not usually think of as such, but which may indeed allow us to understand that home is a place of intimate exchange: it concerns not only what the dead give to the living (what the living receive from the dead), but what the living give to the dead (what the dead receive from the living). Thinking about it in this Vicean way, home may be realized as the primary place where a political struggle and economic exchange between ancestors and descendants occur—and this struggle and exchange have everything to do with our ongoing attempts to live in such a way as to realize ourselves as humans. The conversation between husband and wife may in this sense be understood as an argument about what the proper law of death should be. One might even wonder about Frost: Why doesn't Warren simply say that home is a place that when you go there, they have to take you in, omitting the necessity of having to return ("when you *have* to go there" [my emphasis])? It may be that Frost is signaling to us. The necessity of returning home to die—*you must go there*—suggests that he realizes that the ultimate home is the grave, the ultimate community the graveyard, where we find, as in Mercurio's sad joke from *Romeo and Juliet,* grave men.

So why is Mary arguing with Warren? Something about the notion of not needing to deserve a home, but of others needing to provide one for you, seems to fly in the face of individual autonomy, or what we might call the right to be left alone. Perhaps this is why Mary's response to Warren serves to qualify what he has said, to rid this idea of home of its ironic tone. But her qualification is still mysterious. Home is something you somehow "haven't to deserve"? What does that mean? Does it mean you don't have a right to home?

Not exactly, but close. Imagine it as a question: Does one deserve a right? A right, in language Frost would surely recognize as being from the single most important document of American political history, is inalienable. A right is not deserts, not something somehow earned, but an endowment. Since Mary suggests that we don't need to deserve home, perhaps she is suggesting home is not a compensation for something we may have unjustly been denied, but is a simple human right, like life itself, Arendt's gift from nowhere, secularly speaking. The obligation of the host is absolute, as is the right of the hired hand to have a place called home where he may go to die. Or, put in gentler terms, the generosity of the host is reliable, unconditional. That may be Frost's point; home is so absolutely a part of our human being that to deny anyone a home is to deny that person's humanity.

In *Unforgiven,* the sense of deserving might be illustrated in such a way as to cast another, different light on Frost's understanding of what one deserves.[43] Much of the film revolves around questions of justice and just deserts. The lead character, William Munny, is a retired "bad man," formerly a vicious murderer and thief, now a widower, who through the love of the good woman who married him gave up his criminal way of life. But since the death of his wife he has fallen on hard times, and he is tempted to go on one last job as a hired assassin out of a need for money. To avenge the mutilation of a young prostitute by a cowboy, her fellow sex workers have put up a reward for killing the cowboy and his younger friend, another cowboy, who is mistakenly thought to have contributed to the atrocity. A young man, the self-named Schofield Kid (for the Smith & Wesson revolver he carries with him), having learned of Munny's past, enlists him to help in this assassination.

In the penultimate scene of the film, Munny is in the midst of a final and brutal confrontation with legal authorities in a saloon in the town of Big Whiskey, Wyoming. He has just killed almost all the men in the bar, who had gathered to form a posse to hunt him down. The town's sheriff, named Little Bill Daggett, who by letting the cowboys off with a fine in the first place helped set in motion the cycle of revenge, had earlier that day killed Munny's old friend Ned Logan, beating him to death in an attempt to find out who had shot the cowboys. Little Bill now lies on the floor of the bar, badly wounded. Even though he is flat on his back, Little Bill reaches for his gun in a final and futile attempt to shoot Munny. Munny stops him, pinning Bill's arm to the floor with his foot. He then aims his rifle at Bill's face. Bill says, "I don't deserve this . . . to die like this. I was building a house." Munny responds, "Deserve's got nothing to do with it." Bill responds in turn by saying, "I'll see you in hell, William Munny." Munny agrees, and fires his gun, killing Little Bill.

Little Bill believed he didn't deserve to die by being shot to death on the floor of a saloon. By implication, he seems to think he should be allowed to die in the house he is building, a house that does not yet seem to be a home. Earlier in the film, Little Bill waxes poetic about sitting on his porch in the evening with his coffee, watching the sunset over the mountains, once the house is completed. One of the many telling asides in the film shows him to be a terrible carpenter, building a house with a leaking roof, crooked windows, and doors that won't shut. In other words, as much as he may want to do so, he is not capable of making a home for himself, even as he is capable of imagining what it might be to have one.

But if we reflect on Munny's retort, it would seem that he is saying that dying and its circumstances aren't matters of deserts at all. In an earlier scene, the Schofield Kid has just killed one of the cowboys. Despite his earlier lying and bragging about his qualities as a killer, the Kid is rattled by the experience, in truth having never killed anyone before. In an attempt at self-justification he says,

"I guess he had it coming." Munny responds, "We all have it coming, kid." In other words, we all will die. It is only a matter of the circumstance of our deaths that will distinguish us in the end.

Nietzsche once claimed that it is important to know how to die at the right time. Avoiding an untimely death, not death itself, is the best we can hope for, and then it is only a hope. Perhaps that is the lesson of this film. Perhaps even more than this, Munny may be saying that there is no escaping death, that death is coming to all of us. But why do we need to be reminded of this?

Is this understanding of not deserving to die akin to Frost's sense of not having to deserve a home? It would seem not, at first glance. We all will die eventually, and Little Bill seems only to be complaining about Munny killing him. But there is a way in which the two are nonetheless connected. We might imagine home to lie on the side of the metaphoric line where the unbidden gift is found, and not the side of the line where we find just deserts. It is a place we go to die, or at least our final resting place after we die. This is what is meant by the "long home," the grave, our odyssey back to Earth, from dust to dust. When we have to go there, they have to take us in. Going home is the end, the death of the hired hand, the one who dies with those who take him in. It is not his brother to whom the hired hand goes to die—it is to those kind people who know who he is and who he has been, and who will in the end acknowledge his death and remember him, at least for as long as he will be remembered by anyone. Similarly, in disavowing the idea that deserts have anything to do with dying, Munny is reminding him that regardless of what Little Bill thinks, death is death, and Little Bill does not get to dictate when he will die.

In this sense, the politics of home seems somehow to be beyond justice, or at least beyond our understanding of what justice is, and hence what political life is, an absolute zero from which we begin and end our lives. But that cannot be so. Home as refuge from the struggles of justice is not immune to those struggles, regardless of whether it is deserved or not. In fact, the right to home, the unalienable right to home, is perhaps the cardinal right of all rights, underlying those of life, liberty, and the pursuit of happiness, grounding the human so that we may explore how to realize these other rights. If such struggles do not concern what is just, then what does?

In the penultimate chapter of his massive study of the history of Western attitudes toward death, Philippe Ariès notes that the twentieth century marked a dramatic shift in the way in which people treated the deaths of family and community members, in regard to both dying and mourning.[44] We began to make death invisible, confining the ill to hospitals, becoming more embarrassed by the smells and sounds associated with the dying. The rise of a funeral industry in the United States further removed the dead from the rest of us, and the rise in cremation as well signaled a move toward simply making the bodies of the dead disappear. We eventually reached the point where mourning itself came into question, at least as a public ritual. It may be that making death invisible is a symptom of our larger homelessness, our loss of understanding of home as being beyond desert. Perhaps it is the case that in our desire to live we have forgotten how to die. Perhaps this is what we do not know and need to learn: that we have to go home, not only to live but also to die.

If it is the case that we have become homeless, it may be because we have lost our connection to the dead. We may be like a hired hand who does not know where to go to die. If that is so, we could be facing a terrible situation in which we would be seeking a home that is nowhere, a haven from our terrible losses, a haven that does not exist. But our homes do exist, not as utopian spaces or final resting places but as real sites, containing multitudinous elements of an on-going struggle for a more (or less) moral economy. It is in seeking out a home that we also seek an ethos that would support us in our searches for better ways of being human.

If we reach for an answer to the question concerning our suppression of our knowledge of the dead, then perhaps we may be able to recognize our dread of death, and then perhaps as well we may come to be better reconciled with our dead. And this recognition may lead to other recognitions as well. At the deepest level, we may be faced with the task of rethinking large elements of our humanity as we attempt to re-forge our attenuated relationships with our dead. Reflecting on these matters may help us see how our desires for a home shadow and sometimes overshadow other modes of understanding the world, and how at the intersection of our private home with the more public elements of our existence we can see better how each side reflects and informs the other. The quest for home—whether it be in returning home, leaving home, building a home, discovering home—plays the most important role in shaping our deepest yearnings, and how we make our homes determines our varying ability to see where our yearnings lead us.

In the United States of America, as elsewhere, the unsettled character of what it means to be at home has had consequences for our self-understanding as a culture. But it seems as though our culture is a bit more impoverished than some others in this regard. In *The Liberal Tradition in America,* his 1955 study of the history of American political thought, Louis Hartz infamously argued that Americans have never gone through the terrifically painful changes that our European counterparts did. Having escaped a feudal past, he suggested, we also avoided a socialist future. But the cost, he noticed, was that as a culture we have been in a state of arrested development for centuries now; we have developed a monoculture of

politics in which the strivings of left and right are not as important
to us as embracing those who seem best able to pretend to embody
the American way of life.[45] Hartz has justly been criticized for his too
simplistic reading of the Anglo-American encounter with the natives
of this continent, for his marginalization of the slave-owning South
in American political development, and for his reduction of a complex and contradictory history of capitalism and liberalism into a
monoculture of "the American way of life."

But the mythology of the country fits his thesis, even as he contributed to the myth of American exceptionalism. In the polarized
polity of the early twenty-first century, we can see Hartz's thesis illustrated in how debates in politics devolve into demonological arguments about who is more American, who is protecting the American way of life, and who is undermining it. We may acknowledge
that the language of those who say they are seeking to "take our
country back" is a language of fear and ignorance. But there is also
a language of ignorance on display by those who think they know
better, and who would dismiss the power of fear and ignorance and
underestimate the affective power of the intuited loss of home suggested by such rhetoric. It may well be a consequence of our inse-
curities about being at home that current political issues in the
United States revolve around who belongs here, what it means to
protect the homeland and our homes, at a time when Americans
have been losing their homes at historically high rates by fire, flood,
and bankruptcy.

Still, there are voices and countervoices to be found in the history of the American home, however muffled they may be, however
ghostly they are to us. These ghosts haunt me, and I hope to make
them haunt you: they are speaking, whispering, and singing to us.
Sometimes they are on the margins, and because of that marginality,
they are hard to hear. Sometimes they are buried within the larger

culture as minor notes in a louder major key. When thinking about any or all of these voices, whether from the antebellum South or Transcendental New England, the domestic arenas of the western frontier of the 1870s or the interiors of other New England homes smothered in domestic melodrama over roughly the same period, or even in the claustrophobic confines of a Louisiana prison cell inhabited by a solitary dreamer, in each and every place we try to listen, we should strain to hear something else, about another way of being at home.

TWO

Thomas Jefferson's Monticello

I allow nothing for losses by death . . .

—THOMAS JEFFERSON

Republican Patriarch

Its image is engraved on the US five-cent piece—a faux Greek garden temple topped with a Palladian dome. Balance, grace, proportionality, simplicity masking complexity: it has been long considered the epitome of American Enlightenment architecture, if not in its design then in its architect's imagination. It is in any case a building unique in its departure from the standards of its time and place. So important is Monticello as a historical artifact that it is the only American home designated a UNESCO World Heritage Site, though this inclusion may be a testament to the man who built it as much as to the house itself.[1] It certainly is the most famous and probably the most thoroughly documented home in the history of the United States. And it is among the most visited of all American homes (though Elvis Presley's Graceland seems to win that contest).

People come from around the world to peek into the private spaces of its original owner, to see his library, to look at the clever devices he invented, to see the organization of the space, to think about the separation of his public and private personas, to imagine him living in these rooms.

The Palladian dome is the signature feature of the mansion. And yet there has remained something of a mystery about that dome for most of the history of Monticello. It seems to have had no serious function, but it is too prominent a feature of the house to be merely decorative. One can only reach the large room under the dome via a very narrow staircase. The architect was known for his hatred of staircases, as they disrupted his sense of space and its symmetrical distribution. The room under the dome was not really designed to be lived in. So what was it for?

The grounds surrounding the house—the gardens, the housing for the slaves, the nearby fields—have only in recent years become an important object of interest to those who have preserved this home. The effacement of slavery from the representation of Monticello was perhaps the most important whitewashing in the earlier history of its curation, as earlier generations of Jefferson apologists tried to ignore the central role that slaves played in the life of the plantation, trying to keep that biggest secret which is not, but is, a secret. (Monticello is a place of many secrets.) But things are different now. The most recent keepers of Monticello for the Thomas Jefferson Foundation have made up for this shameful history, now giving the role of slaves in the history of Monticello something closer to the place it deserves.[2]

The beauty of the contemporary version of the mansion allows visitors to forget that the site was almost continuously under construction from 1771 until the time of its owner's death in 1826 (though the bulk of the work was completed by the time of Jefferson's retirement from

public service in 1809). For Jefferson, Monticello was always at
least as much a theory to be explored as a house to be realized.
This sense of incompletion, the idea that the house itself was an
experiment, may be thought of as a suitable reflection of the man
who was the master of the house: it was always being impro-
vised, always being rethought. Yet the house's secrets also reflect a hidden history of a particular kind of American home: the
secret of Jefferson's second, slave family, the hidden (mis)man-
agement of his enormous debt, and yet one other obscurity concerning a feature of the system of supervision that made Monticello a peculiarly modern institution, as much a factory as a
farm. Did these secrets make Jefferson's home an anomaly or an
exemplar? All homes hold secrets, but the secrets of Monticello
were to have an inordinate impact by example, symbolically and
practically, on the course of the private histories of countless
American homes.

Perhaps it is the extraordinary public role of Monticello in combination with this hidden history that makes its study so compelling. As Maira Kalman has noted, "If you want to understand this
country and its people and what it means to be optimistic and complex and tragic and wrong and courageous, you need to go to Monticello."[3] From Kalman's perspective Monticello may be thought of
as a site of primal American contradictions, contained within one
personality. Jefferson was an Enlightenment intellectual who embraced a reactionary patriarchialism; a politician and statesman
who advanced the cause of liberty but enslaved others; a householder
who could minutely calculate and measure and record the details
of his home economy, but who could never balance his books,
leaving behind a crushing debt passed on to his various children.
In short, he was both an exceptional individual and a representative man of the early republic.

Jefferson held his secrets close, and his manner of holding them was to provide a crucially important rationale for a terrible shift in the trajectory of slavery, an unexpected intensification of slavery as an economic force. By the early 1790s, Jefferson was beginning to put in place a business model for his plantation that would allow for the architectural development of the Monticello we now know. But his business model relied completely on the continued expansion of the number of slaves he owned. It also depended on his ability to take on much more debt than he had previously carried so that he could rebuild his home in accord with his desires. All of this was occurring at a time, as Henry Wiencek puts it, of "a transitional moment in American history. Like many other planters, in the South, Jefferson was trying to devise a 'rational and humane' plan not to end slavery but to reshape it and bring it into the new republic as an acceptable, indeed respectable component of the economy and society. This is what slave-holders called 'amelioration.'"[4]

Jefferson was both a moralist of freedom and a practitioner of the most total form of slavery—chattel slavery, which he was to rationalize by embracing his own hybrid ideology of republican patriarchy. Some have long accepted the contradictions in Jefferson's life as simply an inevitability of American history. He was, as they say, a man of his times. But that characterization isn't quite right. Jefferson held his slaves at a time when the question of the morality of chattel slavery was being widely debated, and when many others were active in attempting to end it. So it is too easy to reach "realistic" conclusions concerning what people chose to do or not do during the course of their lives. To suggest that there is a volition, a will, behind acts is not so much a judgment inflecting the memory of those who have passed into history as it is a warning to the living that our lives as well are subject to judgment, that how we live will be subject to future evaluation by our descendants, much the same as our evaluation of our ancestors. Put another way, in probing Jefferson's way of being at home, we are providing grounds for how we may come to judge ourselves in our own homes.

Monticello was the source of Jefferson's fortune as well as his misfortune. He was completely dependent on the slaves whose labor he exploited. But even as we must evaluate him on his own terms, it is too easy to simply point a finger only at him, and others seemingly like him, because in truth the reach of chattel slavery extended far beyond the plantations of the American South. Recent works by American historians demonstrate without a doubt that chattel slavery was deeply tied to the development of industrial capitalism throughout the New World and, as it turns out, was crucial to the emergence of the northern United States as a major economic power.[5] In that sense, it was not simply a way of life, an anachronism destined to fade away, but an economic force that had to be forcibly ended, and that, despite the victory of the United States against the secessionists in the Civil War, has persisted in other forms well through the twentieth century and into the twenty-first.[6]

The eminent historians / biographers Annette Gordon-Reed and Peter S. Onuf have directly addressed the complexity of Jefferson's accommodations to slavery, presenting a nuanced explanation for Jefferson's contradictions, especially exploring this idea of patriarchal republicanism. To do so they develop a complex model of persona that they borrow from the Portuguese poet Fernando Pessoa. They cite him thusly: "Each of us is several, is many, is a profusion of selves. So that the self who distains his surroundings is not the same self who suffers or takes joy in them. In the vast colony of our being there are many species of people who think and feel in different ways." And, more obviously, they cite Walt Whitman: "Do I contradict myself? Very well, then . . . I contradict myself; I am large . . . I contain multitudes."[7] They argue that Jefferson played so many roles in his long life, and played them all so well, that it is an extremely difficult task to probe his thinking.

But Gordon-Reed and Onuf also note something else that goes some distance, if not to resolving the contradictions in Jefferson's psyche, then toward raising the contradictions to a higher level. They refer to him as a "republican patriarch." In their broad understanding, Jefferson thought that what he and the other participants in the American Revolution were attempting to create was a society in which there would be the establishment of an orderly freedom. Everything, from his generational understanding of sovereignty, to the idea of the creation of "ward" republics, the decentralization of power to the states, and the very notion of the yeoman farmer, fed into his sense that patriarchs at home would participate in the affairs of politics. Such a vision of politics feels strangely indebted to ancient Greece, with slavery being an underpinning of the *oikos*—the home economy—as well as the patriarchal republic. Yet this comparison is not quite right, as the ancient institution of slavery was not advanced through doctrines of racial inferiority that rationalized slaveholders' ownership claims to the progeny of their slaves as it was in colonial and postcolonial America.

What does the characterization of Jefferson as a republican patriarch mean for the vision of home that he pursued at Monticello? As patriarch, he had the power of command over all of those who labored for him, both his children by Sally Hemings and the other slaves, and his own legal children, but with the attendant responsibility that also fell upon the father of the plantation. Indeed, Gordon-Reed and Onuf suggest that Jefferson may have thought of *himself*, and not Washington, as being the real father of the country, and believed that the country only became completely realized with the revolution of 1800, which for him fulfilled the promise of 1776, the triumph of a nation of small farmers, artisans, and workers (with slavery in parentheses).[8] As patriarch, he understood his obligation to his slaves to include benign treatment, opportunities for development of skills, and even the possibility of manumission. But all these obligations of the patriarch were defined by the patriarch himself. In other words, it is important to remember that while Jefferson understood himself to be the benign father to his various children, he never ceased to be the master of his house.

And the *republican* aspect? An important dimension of republicanism is the role of dominion and its attendant limits in the range of political authority that the polity can assert. For Jefferson, republican virtue rested on an agrarian base. Ensuring the power of the polity was its uncorrupt character. He famously argued in *Notes on the State of Virginia,* "Corruption of morals in the mass of cultivators is a phenomenon of which no age nor nation has furnished an example. It is the mark set on those who, not looking up to heaven, to their own soil and industry, as does the husbandman, for their substance, depend for it on the casualties and caprices of customers."[9] This stark contrast between the commercial and the agricultural was for Jefferson the key note of the struggle to maintain a republican polity. The virtuous husbandman was always to be in conflict with the commercial interest. Jefferson versus Hamilton was the most famous expression of this conflict. But importantly, it put the institution of slavery itself on the side of republican virtue. No demos here, so much as the power of dominion.

The obligations of the patriarch pressed upon Jefferson not only because of the burden of responsibility he bore but because the substance of those obligations served as a constant reminder that slavery at bottom was in deep conflict with his imagined family values. Hence, it is not surprising that Jefferson had a fraught relationship with those whom he enslaved, especially those who constituted his secret family. (As we will also see, not surprisingly, his relationships with his acknowledged daughters were also complex and difficult.)

The first biography of Jefferson that attempted to address this complexity in full was Fawn Brodie's *Thomas Jefferson: An Intimate History*.[10] Brodie was to anticipate much of the later research that demonstrated conclusively a sexual relationship between Jefferson and Sally Hemings, taking their relationship as a fact and not a myth. Her book traces the enormous sense of guilt that Jefferson felt regarding his continued ownership of slaves, as well as his despair over his debt, and more generally attempts to balance his undoubtedly humane instincts with his pattern of decisions that persistently failed to be humane. More recent histories concerning the Hemings-Jefferson family, starting from Brodie's psychoanalytically oriented study, have come to make the truth of Jefferson's relationship with Hemings the conventional wisdom, even as that truth remains a source of consternation to many of Jefferson's more hagiographic students (and some of Jefferson's white descendants).[11] (It remains difficult to assess that truth in another way: while it is undoubtedly the case that Thomas and Sally had a sexual relationship, it is less clear what the more general character of that relationship was, which is to say, how he felt about her and how she felt about him.)

I am less interested in the specific details of Jefferson's treatment of the members of his secret family—treatment that varied from child to child—than I am in his understanding of the patriarchal form of love that shaped it. To clarify, as important as the treatment of the Hemingses by Jefferson was, as well as his treatment of the many others he enslaved, and the redounding legacy on the succeeding generations of the enslaved, their eventual emancipation, subsequent peonage, and second-class citizenship goes through a trajectory that is better explored (for my purposes) in a later chapter.[12] Here my focus is on Jefferson's understanding of love. My sense is that in trying to understand Jefferson's concept of love, we may gain some larger comprehension of his understanding of what being at home may be.

Two other secrets of Monticello concern Jefferson's struggles with the problem of debt, and the financial innovations he made in the everyday management of the plantation that maximized the efficient use of slaves. These are important to understanding Jefferson's sense of home, if only because the ordinary life of Monticello beyond Jefferson's immediate family was so deeply shaped by the reality of his debt and the stringencies of economy that followed in his perpetual effort to overcome it. The innovations he made and the debt he took on were closely related to each other, in that through innovations, some of them derived from surprising places, he hoped to manage his debt. (It was almost as though he presaged the American cultural trope of the gadget maker, thinking that one new innovation would make his fortune.) The form that debt took for Jefferson further cemented his identity as a slaveholder. In this, he was in some ways typical of plantation owners in Virginia during this era, but in other ways, as in all things Jeffersonian, he was anything but. The management of Monticello, dependent as it was on the most advanced, scientific forms of organization, anticipated much of what was to shape new rationalizations for the continuation of slavery that emerged in the period between the decline of tobacco and the rise of cotton.

In short, by exploring these elements of Jefferson's home life, I will be addressing important aspects of what Michel Foucault once called "the history of the present."[13] That is to say, we may be able to see traces of Jeffersonian patriarchal republicanism in the habits of subsequent generations of home makers. And we may be able to perceive, if only faintly, a residue of that difficult heritage as it is mixed into the foundation of our present.

Love

Jefferson experienced the loss of his beloved wife, who died at the relatively young age of thirty-four in 1782 after giving birth to the last of their six children. Only two of those six children survived past infancy, his daughters Martha and Mary (and Mary was to predecease him in 1804). Jefferson never remarried, though he was to father other children with Sally Hemings. His position as father was not unusual for the times, though he was unusual in the resources he was able to bring to bear in raising his daughters and in the theories of education he was to apply to them.

There are at least two letters he wrote in the years immediately after his wife's death, during his sojourn to France, that express his understanding of love: his famous "dialogue between heart and head," written to Maria Cosway from Paris in 1786, and a less famous letter to his older daughter, Martha (Patsy), who was staying in Philadelphia, written from Annapolis as he was preparing to leave for Paris in 1783 to take his position as a member of the American legation.

Jefferson's letter to Patsy was written when she was eleven years old, immediately after he left her in the care of a Mrs. Hopkinson in Philadelphia before leaving for Paris to assume his diplomatic duties. One striking element of the letter is that he suggested that Patsy consider treating Mrs. Hopkinson as if she were her mother. Martha Jefferson had died only the previous year, but Jefferson didn't seem to consider what he was asking of his motherless child. In fact, the entire letter seems tone-deaf in this regard. In it, he provided detailed instructions to Patsy concerning her daily schedule. Subject to her teacher's approval, she was to devote herself to music, dance, drawing, French language, and writing, on a set schedule, from eight in the morning until she retired in the evening. He exhorted her to do everything to please her host, and never to do anything to alienate this substitute mother's affection. He concluded his letter with the following formulation of parental love:

> I have placed my happiness on seeing you good and accomplished, and no distress which this world can now bring on me could equal that of your disappointing my hopes. If you love me then, strive to be good under every situation and to all living creatures, and to acquire those accomplishments which I have put in your power, and which will go far towards ensuring you the warmest love of your affectionate father,
> Th: Jefferson
> P.S. keep my letters and read them at times that you may always have present in your mind those things which will endear you to me.[14]

For Jefferson, it was of greatest importance that his daughter realize that the love of her father was provisional. If she loved him, she must strive to earn his love in return, which would be demonstrated by her accomplishments. He had provided her with the means to do so, and it was up to her to employ those means. He underlined the point, writing, "I have put in your power." He insisted that he must be a continuous presence in her mind; she must behave as though he were there with her. Or, more accurately, she must keep in mind "those things" that would endear her to him, her accomplishments, her good behavior. This was his way of exercising his patriarchal power. Love is the reward for accomplishment, and withholding love the punishment for failure. (We will see that such a utilitarian system of rewards and punishments, coupled with a technique for continuously being present in the mind of the subjects of these sanctions, is what also shaped his direction of the slaves of Monticello.)

That Jefferson could write such a letter to his beloved daughter—an eleven-year-old child who had lost her mother only the year before—might seem cruel.[15] But within the formal conventions of the time governing the relationships of fathers and children in his class, such a distance may not necessarily have been considered unusual.[16] What perhaps was more exceptional was the explicit calculus of affection he presented to her. And it is here that we run into a serious problem while trying to understand what Jefferson desired, what the objects of his love may have been, because Jefferson engaged in such calculations across every aspect of his life.

This calculus followed his romantic dalliances in the wake of the death of his wife, as expressed most fulsomely in his letter to Maria Cosway in October 1786, written while he was in Paris.[17] Joseph Ellis suggests that it is the most self-revealing document Jefferson ever penned.[18] Jefferson had met Cosway in August of that year. She was the twenty-seven-year-old wife of the portraitist Richard Cosway and an artist in her own right. In Ellis's words, "Within days Jefferson was head over heels in love."[19] For six weeks they were constantly in each other's company. The idyll came to an abrupt end on September 18, 1786. Cosway left for England with her husband on that day while Jefferson was recovering from an injury to his wrist that he had suffered from a fall off a horse. Although Jefferson rallied enough to see the couple off from Paris, he and Maria never saw each other alone again after that farewell.

In his letter to Maria, Jefferson explained his internal struggle. He began by describing how he felt upon her departure. Besides suffering from pain caused by a botched surgery on his wrist, he was depressed and suffering psychically. As he wrote, "I turned on my heel and walked, more dead than alive, to the opposite door, where my own [carriage] was awaiting me" (400). Upon his return to his Paris home, he wrote, "Seated by my fire side, solitary and sad, the following dialogue took place between my Head and my Heart."

The point of the dialogue seems to have been for Jefferson to explain to Cosway what informed his judgments regarding all of the important, and some not so important, events in his life. His examples included giving a person a ride in his carriage, giving money to a woman who may or may not have been a drunkard, and, momentously, joining in the American Revolution. (That his examples culminate in that particular decision makes this explanation particularly significant.) In each example the head advised against. But, consistently, when Jefferson followed his heart, the end result was better than it would have been had he followed his head instead. He suggested that the head should be the source of final judgment only in matters of science, but that the heart should be the source of final judgment in the realm of morals. In the voice of the Heart he wrote to the Head:

> When nature assigned us the same habitation, she gave us over it a divided empire. To you she allotted the field of science, to me that of morals. When the circle is to be squared, or the orbit of a comet to be traced; when the arch of the greatest strength, or the solid of least resistance is to be investigated, take you the problem: it is yours: nature has given me no cognizance of it. In like manner in denying to you the feelings of sympathy, of benevolence, of gratitude, of justice, of love, of friendship, she has excluded you from their controul [sic]. To these she has adapted the mechanism of the heart. Morals were too essential to the happiness of man to be risked on the uncertain combinations of the head. She laid their foundation therefore in sentiment, not in science. (408–409)

This division split Jefferson down the middle: the emotional Jefferson would rule over matters of morals, the rational Jefferson over matters of science. But for Jefferson, determining the boundary between the two domains was to prove problematic. And here we get a glimpse of a frightening aspect of his personality. Were we to imagine that he is in the end a rationalist more than a sentimentalist, then the list of emotions from which he has excluded his rational self—sympathy, benevolence, gratitude, justice, love, friendship— is absolute. But it is the exercise itself that is the root of the problem. We might ask, are there any matters that are not subject to Jefferson's rational calculus? By making rational procedures determine what is and is not rational, a hierarchy of reason over emotion is already established. In making the division between reason and emotion so clear and so absolute in their inclusions and exclusions, it is as though he were describing the inner dialogue of a person who could be suffering from what once was called a split personality and is now known as dissociative personality disorder. On the rational side, a will to dominate over nature prevails. On the sentimental side, a despair over the continued loss of loved objects leads to the contemplation of death. Suppressing this conflict by ruling in favor of the rational over the emotional becomes essential to holding on to a coherent sense of self.

In this sense, the very fact that Jefferson wrote this letter is evidence of this suppression. Ellis provides insight into this moment, and into Jefferson's relationship with Cosway more generally, when he writes:

> So at one level the heart is the unequivocal winner of the debate. Despite the agony he felt at Cosway's departure, the ecstasy of their time together was worth the pain. But at another level it is Jefferson's head that is orchestrating the arguments

and words of the dialogue. The act of crafting the letter allowed him to recover control over the powerful emotions that
the relationship with Cosway had released. . . . In the long run
the head prevails.[20]

The Jefferson of historical fame is not the passionate lover described
in his letter to Cosway. He is instead the Enlightenment figure, the
natural scientist, the political theorist, the intellectual par excellence. We are presented with a relatively cold, calculating, self-
centered, and instrumental individual, a person deeply concerned
with appearance, someone whose desires have been suppressed or
driven into secret channels. This Jefferson is presented as a utilitarian of the worst sort. To the extent that he loved, he loved himself above all. Those he loved were to be but extensions of his self.
If there is a consistency in his life, it may be found in the continued
cultivation of this self, a continued rationalizing of his own behavior,
and the continued bearing of a deeply held private guilt, one he held
while nevertheless doing nothing to ameliorate its deepest causes.
(Thus, the brilliance of Ellis's title, *American Sphinx*. Jefferson is a
mystery of motive because he is unable to acknowledge his motives
to himself.)

In this sense, Jefferson's creation of a second and secret family
fits well with the pattern of control he wished to establish. If, as Ellis
suggests, it is the case that he "preferred to meet his lovers in the
rarified region of his mind rather than the physical world of his bed-
chamber,"[21] the separation of head from heart that characterized
his infatuations with the white women of his class status didn't follow
through to his relationship with Sally Hemings. Here it is secrecy
rather than repression that is at work.

Gordon-Reed suggests that Jefferson followed a different path in
his long relationship with Hemings. Observing that in his *Notes on*

the State of Virginia Jefferson infamously characterized blacks as being intellectually inferior to whites, lacking the same capacity for reason, she writes:

> In the passages in *Notes* in which he casts doubt on blacks' equal intellectual capacity, Jefferson expressed his greatest confidence in blacks, besides his opinion that they had better rhythm than whites in matters of the heart, stating with great certainty that nature had done them "justice" in that department. These formulations about people of African origin— skepticism of their equal intellectual capacity and certainty about the quality of their hearts—were ideas from which he apparently never wavered. . . . Sally Hemings, then, combined what Jefferson regarded as the best in white people with what he regarded as the best in black people, an evidently appealing blend of the head and the heart.[22]

In other words, for Jefferson there would have been no need to engage in any dialogue between his reasoning and his sentimental selves while in the presence of Sally. The relaxing of this fundamental tension would be an enormous relief, providing him with a secret realm of true comfort, a real home. But it would be gained with the cost being borne not by him but by his hidden family who were simultaneously his slaves.

Taken together, Jefferson's relations with Patsy Jefferson, Maria Cosway, and Sally Hemings present us with a man whose understanding of love shifted according to his rational calculation of his needs and desires and how he might best satisfy them. His daughter must earn his love by her accomplishments and appearance; she must not shame him. Cosway could only be imagined as an impossible love, placed safely in the rarefied regions of his mind. Sally Hemings (who, not irrelevantly, was the half sister of his departed

wife) would seem to be the truest love of his life after Martha, involved in a relationship of love, but one that was paradoxical, in that
it could only be sustained because he owned his beloved. In that, it
was but one expression of the more general paradox that was his life,
which could ultimately be thought of as that of living in freedom by
way of the institution of slavery. At Jefferson's death, although several of the children he had with Sally were freed in his will, Sally
was not; in fact, she was never mentioned in his will at all.[23]

Debt

If the head ruled over the heart in Jefferson's calculations concerning
love, what happened when love had nothing to do with it? Consider
the following two sentences, both penned by Jefferson. The first,
I think it is safe to say, is one of the most famous, if not most lustrous,
sentences ever penned in the history of humankind, written and
published in 1776: "We hold these truths to be self-evident, that all
men are created equal, that they are endowed by their Creator with
certain unalienable rights, that among these are Life, Liberty, and
the pursuit of Happiness." The second is obscure and private, a
scribbled note, contained within brackets, on the middle of a page
of a letter sent by Jefferson to a fellow plantation owner in 1792:
"I allow nothing for losses by death, but, on the contrary, shall
presently take credit four per cent per annum, for their increase over
and above keeping up their own numbers."[24]

Enormous celebration has attended the first of these two sentences, which has been widely praised as the opening passage of
the most eloquent and passionate statement in favor of freedom
and equality ever written. Indeed, Jefferson's fame rests more
upon his participation in authoring the Declaration of Indepen-

dence than it does on any other single accomplishment. When he penned his own epitaph, he wrote of his authorship of the Declaration and his role as founder of the University of Virginia as his key accomplishments, not even mentioning his eight years as president of the United States.

That second sentence was inserted as a gloss on a comment made in a third party's letter, which Jefferson sent to that aforementioned fellow plantation owner, who happened to be George Washington. In this marginalia, Jefferson was referring to the percentage of profit he could make simply on the basis of the ever-growing number of slaves he owned. His discovery of this increase over and above what would be needed to sustain their numbers was a timely one, because during this period he was renewing his efforts to figure out how to make his plantation economically viable. Bluntly put, he was constantly hemorrhaging money. The credit he was to leverage by dint of this 4 percent was to be crucial in financing his ongoing expansion of Monticello.

The second sentence could be thought of as a trace residue from a drop of water in a particularly powerful subterranean stream of American economic history. That is the mighty stream of chattel slavery, the labor force so crucial to the economic formation of the United States: chattel slavery, which is also what might be called the secular original sin of this country. To follow the course of that underground stream as it flowed through the Jefferson household is to revisit one of the two original American horror stories, here appearing in the form of the haunting of one of the most famous homes in this country's history. But even to call slavery a horror story is dangerous, in that it risks us pushing away from an American history that we really need to pull closer to us so as to account more fully for the debts America fails to acknowledge, the mortgage we have failed to pay.

Henry Wiencek suggests that Jefferson's discovery of the amount of profit to be derived from the simple breeding of slaves had the force of revelation for him:

> As Jefferson was counting up the agricultural profits and losses of his plantation in a letter to President Washington in 1792, it occurred to him that there was a phenomenon he had perceived at Monticello but had never actually measured. . . . What Jefferson set out so clearly was that he was making a profit of four percent every year on the increasing number of slaves he held as a consequence of the birth of children. These enslaved people were yielding him a bonanza, a perpetual human dividend at compound interest.[25]

Wiencek goes on to suggest that Jefferson's calculation of profit coincided with the decline of his emancipatory fervor, that "Jefferson began to back away from antislavery just around the time he computed the silent profit of the 'peculiar institution.'"[26]

By establishing this 4 percent per annum formula, Jefferson found the solution to the chronic problems associated with the ongoing indebtedness he shouldered as a plantation master. The problem of debt management plagued many plantation owners during the transitional era between the end of the colonial period and the establishment of the Constitution, as the sources of capital for investment were not easily to be found given the precarious state of the new nation's finances. For Jefferson the problem of managing debt was compounded by his constant struggles to balance his intellectual pursuits with his political ambition and his acquisitive desires—for a luxurious lifestyle, for a home worthy of his self-image as the republican patriarch of his fellow countrymen, and for the protection of perhaps the most sustaining relationship of his adult life, his secret affair with Sally Hemings. The dynamic of these internal contradictions was made even more difficult by Jefferson's role as the most prominent public advocate of his generation for the ideal of liberal freedom, a master of slaves who decried the tyranny of England by deftly employing the accusatory rhetoric of enslavement.

Jefferson was a plantation owner during a period of radical transition: tobacco was on its way out as a cash crop, and cotton had yet to come in. Some imagined (or hoped) that with the decline of tobacco, slavery would also decrease in importance. But slavery was to be rejuvenated in American economic development because of the rise of King Cotton, which happened largely after Jefferson's death and the loss of his estate. As with his fellow Virginia planters, the exhaustion of the land through the cultivation of tobacco led Jefferson to a transitional crop, wheat, which did serve to resurrect his fortunes, but only for a time.

At his death Jefferson was a bit more than $100,000 in debt, which in current numbers would be slightly over $2 million (though direct comparisons can be misleading; the relative scarcity of capital during this earlier era exaggerated the amount of debt as a practical matter).[27] But debt had been at the heart of Jefferson's experience as a plantation owner from the time he became the master at Monticello. And in the years of his absence, during the Revolutionary War and his various tenures in the Washington administration and as vice president under John Adams (though he spent far more time at home during that presidential administration), he anticipated making major changes in the organization and business of his plantation, with the idea of turning the debt-ridden place into a profit-making enterprise, including its industrialization, creating a series of localized factories—a nailery, a textile factory, a tinsmith operation, a coopering operation, and a charcoal-burning enterprise.[28] But he also returned to Monticello with the idea of making his house into the grandest home in the United States. These plans required large amounts of money, and to find money was a pressing matter for Jefferson.

His solution to this problem came in the form of a line of credit provided by a group of Dutch merchants and bankers. For collateral, Jefferson put up 150 of his slaves. He signed a deed of mortgage of those slaves to the firm of Van Staphorst and Hubbard on May 12, 1796, in exchange for an open line of credit. As Weincek puts it, Jefferson's slaves became "bundled and collateralized assets in an international banking transaction."[29] By selling off his slaves in this manner, Jefferson bought himself time for the payment of his then current debts. Weincek observes, "He realized he could take on debt to expand, to acquire new machinery and erect a new house. He showed the plans to La Rochefoucauld, who thought 'his house will certainly deserve to be ranked with the most pleasant mansions in France and England.' The Dutch bankers opened an equity line backed by Jefferson's slaves for $2,000."[30] A credit line of $2,000 at that time would be the equivalent of approximately $300,000 today.

This transaction marked the beginning of both Jefferson's grandiose expansion of Monticello and the leveraged debt that would result in the estate's ruin upon his death. If not before, from that moment on Jefferson's continuing debt management became a central element in his planning for Monticello. The debt informed all his attempts to develop various industries on the planation in order to raise money, but it also, paradoxically, enabled the sinking of extraordinary funds into the luxuries that he now could seemingly afford, and the hospitalities that as a gentleman he could not deny his visitors and family. (While in the end it would be his cosigning onto the debt of other family members that would prove the proverbial straw that broke the camel's back, sinking Monticello, the level of luxury in which he lived certainly was a major contributing factor to his debt.)

Jefferson's ability to shoulder such massive debt depended almost exclusively on the hidden equity provided by his slaves. In this sense, Jefferson was participating in a major transition in the system of slavery that positioned it more firmly in the larger capitalist world. Weincek writes, "The slaveholders were fashioning a transition from a system of slavery they had inherited, which Jefferson portrayed as a burdensome legacy bequeathed by the dead hand of the past, to a new, refined system of deliberate enslavement."[31] Jefferson's fate was tied to this larger flood, the enormous expansion of debt that fueled the rise of industrial capitalism, not only in the United States but throughout the western world.

If Jefferson failed to recognize the hold that debt was to have over him personally, he was acutely aware of the power that debt could play in the expansion of empire. In a personal letter written to the governor of the territory of Indiana in 1803, he discussed the role that debt could play in the pacification of native tribes: "To promote this disposition to exchange lands, which they have to spare and we want, for necessaries, which we have to spare and they want, we shall push our trading uses, and be glad to see the good and influential individuals among them run in debt, because we observe that when these debts get beyond what the individuals can pay, they become willing to lop them off by a cession of lands."[32] The inclination toward debt, and the exchange of land to pay for debt, was a device to be used against those who could not rely on an increase of value as a consequence of any growth similar to that of his 4 percent per annum.

In a sense, despite his exceptional circumstances, Jefferson was an example of what Maurizio Lazzarato has called "the making of the indebted man."[33] Ironically, while Jefferson's Monticello may appear, at least partially, to be a historical anachronism, in his assumption of such a massive debt he anticipated the development of a primary instrument of modern capitalism—the rise of financialized debt as the primary instrument of industrial capitalist development.

Lazzarato notes that there is an intimate historical relationship of debt to modern subjectivity. The roots of this relationship burrow deep into the foundations of Western life. Citing Nietzsche's observations in the second essay of *On the Genealogy of Morals* concerning Christianity's introduction of the infinite into common life, Lazzarato glosses:

> Christianity, by introducing the infinite, completely rein-vented the system of debt which capitalism would inherit. In imperial configurations prior to Christianity, debt was indeed infinite, since thanks to their "state" apparatuses, and unlike in primitive societies, one could no longer reimburse, one could no longer balance the power differentials established through an ever-unequal exchange. Still, the debt remained "exterior" to the individual. The particularity of Christianity lies in the fact that it places us not only within a system of debt, but also within a system of "interiorized debt." [Quoting Nietzsche]: "The pain of the debtor is interiorized, responsibility for the feeling of debt becomes the feeling of guilt." (78)

The power of guilt that we see in Jefferson is that of the self-possessed individual who is constantly in danger of losing this crucial possession—his very self—to his creditors. In other words, the distance that Jefferson exhibited in his personal relationships could have been a reflection of his persistent worry over his debtor status, his ongoing attempt to construct a facade of confidence to cover up the precarious state of his increasingly mortgaged estate, his beloved Monticello.

Lazzarato is referring to the contemporary condition created by neoliberal capitalists when he writes, "This is how the debt economy institutes economic and existential precariousness, which is but the new name for the old reality: proletarianization—especially of the middle class and the class of workers in these new fields of what was once called, before the bubble burst, the 'new economy'" (93). But he also is describing what he sees as being the contemporary culmination of processes long at work in Western capitalism. The process of becoming indebted now bears an uncanny resemblance to the social relationships at work in the plantation economy of Jefferson's day. Lazzarato writes:

> The transformation of social rights into debts and beneficiaries into debtors is part of a program of "patrimonial individualism," "whose basis is the assertion of individual rights, but according to a completely financial conception of these rights, rights understood as securities." Unlike what happens on financial markets, the beneficiary as "debtor" is not expected to reimburse in actual money but rather in conduct, attitudes, ways of behaving, plans, subjective commitments, the time devoted to finding a job, the time used for conforming oneself to the criteria dictated by the market and business, etc. Debt directly entails life discipline and a way of the life that requires "work on the self," a permanent negotiation with oneself, a specific form of subjectivity; that of the indebted man. (104)

Lazzarato is describing processes at work in neoliberal political economy, but, as he notes elsewhere and as has been abundantly documented by political theorists, the psychology of debt is rooted in the very foundations of Western liberalism. The political psychology of liberalism, a logic at the root of modern ownership, is shaped by what C. B. MacPherson once called "possessive individualism."[34] The philosophy of freedom espoused by liberal thinkers such as John Locke is premised on this understanding of the self as being "self-owned." The free individual is what might be called a behavioral self, someone who understands being itself as a form of having. (Being and having are compounded into the very word *behave*.)[35] Hence the demands for behavioral change by the creditor, for the constant reexamination of the debtor's integrity, for reassessments of the quality of the work on the self that makes the debtor struggle with himself, in guilt and responsibility.

This form of indebtedness is deeply tied as well to the form of time that is entailed in trying to manage the infinite. Debt is forestalled, here, by the assumption of an open and infinite futurity. No debt will ever be paid in full, but no debt ever needs to be paid in full. Jefferson would later attempt to limit debt in his thinking of generational limits, as we will see. But his anxiety concerning his own debt never stopped him from acquiring new debts. As a deeply indebted man, Jefferson was at risk of losing his freedom because of his indebtedness, in this complex economic and moral sense. He acted in response to these pressures by constantly working, constantly innovating, constantly reinventing the disciplinary systems of his slaves in order to extract ever more production from their labors. (While it may be too glib to make this comparison, it is as though he was a part of the gig economy of his time.) This was his way of working on his self, of becoming an entrepreneur of his self. (We may be reminded here that Jefferson's sensibility was that of an Enlightenment man, someone who was deeply committed to the management of his time. Famously, there is an advanced clock in the main entry room of Monticello, powered by cannonball weights. It kept track of time from the second to the hour to the day of week. Jefferson would record the weather twice daily, in sync with the clock. His punctuation, in this sense, extended to all of his activities.)

But, of course, Jefferson was also the owner of these other human beings who were the instruments of his work. Hence, they bore the brunt of his indebtedness, even as he bore the guilt of being their master. His famous Memorandum Books (including his Farm Book) record these efforts, showing in the most acute detail his obsessive accounting for every bit of flora and fauna, every bushel of wheat, every barrel of nails, every piece of clothing, every case of wine, every human being under his power. He daily surveyed his plantation on horseback, up to the months preceding his death. How could he have done otherwise? As an indebted man, Jefferson could not cease in this activity: it would have been to concede the meaning of his own identity, to have given up, to have begun to die.

Power

One might think that the management of Monticello would have forced Jefferson to confront the contradictions between his philosophy of freedom and his practice of enslavement. As an Enlightenment thinker, Jefferson relied on his faith in natural reason to guide his decisions. But his rationality was in many ways his bulwark against ending his existing position concerning slavery, providing him with the ability to rationalize his practice. Lucia Stanton illuminates Jefferson's sense of certitude:

> In the age-old debate over the relationship between self-interest and moral duty, Jefferson was emphatically certain: "So inevitably do the laws of nature create our duties and interests, that when they seem at variance, we ought to suspect some fallacy in our reasoning." His confidence in this "law of nature" and its broad application is also revealed in his Second Inaugural, where he stated, "We are firmly convinced, and we act on that conviction, that with nations as with individuals, our interests soundly calculated will ever be found inseparable from our moral duties."[36]

Jefferson seems to have convinced himself that his interests and duties coincided in regard to the question of slavery. By 1805, any doubts he may have had about his practices would have been gone, the head having prevailed over the heart. One of the ways he rationalized his ownership of slaves was by insisting that for him their well-being was more important than were the fruits of their labor. Stanton notes, "For Jefferson, maximizing the efficiency of his plantation must go hand in hand with watching 'for the happiness of those who labor for mine'" (76–77). How well he was to meet that test is a puzzle, not only because his standards of "care" could often be honored only in the breach (though he was certainly not as cruel, in the conventional sense, as most masters), but because of the inherent contradiction to be found in the idea that one could hold people in servitude against their will and still be caring for them.

Jefferson was to establish incentives for his slaves to encourage them to labor more efficiently. He also believed that by establishing such a system he would contribute to the development of the slaves' character. He began putting these ideas into practice during a period when he was turning his attention back to the management of his estate after years of political activity and relative neglect of the plantation. After an unsuccessful attempt at making potash, late in 1793 he established a nailery on the grounds of Monticello.

The nailery was an enterprise that would more fully employ the labor of some of his younger male slaves and also provide a source of income other than agriculture. It was organized in accord with principles that had recently been employed in Philadelphia at the Walnut Street jail as a part of the penal reform efforts initiated by some prominent citizens of that city, including Jefferson's friend and Revolutionary War colleague Benjamin Rush. More directly, Jefferson made his initial purchase of a ton of nail rod from another Philadelphian, someone closely associated with Rush, Caleb

Lownes, who was the leader of the reform movement that turned the Walnut Street jail into the world's first penitentiary.[37] Jefferson was quite familiar with these reform efforts and was, like these reformers, also a reader of John Howard and Cesare Beccaria, the famous European penal reformers.

The core prison reform in that period was ending corporal punishment and replacing it with a system of graduated sentences of time. Time served in prison replaced such punishments as pillories and stocks. In Pennsylvania, prisoners were to spend their time in strict solitude, often being assigned work within their cells to avoid contact with other prisoners. When they were with others, they were to work in silence, and at all times they were to reflect on the wrongs they had committed, so that upon their release they would be able to resume their roles as citizens. The development of work habits was at the core of rehabilitation. Without work, the constant solitude was unbearable.[38] (Indeed, this emptiness of time is one important aspect of modernity itself.) Benjamin Rush referred to the ideas behind this reform, as well as the reforms of educational and mental institutions, which emphasized discipline and silence, as a part of a more general effort to effort to create "republican machines."[39]

While the penitentiary in Philadelphia used solitary confinement as a primary means of rehabilitating prisoners, it also employed prisoners in a variety of labors during the daytime hours, including, eventually, working in a nailery. It may have been this model of a nailery that inspired Jefferson. Obviously, a system of graduated sentences and solitary confinement would not work in the context of a plantation. Slaves rarely were to be given the incentive of their eventual freedom, and the plantation itself remained a place where slave families were integral to the social structure, however threatened they might be with being sold piecemeal into the Deep South. To

his (relative) credit, for the most part Jefferson focused his efforts
on providing more straightforward positive and negative sanctions
to the boys who worked in the nailery. Techniques included providing them with uniforms to distinguish them from other slaves,
making them compete against each other for rewards, providing
them with better food than other slaves, and even giving them small
payments of cash.[40]

The use of solitary confinement in the Pennsylvania system of
punishment was designed to make the prisoner reflect upon his bad
behavior, but it also was intrinsically a terrible punishment. Much
as it does now, it would often reduce those suffering it to psychotic
states. There was no way for the plantation system to accommodate
solitary punishment as an ordinary sanction. Instead, the constant
threat facing a slave was to be sold away, usually farther south. "This
was the Monticello equivalent to sending a prisoner into solitary
confinement," writes Stanton, "which Caleb Lownes had described
as 'an object of real *terror*' to all in the Walnut Street jail."[41] One
cannot overestimate the force of the terror of being sold farther
south. Like solitary confinement, it operated as an intensification
of the loss of freedom already being experienced.

Stanton describes the nailery and prison reform as examples of
the more general wedding of interest and duty advocated by utilitarian thinkers such as Jeremy Bentham. For Jefferson, she writes,
the nailery "was an experimental laboratory for working out new
ideas for exercising power, a place to try to manage enslaved labor
in harmony with current ideas of humanitarian reform" (79). The
establishment of systemic incentives would be extended to many of
the enterprises at Monticello, including the making of charcoal necessary to fuel the nailery. But there was one more element of prison
reform that was to be applied to Monticello, a more general model
adopted for the entire planation.

The most important innovation Jefferson derived from Bentham turned out to be easily transferred from the prison system to the plantation, namely, the more generalizable and abstract architectonic of the panopticon. While Bentham's *Plan for the Panopticon* emphasized the architectural form of a central tower surrounded by cells, the principle of panopticism was less reliant on a specific architectural form than it was on establishing realms of constant surveillance over those who are to be subjected to its power. The most famous contemporary characterization of the power of panopticism is to be found in Michel Foucault's *Discipline and Punish,* in which he writes, "The domain of panopticism is . . . that whole lower region, that region of irregular bodies, with their details, their multiple movements, their heterogeneous forces, their spatial relations; what are required are mechanisms that analyze distributions, gaps, series, combinations, and which render visible, record, differentiate, and compare."[42] Foucault's description of the power of panopticism closely fits the model of enlightened slave discipline that Jefferson began to practice at Monticello. His point is that there need not be the physical presence of a panopticon for the principle of panopticism to be realized. Indeed, very few panopticon prisons were ever built. But the core principles of panopticism have informed architecture for centuries now, making those who are subjected to it visible while those who observe are invisible.

Evidence of the systematic use of the principles of panopticism as well as a more general concern with disciplinary techniques is to be found in Jefferson's record books, with their detailed measurements of every aspect of labor, but the principles also can be observed in the very geography of the plantation itself, including siting the main building on the hilltop that he had had flattened for the building of the house. The architecture of the house, with the low-slung Palladian dome used as a platform for Jefferson's surveillance of his slaves, was clearly intended for such oversight. His use throughout the house of venetian blinds—then a new innovation—was strikingly similar to the louvered window shades prescribed by Bentham in the original plan for the panopticon. The blinds allowed Jefferson to see without being seen. Stanton makes the connection to Bentham explicit in her description of Jefferson's management of his slaves:

> There is no question that the African Americans within the Sage of Monticello's extensive panorama were acutely conscious of an all-seeing Jefferson and his Enlightenment optical equipment. In his recollections late in life, Peter Fossett, who was a child of eleven when Jefferson died, combined the telescope he could see every day on Monticello's North Terrace with the Revolutionary War events he had heard about from older family members: "One day while Mr. Jefferson was looking through his telescope to see how the work was progressing over at Pan Top, one of his plantations, he saw 500 soldiers, headed by Col. Tarleton, . . . coming up the north side of the mountain to capture him." It is curious that Fossett chose Pantops, which means "all-seeing," as the quarter farm Jefferson was inspecting. Similarly, a black man who had worked on the construction of the University of Virginia, three miles distant from Monticello, recalled Jefferson standing in the yard, watching "we alls at work through his spyglass."[43]

"Pantops," etymologically related to *panoptics,* makes the connection to Bentham even clearer. In short, Jefferson acted as the all-seeing eye, the invisible but ever-present master of his domain.

That Jefferson's slaves understood him to have the ability to watch them constantly is reinforced by his unending improvements of Monticello, including the slave quarters along Mulberry Row. Jefferson was acutely aware of the lines of sight on his plantation, and in his plans for Monticello he reduced the height of the central building in part to improve those sight lines. In his review of the landscape architectural design of Monticello, Terrence Epperson has argued that both Monticello and George Mason's nearby Gunston Hall "were preeminently designed as observation posts. Power was embodied in, and expressed by, the ability to see rather than to be seen."[44] In other words, the very siting and placement of buildings were part of the plan to render lines of visibility throughout Monticello, even as the living quarters of slaves were to be tucked away, out of sight of the guests to the plantation. As Epperson puts it, "Jefferson was able simultaneously to preserve his view of the surrounding landscape, mask the dependencies from view, yet still incorporate them into the rigid, symmetrical space of the immediate plantation nucleus."[45] Visibility is a trap, Foucault once observed. This is the system of power Jefferson embraced. (Jefferson went so far as to draw plans for the construction of a watchtower for the summit of Montalto, the land adjacent to Monticello that he acquired in 1777. That land looked down on the smaller mountain and would have afforded him a clear view of the entirety of the plantation.)

Jefferson at home could be thought of as someone who was so concerned with controlling his environment as to find ways to dominate the lines of sight all around him. But, just as Foucault noted how the sovereign power of the monarch that emphasized the pageantry of being observed was transformed, as sovereignty migrated into the more generalized power of observing and shaping the subjectivity of workers, so too was Jefferson obsessively concerned to see, and not to be seen. In this, he showed one way to pursue democracy, by making the democratic life one of appearances, in which the public face is what counts, and the private is hidden from sight.

Jefferson's effort to sustain this form of power was consistent across the various dimensions of his life. He was a very public man, but he was so inscrutable as to be labeled "American Sphinx" by one of his most important contemporary biographers. He was a father who instructed his daughter to act as though he was always watching her, so as to encourage her in behavior of which he would approve. But he also kept hidden one of his most important relationships, conducting a lifelong affair with one of his slaves. He was constantly on the verge of bankruptcy but was able to keep the appearance of grand riches throughout his life, a benevolent statesman and gracious host. Even in his dress he projected his democratic ethos, adopting plainer clothing the higher he rose in politics.

Jefferson's home, then, was a realm of privacy in which the principles of freedom to which he was so firmly committed somehow did not matter. The interior life of home was to be a great exception to the public freedoms that democrats would espouse in ending the tyrannies of the British over Americans. And that is in keeping with the ancient understanding of the home as being a realm of privation, of the dominion of the patriarch.

In this sense, many of us are the descendants of Jefferson. Our homes too are places of secrecy, of hidden desires and frustrated wishes, of embarrassing debts and the constant balancing of books, which never seem to balance in the end. He acted out on a grand scale the desire for convenience we seek, the desire for a repose we will never quite achieve. This strange man built a house that is our national symbol of home, not because of its grandeur, but because of its representativeness.

But to note the representativeness of Monticello would also be to understate the destructive power of that vision of home. Monticello was built on blood, on misery, on what Jefferson knew to be a hateful system of human bondage. Other homes will teach us something of that burden, of that haunting, of that heritage. Our question persists into our present: In what sense do we remain Jefferson's children?

And who, in the end, constitutes the "we" that I am trying to summon? Jefferson had his own sense of who that "we" might be.

Coda: Generational Usufruct

In 1789, Jefferson wrote to James Madison, using him as a sounding board to expound upon an idea that had just occurred to him, namely, *"that the earth belongs in usufruct to the living;'* that the dead have neither power nor rights over it."[46] He extrapolated that since the rights of a living person to have property, to harvest the goods of the land, and so forth, end when that individual dies, there is no natural right to property that extends beyond the life of a single person. Everything that determines the disposal of these goods is by convention, by rules laid down by the members of society.

This formulation of usufruct echoed that being advanced around this time by thinkers like Kant and Hume. But Jefferson went one step further. If the principle of usufruct applies to individuals, he suggested, there is no reason why it should not apply to generations as a whole. Relying on a series of calculations based on mortality tables and other materials, he believed he would be able to determine the length of time a generation would live, starting from the point in time at which each person attained the age of twenty-one, the age of majority, until death. He determined that time length to be another thirty-four years. As Jefferson elaborated:

> What is true of a generation all arriving to self-government on the same day, and dying all on the same day, is true of those on a constant course of decay and renewal, with this only difference. A generation coming in and going out entire, as in the first case, would have a right in the 1st year of their self-dominion

to contract a debt for 33. years, in the 10th. for 24. in the 20th. for 14. in the 30th. for 4. whereas generations changing daily, by daily deaths and births, have one constant term beginning at the date of their contract, and ending when a majority of those of full age at that date shall be dead. The length of that term may be estimated from the tables of mortality.

Both the rights and the obligations—to incur debts and to repay them—of one generation would end with their departure as a generation from the earth. As Jefferson writes, "For if the 1st. [generation] could charge it [the 2nd] with a debt, then the earth would belong to the dead and not the living generation."

Practical exigencies aside, Jefferson's idea of this truncated relationship between the living and the dead is worth some reflection. Gordon-Reed and Onuf suggest that this idea allowed Jefferson to withdraw "from the noisy and contentious world of the 'living generation' into the 'tranquility' of retirement" and also provided him with an excuse not to endorse the plan of a young neighbor, who wanted to emancipate his slaves and move with them to Illinois, and sought Jefferson's endorsement for his plan. Having become civilly dead, Jefferson suggested that he had no voice in the matter.[47] But the idea of generational sovereignty did more than conveniently absolve him from taking a stand on emancipation. It allowed him to imagine that each new generation would begin de novo, making its own decisions, its own laws for itself. Moreover, this idea of generational usufruct may have also allowed Jefferson to think that the succeeding generation of his family could be relieved of the debts he had incurred, though this is certainly not clear, as his rule of generational sovereignty included the idea that no generation could borrow more than they could pay during their civil lifetime.

This concept is perhaps the most radical of all of Jefferson's ideas. But it is not simply the somewhat absurd notion that one could determine with precision the life span of a generation that renders it so. Here we may recall the intimate relationship of the living and the dead that Vico insisted upon as being at the heart of the emergence of humanity. The attempt to honor the dead, the core obligation of the living to the dead, is at the heart of what it means to be human. For Vico, to sever that relationship, which seems to be the very idea at the heart of Jefferson's argument—"the dead have no power or rights over the living"—puts us in a place of great peril, making it more likely that we will lose our sense of the human. One might say that this doctrine reflects what Vico understood to be the dynamic of degeneration coming about through de-generation.

But was this actually Jefferson's intention? I doubt that he consciously had such a goal in mind. Perhaps he simply didn't think it through. His Enlightenment vision—the triumph of his head over his heart—set up a utilitarian calculus. In this case it would mean that happiness is best achieved through the relief of those generational obligations that require the shouldering of the dead's debt, evading the pain that such obligations would entail. After all, the weight of the dead is what revolutions are designed to lift off of our shoulders. Allowing us to begin anew is the modern vision of progress. If the dead have no claim over the living, then the haunting of the living by the dead will not occur; we will not bear any responsibility to them. The elimination of debt, after all, is the elimination of guilt. And Jefferson had a large debt.

But what of the next generation? Jefferson's dream was for there to be a constantly new beginning for each generation of Americans, an assurance of a constantly unfolding future, with no debt to the past. This is his understanding of the American dream. This is our inheritance from Jefferson: so busy are we in the pursuit of happiness that we leave all sense of the past behind. It is a dangerous idea, this notion of generational sovereignty, one that too easily allows one generation to forgive itself for its sins, in the name of a constant futurity that cannot be compared to a powerless past. But what it does in the long run, rather than allow a constant refreshing, is to sweep under the rug the devastating wastes that we continue to leave in our generational wakes. And the long run has now become short.

Jefferson's home did not and could not exist outside of history. But that he was tempted by a theory of generational usufruct suggests that he wished Monticello to be exempt from history's claims, its privacy preserved so as to serve as his *oikos,* from which he could occasionally emerge into the *polis* to make history. History seems to have caught up in recent years. A visit to Monticello reveals what we can imagine he would have wanted effaced—the nail factory, the panopticon, the slave quarters, the second family, yes, the qualifications of his love for any and all, all of them and all of those things, all designed to promote his pursuit of happiness, all of them his children, he the patriarch, the real father of his country, but perhaps not as he intended to be remembered.

After Jefferson died in 1826, his estate had to pay for the enormous debt he had accumulated. Several months after he was buried, on the south lawn of Monticello, there was an estate sale. Most of his furniture, his books, and his collection of art was sold. His slaves were auctioned, with families being separated, and eventually Monticello itself fell into the hands of its creditors. (Eventually a man named Levy, a Jewish plantation owner, bought the home, in part out of admiration for Jefferson's stance on religious freedom.)

We might say that Jefferson's attempt to manage the infinite was in the end defeated by finitude. And yet his model of amortizing debt, his leveraging of his assets in order to delay the due date, may be understood as the spiritual predecessor to the modern system of collateralized debt bonds, futures, and all the other imaginative ways of expanding capital that have succeeded him. In this sense, Jefferson's spirit persists in the continued crisis of debt today afflicting the world made by modern capitalism.

THREE

Henry David Thoreau's Walden

Should not every apartment in which man dwells be lofty
enough to create some obscurity over head?

—HENRY DAVID THOREAU

Slaves

Henry David Thoreau was acutely aware of the fact that most homes
were, are, and are destined to be sites of unforgivable debt. He saw
how deeply entangled American prosperity was with the economic
and political morass of slavery, whether it be chattel or otherwise.
Rather than accommodate himself to such indebtedness, he sought
a way to rethink what a home could be or, if failing in that endeavor,
to imagine what alternatives to home could exist. Rather than live
as a debtor, as did Jefferson, Thoreau believed that to be free one
needed to reduce one's debts to a bare minimum. A borrowed ax
might suffice as the most minimal debt, but if returned to its owner
well sharpened, perhaps the debt will have been repaid.

Thoreau was convinced that most men labor under a false necessity, that they have condemned themselves to a meaningless, and

hence deadening, existence because of their failure to face the truth of their lives. But what *is* that truth? It is difficult to say. He is presumed to have been hectoring to his neighbors, characterizing them as ignorant and, worse, of being unwilling to learn. He sometimes gave the impression that they did not have the depth—of character, of thoughtfulness, of care—that he did. For example, he wrote of the farmers he observed in Concord village, "Who made them serfs of the soil? Why should they eat their sixty acres, when man is condemned to eat only his peck of dirt? Why should they begin digging their graves as soon as they are born?" (I, 4).[1] Was this condescension? Or concern? And if he was suggesting that they were the living dead, zombies so to speak, to what extent was he to think about how they lived their deaths?

Thoreau alternatively suggested that these men were enslaved by their possessions—perhaps another way of saying they were zombies—trapped in prisons of their own making, burdened, needlessly indebted. In this sense, they were not unlike Thomas Jefferson. If this is what he saw, how could he not speak out? He makes this deliberately shocking and explicit comparison of slavery to self-possession: "I sometimes wonder that we can be so frivolous, I may almost say, as to attend to the gross but somewhat foreign form of servitude called Negro Slavery, there are so many keen and subtle masters that enslave both north and south. It is hard to have a southern overseer; it is worse to have a northern one; but worst of all when you are the slave-driver of yourself" (I, 8). For those who have read Thoreau, this is an infamous passage. Even as he qualifies the harshness of the comparison—"I may almost say"—he seems to be saying that it is worse to be self-possessed than to be possessed by someone else. How could he make such a claim?

Thoreau was a radical opponent of slavery, and he knew of its terrible cruelty. So why would he seemingly diminish the terribleness of that institution? If we reflect on the idea of "the slave-driver of yourself," we may come to sense that this phrase accurately describes the slave owner, the overseer of the plantation. The person who bears the psychic weight of attempting to rationalize the ownership of others, to the extent that he thinks about it—and, above all, Thoreau demands that people think—may find himself in an unbearable position, the worst of all. Indeed, the position of such an owner is the position inhabited by Jefferson.

The house Thoreau built near Walden Pond was by design an experimental habitation, much as was Jefferson's house. But Thoreau's house was built on a different temporal scale and with a different end in mind. If Jefferson wanted to secure freedom by maximizing his possessions, Thoreau wanted to become free by minimizing his. This is what we may reasonably surmise was the task Thoreau set for himself when he went to Walden Pond. His experiment was limited by design. He wanted to swap possessions for time. His was an experiment with finitude, recognizing the limits of life, trying to stretch them, perhaps, but remaining within life's bounds.

Thoreau had, as he put it, many lives to lead, and his time at Walden was necessarily both focused and transitory. But then again, in part his point was exactly that: life itself is a sojourn, transitory. Hence the importance for Thoreau of understanding what it means to live. And hence the importance for him to think of time—his finitude within it, and the infinite as he understood it—as an element of his sense of home, his sense of economy.

But how does one find a way to be at home when one believes that life is a journey? How does one square time with space? Questions such as these give me pause because they are in the end unanswerable, but paradoxically, they remain important. When he built his house on Walden Pond, Thoreau was acutely aware of these questions, and he sought to answer them. One could consider *Walden* his book-length answer, in the sense that he was responding to neighbors who kept asking him about the way of life he was pursuing. However, his response to their pertinent questions was to be impertinent, in the sense that he would not provide them with the answers they wanted. Instead, he thought he was giving them answers they needed.

Explaining to them what they needed and how he could provide answers to their needs makes up the bulk of *Walden*, though we usually think Thoreau is so self-absorbed that he is forgetful of his initial insistence that he is responding to their questions. His insistence makes *Walden* a difficult book to read. In trying to think with Thoreau about his home, in considering his various formulations of what a house is and of what a home consists, we risk losing ourselves in the ambiguity of his language, in his proclamations concerning the mysticism he embraced as an element of his everyday life, but perhaps, most of all, in the sense we get that he seems at times to forget us, who we are, why we are who we are, in short, in his relentless judgment concerning our imperfections. His account of his experience may be more foreign to us than that of Jefferson for that judgmental stance, his distance from us greater, even as Jefferson held his secrets close. For while Thoreau wrote that his secrets were unwillingly kept, they nonetheless remain secret. (Is it important to note that their lives overlapped? Thoreau was nine years old in 1826, the year that Jefferson died [in a historical rhyme, on July 4, the day of the year that Thoreau chose to move into his house on Walden Pond some years later.])

The language he used to describe his house does not seem to evoke the idea of trying to be at home at all. Sometimes, house and home are confounded, one for the other. For instance—to mention again that fateful date—when noting when he moved into his new home, he wrote, "I began to occupy my house on the 4th of July"

(I, 64). Occupying a house does not sound like living in a home. On the other hand, when he titled the second chapter of *Walden* "Where I Lived, and What I Lived For," we might have occasion to ask if he considered it possible to live without a home, and the provisional answer is that he did not believe it possible at all, that he did, in fact, understand his house in the woods to be his home.

When is a house not a home? For Thoreau, it is when one finds oneself confined by it, through ownership as much as through mortgage.[2] Finding oneself confined is finding a truth about oneself and one's circumstances. But his hope was not that his neighbors find *the* truth, only that they prepare the way, by facing—or, to use his term, *fronting*—their condition of confinement, a prerequisite for searching. Thoreau's assumption was that searching for the truth of life is the best, perhaps only, worthwhile pastime that there is. When he suggested that people are digging their graves as soon as they are born, it is not as though he is unaware of the Earth or our mortal place upon it. He realized instead that we have come to be at home through a form of homelessness, a repudiation, whether conscious or not, of the connection between Earth and home, humanity and humus. It is within the complex simplicity of our homeless homes—"Simplify, simplify, simplify!" (II, 17), he famously wrote, though the triple repetition of the word makes even that exclamation more complicated than it might otherwise be—that his way of being at home might be recovered. So it is to Thoreau's complicated quest for simplicity that we now turn.

Specifications

The house Thoreau built near Walden Pond was ten feet wide by fifteen long, with a garret and a closet, a large window on each side, a door at one end, and a fireplace at the other. It had two trapdoors and a woodshed by the side. Nearby there was a cellar for keeping root vegetables. It was furnished sparsely, with a bed, a table, a desk, and three chairs, all constructed by the hand of the house builder. Belongings gathered there included a looking glass (three inches in diameter), a pair of tongs and andirons, a kettle, a skillet, a frying pan, a dipper, a washbowl, two knives and forks, three plates, one cup, one spoon, one jug for oil, another for molasses, and a japanned lamp. There were some books on the desk, primarily classical works and dictionaries and lexicons. Excluding the lumber, sand, and stone, the materials used to build the house cost the owner $28.12 ½.

Let us imagine that we are visiting Thoreau's house. We may not immediately notice—he in fact must draw our attention to them—but the house has some very unusual features. The door, for instance, appears to be like any other door, but Thoreau insists that it is not. He has told us that one walks through the door to enter, and *then* one walks through it to enter. In other words, his door is an entry to an entry. How is that possible? Thoreau explains when he describes the experience of being alone during a storm: "I sat behind my door in my little house, which was all entry, and thoroughly enjoyed its protection" (V, 5). Perhaps it is not the door itself but his entire house that is all entry, although it would seem even more unlikely that a house could be all entry. Doors, when open, are thresholds, but usually between inside and out, entry and exit all at once. But this door seems to be a threshold of another kind, from outside to outside. Thoreau suggests that his drawing room is actually the woods behind his house. And here it seems as though the entire house actually is an entry as well, because the house itself is an entry, and the woods surrounding the house are a part of the house, all entry as well, his living room. Interior and exterior are both contained by this house. Rather than the closed rooms of a Kafka, Thoreau gives us nothing but opening.

As seems somehow appropriate for a house with a door that is all entry, one may go outside of this house without going through the door. Then how do we leave? We do not. Because his door is all entry, he is also completely outside. "I did not need go outdoors to take the air, for the atmosphere within had lost none of its freshness. It was not so much within doors as behind a door where I sat, even in the rainiest weather" (III, 8). All doors are open doors in Thoreau's house, even though there is only one of them, and even as he sits behind it.

This exercise in spatial absurdism may allow us to think through the generosity, the hospitality, that Thoreau wishes to communicate to us. His house is open to us; perhaps we could say it is an open book. This is surely not what Jean-Paul Sartre had in mind when he wrote *No Exit*. Or was it? For Sartre, entry is inescapable, the essence of existence is such that we cannot leave ourselves behind. But for Thoreau there is another way of thinking about this question of entry. Each time we cross a threshold, we are entering a world: each entry is the birth of a new experience. Throughout *Walden*, Thoreau insists on being born, insists on becoming as human as possible, being reborn every morning of his life, providing an exemplary existence for himself. Because he is generous, at least with his words, he grants us permission to observe him as he makes his home in the woods. If his house is a place that aids him in his ongoing quest to be reborn each day, to be constantly and fully awake, then all the better for those who hope to awaken.

Thoreau knows how arduous this process of awakening is. It is to strive to become godlike, without the advantage of ever becoming a god. As he puts it:

> Morning is when I am awake and there is a dawn in me. Moral
> reform is the effort to throw off sleep. . . . The millions are
> awake enough for physical labor, but only one in a million is
> awake enough for effective intellectual exertion, only one in a
> hundred millions to a poetic or divine life. To be awake is to
> be alive. I have never yet met a man who was quite awake. How
> could I have looked him in the face? (II, 13)

Poetic or divine life is his telos, reached through an awakening that
is every bit as real as a religious conversion. How real is that? One
does not look a god in the face. But when you are yourself godlike?
What then?

Thoreau is careful to make sure that his house is properly sited
for just such an awakening. Unlike other sites, his house keeps him
as close to or as distant from others as he wishes. Thoreau's site may
be thought of as being placed nowhere and everywhere, because
anywhere in this universe is potentially a good place to be. He asks,
"What is a house but a *sedes*, a seat?—better if a country seat" (III, 1).
(Better a country seat simply to minimize the distractions that
would impede one's awakening.) The seat he found for himself is as
distant from the world as the celestial corner behind the constella-
tion Cassiopeia's Chair: "My house actually had its site in such a
withdrawn, but forever new and unprofaned, part of the universe"
(III, 12).

Every house has the potential to be so sited, if only its inhabitants would learn to sit properly. Sitting properly is to be the discovery each of us makes for ourselves. We are all of us potentially
sitters upon a throne. "There is only one way, we say; but there are
as many ways as there can be drawn radii from one center" (I, 15).
And while his house is readily available to any visitor who might
come by, while his door is always open, Thoreau's sense of having
an open house was less social in character than it was metaphysical.

He wrote, "I have a great deal of company in my house; especially when nobody calls" (V, 15). For Thoreau, to truly be alone is to be able to think, and "With thinking we may be beside ourselves in a sane sense" (V, 9), that is, to be able to continue one's ongoing inner dialogue, with oneself and with all of those others who may fill your head. So despite its simplicity of appearance, this is a very complicated house. It contained Thoreau's dialectic, what he was to call thinking beside himself in a sane sense. His hope for his house was that it would be a reflection of his thinking and his writing. Together they were to constitute his handicraft, to use a term for thinking used by Heidegger a century later, a term that ultimately leads one back to Concord.[3] One is seal, the other print, to paraphrase his friend Emerson.

How are we to understand such a house? Will we ever be able to think about its building and habitation as a way of being at home? When we read about Thoreau's house, we are made aware of the fact that it is as much a house of words as it is a house of wood, stone, and sand. It is a repository of words, and it is the making of this house of words that turns it into a home.

Economy, Purified

Thoreau begins *Walden* with a chapter on economy. His is not really the conventional understanding of economy, though he does write of such matters as the production of goods, the balance of trade, the division of labor, and the ownership of things. But his sense of economy is rooted deep in its history, in its etymology, in that Thoreau seeks to go back to the origin of things by tracing the history of the words that compose them. Economy is rooted in the *oikos* as opposed to the *polis*, always being concerned first with determining what is necessary to live. Stanley Cavell has suggested that for Thoreau, economy is synonymous with philosophy, that he put his chapter on economy at the beginning of *Walden* as the clearest possible expression of the beginning of that philosophy. In short, his economy is a philosophy of life, in both a profound and a banal sense, in that the cardinal concern of philosophy is to understand the meaning of life.[4] (As we will see, Cavell also suggests that it is as a writer of words, words as the systemic metaphor for the woods within which Thoreau lived, that we can more deeply come to understand Thoreau's intent.)

If Thoreau is thinking philosophically, we may consider that he reduces the idea of economy to its essentials in order to get a clearer view of what life is beyond its costs. Economy is no more and no less than the set of practices that sustain the life of a human being. Thoreau's constant question throughout "Economy" is: What do we need to live? This first chapter of *Walden,* one might even say the entire book, is an ongoing exploration of costs, and in that sense it is a philosophy that measures our losses as they mount, as we approach life's extinguishment. For him, true cost is not to be found in the price of things. It is instead "the amount of what I will call life which is required to be exchanged for it, immediately or in the long run" (I, 44). This formula resembles the labor theory of value, shared to an extent by both Marx and Locke, but there is one crucial difference. Life is more than labor for Thoreau.[5] It is a good in itself, and it is the worth of life that is exactly what he is testing. He puts it this way: "I did not wish to live what was not life, living is so dear; nor did I wish to practice resignation, unless it was quite necessary" (II, 15).

What is the cost of a house when it consists of the amount of life that we are required to surrender in order to build or acquire it? How much of our life are we to devote to our houses (imagining that such devotion will lead to their becoming homes)? Thoreau suggests that we should give as much life as we need so that it will provide adequate shelter, and no more. He thinks that we put too much of what should be our own lives into the life of our institutions "in which the life of the individual is to a great extent absorbed, in order to preserve and perfect that of the race" (I, 45). In contrast, he believes that we can have the benefit of civilized life without the sacrifice of our individual lives to that end: "But I wish to show at what sacrifice this advantage is at present obtained, and to suggest that we may possibly so live as to secure all the advantage without suffering any of the disadvantage" (I, 45).

Thoreau lists our essentials as food, clothing, and shelter. But in imagining these essentials he realizes that life itself is the essence of these essentials. The shelter he builds is to support life, and as much as possible not to diminish it. Because of this entanglement, in many passages *Walden* comes across as a work that can be, to some ears, aggravatingly moraline in tone. But it may be that the tone Thoreau projects is most likely a consequence of the urgency he senses, a feeling that whatever else we may be doing, we are not properly attending to our lives, that we are not living as though our lives are worth the effort, but instead as though we did not care about ourselves, as though we are not taking ourselves seriously. How do we get to a proper understanding of the essence of life? This is what a good practice of economy enables us to do. This is why Thoreau is so emphatic—we are so very close to what it is we may become, but we will not wake up. Hence he must crow like Chanticleer, "if only to wake my neighbors up" (II, 6).

To front the tragically false sense of worth held by so many of his fellow citizens is thus to address the ongoing motivation underlying Thoreau's effort to explain how he lives and wants to live. He knows that economy is separate from and opposed to the life of the *polis*, the realm of public deliberation and action. He knows this separation and appears to repudiate it; such a separation blocks our larger understanding of who we are and who we may become. If we fail to break through the walls of this separation, we will be condemned not to public life but to private life, not to publicity but to privation. This is the political imbalance he discerns, the danger to the fate of the republic against which he launches his jeremiad. The tragedy does not consist of the fact that so many will never learn to recognize this danger; it consists of the truth that so many who do recognize it will pretend that they can live their lives unchanged by that knowledge.

It may be ironic to imagine Thoreau as a thinker who seeks to rebalance the weight of difference between the private and the public by emphasizing the need to open the private to the public. For while it is true that as much as the image of Thoreau as withdrawn from society is overstated, he often resists the company of others, desiring to walk in the woods by himself, welcoming solitude as the sanest time of all, when the derangement of loneliness turns into a finer lunacy. He reflects most explicitly on this understanding in his chapter on solitude, when, in the evening hour, he imagines, "I have my own sun and moon and stars, and a little world all to myself" (V, 3). And he compares his alleged loneliness to that of the loon, to Walden Pond itself, the sun, the dandelion, even God. "God is alone—but the devil, he is far from being alone; he sees a great deal of company; he is legion" (V, 15).

But all the same, from the very first page of *Walden* to its final admonitions, he is exposing himself to the members of the community of Concord. All of the "pertinent questions" his neighbors and fellow townsmen ask of him—what he got to eat, whether he was lonesome, or afraid, what portion of his income he devoted to charity, how many poor children he may have maintained—he considered to be economic questions (I, 2). Underlying all these questions is the most important one: How is one to spend one's time? How one spends one's time is more important for him than how one spends one's money.

In this sense, Thoreau is as deeply modern as those who worked on constructing that amazing clock in Copenhagen.[6] He is concerned to account for his time, so as to slow himself, to empty himself of the need to do anything other than to be in the moment. Giving an account of his time is giving an account of himself.[7] But Thoreau's desire for control is not of the same order as is Jefferson's. He hopes to minimize his labor so as to maximize his living time. Jefferson sought to maximize the labor of others so as to maximize his living time. And, obviously, *Walden* is an account in more than one sense—it is an account as a story, an account as an assessment of himself, and an account of the balance sheet of life itself. Here his balance sheet is to be found in his experiences, not in the entries on buying and selling that constituted Jefferson's daily ritual.

From the beginning of his exploration into economy, Thoreau understands his fellow citizens to be deeply in debt not only financially but spiritually. He understands indebtedness to be a state of hopelessness, not unlike what Thomas Hobbes in *Leviathan* once referred to as the estate of the desperate debtor. This is something he claims to have special insight into, as it is one of his own experiences, not necessarily having been materially in debt, but something perhaps worse. He writes (in what I believe is the longest sentence in *Walden*):

> It is very evident what mean and sneaking lives many of you live, for my sight has been whetted by experience; always on the limits, trying to get into business and trying to get out of debt, a very ancient slough, call by the Latins *æs alienum,* another's

brass, for some of their coins were made of brass; still living, and dying, and buried by the other's brass; always promising to pay, promising to pay, tomorrow, and dying today, insolvent; selling to curry favor, to get custom, by how many modes, only not state-prison-offenses; lying, flattering, voting, contracting yourselves into a nutshell of civility, or dilating into an atmosphere of thin and vaporous generosity, that you may persuade your neighbor to let you make his shoes, or his hat, or his coat, or his carriage, or import his groceries for him; making yourselves sick, that you may lay up something against a sick day, something to be tucked away in an old chest, or in a stocking behind the plastering, or more safely, in the brick bank; no matter where, no matter how much or how little. (I, 7)

Thoreau's sight is sharpened not by what he observes but by what he himself had gone through, for experience is not constituted by observation alone. At this point in his life he has been, so far, unable to free himself to be himself, and *Walden* is a record of his new attempt, his new essaying, the new evaluation of his current account. He knows how shameful this accounting for himself can be. *Æs alienum,* another's brass, coins made of brass, suggests something tawdry. The meaning of the term *sound money* comes from the ringing that coins make when dropped on a hard surface to determine their worth; brass is cheap, and another's brass is cheaper still. Sound money has the ring of gold and silver and copper. It rings true. The term also gives a material sense to the alienation one may feel from the accrual of debt. Underneath all of this alienation we see the fundamental unsoundness of the estate of the sick man, getting sicker all the time by saving up for a rainy day when he imagines he might be sicker yet. In *Walden* the rain will fall, but it will be welcomed. Its replenishing of the pond and its musical rhythm on the roof of the house are both sounds and events that remind us of life worth living.

Shame, Cavell once suggested, is the most public of emotions.[8] It comes into play when someone is confronted with the consequences of his or her own actions, and when those actions are found wanting by those who are aware of them. To be ashamed makes one want to hide. (On the other hand, one can be guilty, Cavell suggests, while remaining visible to those around oneself.) Actions, in this sense, not only reflect who we are but shape us into who we are to become. But they do so in ways we cannot predict or control. For this reason, actions that lead to shame carry with them great risk not only for those who are shamed but also for those who shame them. Shame can turn to rage when those who are so shamed cannot bear to admit those consequences of their actions that they have been confronted with.

Whom is Thoreau ashamed before? Whom may he be trying to shame? It seems as though he understands shame to be a failure to live as fully as one could live. And yet he has met no one who is fully awake, before whom he might properly be ashamed. He holds hope for his fellow citizens, in answering their questions, but that is primarily a hope for the future. Again, as he writes, "To be awake is to be alive. I have never yet met a man who was quite awake. How could I have looked him in the face?" (II, 13).

If life becomes something worth living, then to live it we must think of the least obtrusive ways that we can sustain our lives so as to be free to become who will be more fully awake. This is the ethical stance Thoreau takes in *Walden,* a reexpression of a kind of care for the self that precedes and enables us to join into the larger conversation of justice. "Our whole life is startlingly moral," he writes. "There never was an instant's truce between good and evil. Goodness is the only investment that never fails" (XI, 10). Available to all of us, indefinitely, his work is to aid us in thinking about the way forward, to find another way home.

Deliberation, or Building a House of Words

Thoreau lived in his house by Walden Pond for less than two years. The experiment, as he called it, sometimes seems like an extended camping trip, with visitors arriving frequently from Concord and elsewhere, with his regular trips to the village, and with the general society of others intermittently punctuating his time there. Again, it would be a mistake to imagine that his withdrawal to the woods is a retreat from society. It is instead a confrontation with the society into which he was born. Another way of putting it is to say that Thoreau's time in the woods by the pond is a life of resignation from his prior life, a time of reflection, surely, but not simply that. As Shannon Mariotti has suggested, it was an instance, one of many, of his "democratic withdrawal."[9] Thoreau's account of his life in the woods as directed to his readers, in both Concord and the world for which he makes Concord stand, constitutes a set of instructions on how to similarly test their lives.

For Thoreau, resignation is of two kinds. The first, more obvious form of resignation is that which I have already referred to—the hopelessness, the despair of the desperate debtor. This is the meaning of resignation we may find in these famous sentences: "The mass of men lead lives of quiet desperation. What is called resignation is confirmed desperation" (I, 9). This familiar passage suggests his verdict over and repudiation of the conventions of living that force people to despair, burdened by their possessions, slaves to their own false desires. Resignation is the plight of those who have given up, who succumb to their despair, who swallow it whole. They are in the end burdens to themselves, leading lives that are not worth living and, even worse, doing so thoughtlessly.

But there is another kind of resignation, requiring an explicitly reckoned evaluation of the worth of living, what Thoreau calls necessary resignation.[10] He explains, "I went to the woods because I wished to live deliberately, to front only the essential facts of life, and see if I could not learn what it had to teach, and not, when I came to die, discover that I had not lived. I did not wish to live what was not life, living is so dear; nor did I wish to practise resignation, unless it was quite necessary" (II, 15). This is Thoreau's test—of himself, of the world—his experiment in living as fully as he can. What living *means* for Thoreau is part of the plain and open mystery that unfolds in *Walden;* it is his time there, a time he describes as the experience of two years folded into one. This semifictive compression of time is a part of the complexity of his simplicity, an intensification of the meanings that accrue in the present by dint of repetition. Only by testing his ability to be present over time could he assess the value of his life at Walden Pond. Once his experiment was complete, he was able re-sign his contract with society, to become "a sojourner in civilized life again" (I, 1).

The conditional character of his return to civilized life—as a sojourner—is not to be taken lightly. Jane Bennett has provided a useful summary of the idea of the sojourner that describes Thoreau's posture toward civilized life:

> Sojourners are artificial beings who come to construe themselves—through minute observations of plant and animal cultures, through writing about wilderness, through bodily disciplines—as belonging to a universe that articulates through them and extends beyond them. But sojourners also court what Thoreau calls *the Wild,* that which disturbs and confounds settled projects, techniques, and myths. . . . Sojourners are on the road, moving through places, and those particular somewheres are essential to what they become. So-

journers are in search of a home but also value the sense of
estrangement that propels them.[11]

This sojourner in civilized life is also a sojourner in the woods. It is
important to keep this in mind as we think about the house Thoreau built and the implications of his eventual departure from it, especially if we are to understand what being on the road may mean
for one who is making a home. Is this a simple reflection of the paradox of home and homelessness with which we are concerned? If
we continue on the road, how are we ever to be at home? Or is it but
another odyssey, another way of being on the way home?

In order to understand Thoreau's intent, Cavell suggests that we
directly receive Thoreau's instructions on how to read. Cavell points
us to chapter 3 of *Walden,* entitled "Reading," and suggests that
Thoreau is telling us that he is writing a sacred text, a heroic book.
The relevant passage: "The heroic books, even if printed in the
character of the mother tongue, will always be in a language dead
to degenerate times; and we must laboriously seek the meaning of
each word and line, conjecturing a larger sense than common use
permits out of what wisdom and valor and generosity we have"
(III, 3). For Cavell, "This commits him, from a religious point of
view, to the claim that its words are revealed, received, and not
merely mused. . . . From a critical point of view, he must be read-
able on various, distinct levels."[12] To imagine *Walden* as a liturgy
requires a sort of hermeneutics that will enable us to explore it
more fully. Such is not an easy task, for, as Thoreau puts it, "You
will pardon some obscurities, for there are more secrets in my trade
than in most men's, and yet not willingly kept, but inseparable from
its very nature" (I, 22).

It may take a heroic reader to understand *Walden* nearly as well
as its writer does. But for Thoreau, to be a hero is not anything other

than to try to become the person we aspire to be, rather than becoming another person whom we imagine as being greater than ourselves. He sought to understand a democratic mode of hero, one
who, to paraphrase Emerson, will descend from his own faraway
place to meet with his fellow citizens. This person will not be a
demigod, as Heidegger would have had it, but simply a human being.
That is another way of saying that Thoreau sought exemplars, not
idols.

While Thoreau wrote that he wished to live deliberately, he also
wrote, "Books must be read as deliberately as they were written"
(III, 3). Deliberateness extends in both directions. Cavell cites this
sentence and others following it to suggest that "every word the
writer uses will be written so as to acknowledge its own maturity,
so as to let it speak for itself; and in a way that holds out its experience to us, allows us to experience it, and allows it to tell us all it
knows" (16). Hence, the question, What does it mean to live deliberately? is joined to the question, What does it mean to read and
write deliberately? Here we know that at one level to be deliberate
is to be intentional (we do things deliberately or by accident), at another, related level it is to be careful (his calculations were deliberate), and at yet another it is to think (he deliberated before he
acted). Living deliberately is living with intent, not accidentally;
living carefully, not carelessly; and living thoughtfully, not thoughtlessly. Thoreau suggested that we read and write this way as well,
at all these levels. He went to the woods to write, so his life as a writer
was to be deliberate, to deliberate, and he went to the woods to
read—not only books, but sounds, plants, ice, even the raw earth
exposed by railroad cuts. The life that is to be determined as worthy
or not worthy of living is that of a reader and writer. It is also the
life of one who in writing and reading understands that his life—and
the lives of those he cares about—is to be one that is engaged in a

constant reevaluation of the conditions of life, for him, for them, but also for his other fellow citizens.

The idea of deliberation is connected to writing in several other ways in *Walden*. For instance, Thoreau urges us to spend one day as deliberately as Nature (II, 21). And, he suggests, "With a little more deliberation in the choice of their pursuits, all men would perhaps become essentially students and observers, for certainly their nature and destiny are interesting to all alike" (III, 1). For him, deliberation is a way of thinking, and the process of learning nature, observing, is also a matter of thinking, of knowing.

This way of thinking also extends to writing, to marking. Early in *Walden* Thoreau writes, "In any weather, at any hour of the day or night, I have been anxious to improve the nick of time, and notch it on my stick too" (I, 23). Cavell notes that this writing on wood, notching it, marking time by marking the wood, is an exercise in writing down the experience of the present. This is Thoreau's intent, to experience the present and write it. He is writing on wood, and he is writing in the woods. His references to the woods are also and simultaneously references to the words. "Finding that my fellow-citizens were not likely to offer me any room in the courthouse, or any curacy or living anywhere else, I turned myself more exclusively than ever to the woods, where I was better known" (I, 31). He later notes, "My residence was more favorable, not only to thought, but to serious reading, than a university; and though I was beyond the range of the ordinary circulating library, I had more than ever come within the influence of those books which circulate around the world, whose sentences were first written on bark, and are now merely copied from time to time onto linen paper" (III, 2). If *Walden* aspires to be a book influenced by books first written on bark—books presumed to be permanent additions to the wisdom of humanity, religious books—then it too would be written on bark.

Books such as this attempt to achieve a timelessness. Their words on bark predate and postdate what we may presume to be history. This sense of timelessness is a strand of Thoreau's mysticism of the present, his sense of eternity. (One wonders what he would have thought of redwood trees had he had a chance to see them.) When one goes to the woods, then, one goes to the words, to what has been written and is being written, permanently. Consider this sentence: "Our outside and often thin and fanciful clothes are our epidermis, or false skin, which partakes not of our life, and may be stripped off here or there without fatal injury; our thicker garments, constantly worn, are our cellular integument, or cortex; but our shirts are our liber, or true bark, which cannot be removed without girdling and so destroying the man" (I, 36). Our liber is our true bark. If we write words on our bark, we are, in a complex pun, actually writing the experience of our *liberty;* we are writing on ourselves, our inner selves, under the skin. Because our shirt is our liber, moreover, we may be wearing our words on our sleeves. This is writing on the bios, a bio-graph of the self, auto-bio-graphy. This is what it means to de-liber-ate.

Thoreau intends this inner writing to be read by someone. We already know that he is interested in sharing his experiences with his Concord public. But he also suggests early on in *Walden* the infinite distance that extends between himself and others, a distance that is shared by all writers. He writes, "Moreover, I, on my side, require of every writer, first or last, a simple and sincere account of his own life, and not merely what he has heard of other men's lives; some such account as he would send his kindred from a distant land; for if he has lived sincerely, it must have been a distant land to me" (I, 2). He later suggests, "Where I lived was as far off as many a region viewed nightly by astronomers" (II, 12). Presumably, then, the readers of this inner bark, this liber, are to be all of those who honestly give an account of their lives, including the writer, but also the reader, whether the reader be a writer or someone else (though it is almost impossible to imagine such a reader not being a writer—this, in short, is the problem represented by Socrates and his relationship to Plato that inspired some of Jacques Derrida's best insights). The cosmic distance of each from the other is to be bridged by the integrity of both, their mutual and impersonal attraction to the inner skin of the other. In this sense, our liberty is internal to the process of writing our experience. If we do not write our experience, then we will fail to understand our own words, and, moreover, we will be incomprehensible to others, unable to explain ourselves.

Thoreau writes that he is confined to the theme of his own self by the narrowness of his experience (I, 2). Yet he also insists that with his words he is creating a world. Those who are able to give an account of their lives, then, are the heroes he is writing to and for; like him, they are philosophers. All of us are potentially philosophers, were we only to take ourselves seriously enough as the authors of our lives. The explication of this way of deliberate living, reading, and writing is Thoreau's way of encouraging us to take ourselves seriously, his way of encouraging us to write, to engage in creating our own lives, our own autobiographies. Either way, he demands sincerity, that every writer speak the truth as she understands it. This is one reason he is such a pain in the ass to us, because to meet this test is to attain to something much more than quiet desperation. It is to confront that form of resignation that is constituted by despair with the power of the words as found in the wood we mark. We will mark ourselves indelibly (in yet another variation on our liberating deliberation). This could be considered Thoreau's way of returning to the forest, his transcendental response to Vico's understanding of our emergence from it.

If we accept Thoreau's model of writing, that when he goes to the woods, he is going to the *words,* we must then ask another pertinent question. The mixture of sound and substance presents us with an ongoing paradox: When are the words wood, and when are the woods words? If we are to understand, how are we to begin to read such words? It is not only that writing and reading are of woods; the house on Walden Pond is built of wood and words. The house at Walden Pond closes the gap between inner and outer, self and other, reading and writing, inside and outside, and an indefinite number of other couplets. If we read *Walden* as a study of the making of a home as well as a house, we may see the complicated heritage that he has bequeathed to us in the form of that test. How do we read home? How do we write it? How do we come to know the builder of the house by the pond, if not through the house he built? In this sense, as well as many others, we can continuously read Thoreau's house as a response and rejoinder to Jefferson's imagining of Monticello.[13]

A Living House

If our shirts are our liber, then what are our houses? Thoreau notes, "The necessaries of life for man in this climate may, accurately enough, be distributed under the several heads of Food, Shelter, Clothing, and Fuel; for not until we have secured these are we prepared to entertain the true problems of life with freedom and a prospect of success" (I, 17). Why is shelter necessary? Thoreau is cautious in his response, qualifying: "As for Shelter, I will not deny that this is now a necessary of life, though there are instances of men having done without it for long periods in colder countries than this" (I, 41). A house is a convenience, designed for domestic comfort, but this comfort is sometimes uncomfortable, coming out of our luxury, our version of false necessity. "From the cave we have advanced to roofs of palm trees, or bark and boughs, of linen woven and stretched, of grass and straw, of boards and shingles, of stone and tiles. At last, we know not what it is to live in the open air, and our lives are domestic in more senses than we think" (I, 42). Thoreau's worry about the domestic is that it may come to dominate what we think is necessary, and to confine us in various ways. He advises the builder "to exercise a little Yankee shrewdness, lest after all he find himself in a workhouse, a labyrinth without a clue, a museum, an almshouse, a prison, or a splendid mausoleum instead" (I, 43).

Is it possible to build a house without it becoming subject to the rules of institutions, that is, without it becoming a mausoleum? Thoreau suggests that in building a house that is all entry, we may find a way to refute the notion of a house as an enclosed space and think of it instead as a space that is a part of nature, or at least closely adjacent to it. Here, as he does in other essays, Thoreau implicitly challenges what Vico would call our "basic institutions," suggesting that while we may need to respect the boundary between the wild and the civilized, we ought not ignore the wild as a valuable perspective for seeing the limitations of such confinements as the civilized may give rise to. At one point, he suggests that architecture itself is foolish, in that the architect does not engage in the act of building. "It would signify somewhat, if in any earnest sense, *he* slanted [the sticks] and daubed [the wall]; but the spirit having departed out of the tenant, it is of a piece of constructing his own coffin,—the architecture of the grave—and the 'carpenter' is but another name for 'coffin-maker'" (I, 66).

Unlike the architect, the advantage Thoreau derives from his house is intimately tied to the amount of *his* life that goes into it. He is in tune with Vico in his realization that we build our own coffins, that our homes are mausoleums, and yet at the same time he holds life dear. If we follow him on this understanding of cost, the dimensions of his words expand. The mausoleum he refers to is a splendid one. Is there another mausoleum that he might repair to, a simple one, a plain wooden box, perhaps?

> I used to see a large box by the railroad, six feet long by three wide, in which the laborers locked up their tools at night; and it suggested to me that every man who was hard pushed might get one for a dollar, and having bored a few auger holes in it, to admit the air at least, get into it when it rained and at night, and hooked down the lid, and so have freedom in his love, and in his soul be free. (I, 43)

A box, a coffin, a grave—he sees a need to build a house that reflects his concern for the dead but also, in his case, to allow those of us who are already dead, that is, living a ghostly existence, to be reborn. He writes, hopefully, "But perhaps man is not required to bury himself" (I, 45).

Perhaps it is not a matter of rebirth but simply of birth. Thoreau's presence in the entryway, his presence in the present, is not so great as to allow him to avoid the thought of death, though he skirts the matter mightily. Thoreau's final words are said to have been a response to a question as to whether he could discern the outline of the next world as he slipped away from this one. His answer: "One world at a time." He understands that one does not really die until one has lived. Only living is the true preparation for dying. Those who died before him are those who have truly lived, who have written their words with an aim toward the same permanence that he tries to achieve, those who are, in their deaths, still alive to us, their liber always potentially liberating us. In this way, the world is our home, as long as we truly live in it.

Thoreau meticulously accounts for the cost of the materials of the house he builds, the boards, shingles, brick, nails, and so forth, reaching a final cost of $28.12 ½. But in the sentence that precedes this listing we may note something more. He writes, "The exact cost of my house, paying the usual price for such materials as I used, but not counting the work, all of which was done by myself, was as follows; and I give the exact details because very few are able to tell exactly what their houses cost, and fewer still, if any, the separate costs of the various materials which compose them" (I, 68). To tell exactly what something costs, down to the various materials that compose that thing, is at the core of Thoreau's economy.

Very few can tell the cost of a thing. Why is it so hard to account for costs? Surely, most people keep accounts. But they are not of the sort that Thoreau is keeping. Cavell notes the import of Thoreau's accounting:

> This is what those lists of numbers, calibrated to the half cent, mean in *Walden*.
> They of course are parodies of America's methods of evaluation; and they are emblems of what the writer wants from writing, as he keeps insisting in calling his book an *account*. A true mathematical reckoning of the sort he shows requires that every line be a mark of honesty, that the lines be complete, omitting no expense or income, and that there be no mistake in the computation. . . . Among written works of art, only of poetry had we expected a commitment to total and transparent meaning, every mark bearing its brunt. The literary ambition of *Walden* is to shoulder the commitment to prose. (30–31)

The care that Thoreau devotes to building his house is the care that attended his desire for perfection. That he falls short of perfection is to be expected—what is surprising is how close he comes.

"The separate costs of the various materials that compose them. . . ." This formulation suggests that it is not only a house that is being accounted for, but the self who builds it. Few can do it. All may try. But not all of us keep accounts, or the accounts we keep, our ways of giving accounts of ourselves, are at best incomplete and at worst fraudulent. Economy, then, is an attempt by Thoreau to give an account of himself, one that will be read by other writers who are also giving their own accounts in the distance between themselves and him. The economy that Thoreau embraces will result in a house fitting for him, one in which he was to dwell as himself. Being yourself acquires a mythic significance. For Thoreau, home is where the self is.

But Thoreau also excluded something from his accounting: "not counting the work, all of which was done by myself." He could pay himself a wage, or imagine a wage for his work, but he doesn't. His account is the book itself. The book itself is the work he does, the work is the accounting for his work, all done by himself, all placed inside the book, recording costs and benefits. But the book is to be beyond account, even as it is an account. If this is an exclusion or exception Thoreau is making, it is also an assessment of the worth of true work, which attains to the sort of permanence that we associate with sacred texts and their infinitely indefinite depth (like the legend that Walden Pond itself is bottomless). Another way of putting the matter is to suggest that Thoreau's home must be able to withstand the test of time.

The simplicity of the house is the open secret of Thoreau's extravagant claims regarding his life at Walden. It is the end of his writing. Sitting by the shore of Walden Pond, he converts experience into truth by focusing chiefly on the words, the woods, and the volatile relationship that words and woods have with the truth:

> I fear chiefly lest my expression may not be *extra-vagant* enough, may not wander far enough beyond the narrow limits of my daily experience, so as to be adequate to the truth of which I have been convinced. *Extra-vagance!* It depends on how you are yarded. . . . I desire to speak somewhere without bounds; like a man in a waking moment, to men in their waking moments; for I am convinced that I cannot exaggerate enough even to lay the foundation of a true expression. . . . The volatile truth of our words should continually betray the inadequacy of the residual statement. Their truth is instantly translated; its literal monument alone remains. The words which express our faith and piety are not definite; yet they are significant and fragrant like the frankincense to superior natures. (XVIII, 6)

The uncertainty of words, their indefinite character, just as they are themselves composed of characters, is not a shortcoming, since words are always inadequate to the task of unlimited speaking. Chosen well, our words remind of us of this truth continually. What they offer is a gift worthy of a god—frankincense is one of the gifts of the Three Wise Men—the gift of truth, however volatile, however fleeting, like a fragrance. And the account will have a surplus, an extravagant excess, in the form of his expression not hemmed in, but outside, wild.

Sitting

Thoreau could have built his house anywhere, and it would have been as fine a house as any other house, wherever he eventually built. He as much as says he could build anywhere. But we need to understand what he means with his reference to site: his choice is something that seems casually chosen but upon closer examination is

casual in the sense that Emerson understood the term, in relation
to casualty. ("We thrive by casualties," Emerson wrote.) Thoreau
considers "every spot as the possible site of a house." He visits all
the farms, discusses with the farmers the purchase price, and even
buys each farm; but he does this all in his mind. He "took everything but a deed to it—took his word for his deed, for I dearly
loved to talk—cultivated it, and him too to some extent, I trust."
This exercise enables Thoreau to learn more of the surrounding
landscape and his neighbors than would any other method, and
it also relieves him of the burden of ownership proper. He sur-
veys every spot and concludes that he would do well no matter
where he might choose to build. The site or seat is not dependent
on any given place but is the achievement of a sense of closeness
to the imagined place of one's fullest existence, at a distance from
all others.

We might note that the house at Walden Pond is not Thoreau's
first house. But that other house?

> The only house I had been the owner of before, if I except a
> boat, was a tent, which I used occasionally when making ex-
> cursions in the summer, and this is still rolled up in my garret;
> but the boat, after passing from hand to hand, has gone down
> the stream of time. With this more substantial shelter about
> me, I had made some progress in settling in the world. This
> frame, so slightly clad, was a sort of crystallization around me,
> and reacted on the builder. . . . It was not so much within
> doors as behind a door where I sat, even in the rainiest weather.
> (II, 8)

This crystallization of the frame recalls a reference that Robert
Pogue Harrison makes to Wallace Stevens's "Anecdote of the Jar."[14]
In a chapter that is concerned with how humans create spaces, he

cites Stevens to demonstrate how the humblest of human artifacts may transform the world surrounding it:

> I placed a jar in Tennessee,
> And round it was, upon a hill.
> It made the slovenly wilderness
> Surround that hill.
> The wilderness rose up to it,
> And sprawled around, no longer wild.
> The jar was round upon the ground
> And tall and of a port in air.
> It took dominion everywhere.
> The jar was gray and bare.
> It did not give of bird or bush,
> Like nothing else in Tennessee.[15]

The simple placement of the jar by the hand of the poet transfigures the wilderness around it, crystallizes it, as it were, makes that space a place, a site, a *sedes*, to use Thoreau's ancient reference. If for no other reason, this is why it is so important to site oneself with care, to build as deliberately as one can.

There is another sense to this description that reinforces Thoreau's sense of home. "The crystallization around me" suggests the construction of a chrysalis, site of the metamorphosis from caterpillar to butterfly. The construction of a house as figuratively the making of a chrysalis suggests that home is a site of radical transformation, a protective space within which one *becomes*, while being perfectly still. And Thoreau appreciates stillness. He lives by gathering the world around him: "Wherever I sat, there I might live, and the landscape radiated from me accordingly" (II, 1). Sitting is a human thing to do. It is a part of our upright posture, the pose of study, or contemplation, and a perspective from which we can view.

It is the counterpart of standing, of being on two feet, not four, of walking.

Sitting is also something that keeps us close to our animality, our basic function. It is how we are close to the ground. It is what we do when squatting to defecate. Of this he writes: "The better part of the man is soon ploughed under the soil as compost. By a seeming fate, commonly called necessity, they are employed, as it says in an old book, laying up treasures which moth and rust will corrupt and thieves break through and steal. It is a fool's life, as they will find when they get to the end of it, if not before" (I, 5). It is as compost, both in our waste and in our decaying bodies, that the better part of the man may be found. Our humanity is in our humus. In referring to "an old book," he is referring to Matthew 6:19–21: "Lay not up for yourselves treasures upon earth, where moth and rust doth corrupt, and where thieves break through and steal: But lay up for yourselves treasures in heaven, where neither moth nor rust doth corrupt, and where thieves do not break through nor steal: For where your treasure is, there will your heart be also." (Cavell makes note of this reference.) We foolish humans do not know our hearts, and do not know in what our treasure consists.

We might contrast this notion of value with that proposed by John Locke, who in his *Second Treatise on Government* explained how, with the invention of money, we are able to preserve what otherwise we would consider to be wasted labor. The nuts that we gather—and that our servants gather, for their labor was somehow owned by the master—will rot, but not gold. The fact of money thus encourages us to produce more things than we need.[16] But Thoreau asks, why make more than one needs to begin to live in the first place? Ultimately, the pursuit of money is an interference with true economy: it is a waste of life. What appears to be extravagant is a token of the poverty of the mass of men.

We should instead sit still and achieve riches. Sitting still is required of us if we are to see nature as clearly as we are meant to see it. We must see through our eyes, but we must also experience nature through our other senses, as other animals do, with smell and touch and taste and hearing. The patience of stillness is the boring part of *Walden* for those of us who have never been able to sit still. It is a book that has, I suspect, become more boring for each succeeding generation of readers. This boredom may be thought of as a measure of how far we have gone and how far we have to go if we are to reimagine our way home, for underlying boredom is a deep anxiety. Boredom will not help us unless we use it to achieve another state of mind. We must sit still because if we don't we will miss most of what is before us, we will be frightened by what we cannot see. There is a quiet that we do not achieve by ourselves, but that is composed of those sounds we hear only in stillness, and that is how we can realize that we cannot only be human if we are to be here, in this world, and on this Earth.

Among other things, the stillness of sitting is preparatory for thinking. Thoreau is above all else a writer who is a thinker. Writing and thinking are two aspects of the same thing. His dwelling by a pond is for good reason. As Cavell notes, ponds saturate, drench. Walden Pond is a place that sits, as opposed to, say, the Ister River, which is never still, a place of constant commerce, always flowing.[17] The pond's waters reflect light. And the light of Walden Pond enables Thoreau to write his words on wood.

Obscurity Overhead

In building his house, Thoreau was preparing for his move into the woods. Even before his chimney was finished he moved in, on July 4, an auspicious day we might think, but one he deliberately notes as not being so special a day at all, only moving in that day by coincidence. Perhaps he fails to mention the import of the day because of his sense that the Revolution had not been won as yet, that the enslavement of others in the South and the self-enslavement of property holders in both the South and the North deny the promise of that declaration. Unlike Jefferson, he is unable to live peacefully with that contradiction—though he is able, however crankily, to live with others. In the meantime, his life at Walden, his experiment, proceeds *deliberately,* as an exercise in achieving freedom by learning a way to be at home.

Thoreau is clearest about this matter when he reflects upon the building process itself. But when it comes to deliberation, the final turn is not to the solid foundation of a house but to the singing that is to accompany the building process, the release from the forces that would otherwise hem in the builder, the builder who would not build for himself, that is, who would be unable to know himself well enough to realize the sort of home he wants. This meditative state of deliberation, if perfected, would lead to the suspension of time itself. But we are far from perfect, and we do not need to be. We only need to build more deliberately.

Following his description of how he built his house, Thoreau suggests the following:

> It would be worth the while to build still more deliberately than I did, considering, for instance, what foundation a door, a window, a cellar, a garret, have in the nature of man, and perchance never raising any superstructure until we found better reason for it than our temporal necessities even. There is some of the same fitness in a man's building his own house that there is in a bird's building its own nest. Who knows but if men constructed their dwellings with their own hands, and provided

food for themselves and families simply and honestly enough,
the poetic faculty would be universally developed, as birds
universally sing when they are so engaged? (I, 65)

A purer deliberation would exclude "temporal necessities," finding
a better reason to build, the development of the poetic faculty.
Thoreau is insistent on this point: the work of the hand leads to
poetry. Here he anticipates Heidegger, who, as we have already
seen, suggested that to dwell is to think, that we dwell poetically on
this earth.

But poetic expression depends on the riches available to those
who will learn to be as close to being whole men as possible. Thoreau is aware of how rare it is to find anyone who will deliberate at
the level of slowness required, who will embed himself in the liber,
building that house of words and wood. He notes the difficulty of
this work and its relationship to the division of labor to which we
have subjected ourselves. It is a division that prevents the realization
of home, of self-understanding, of being able to think for oneself.
Instead, we fail ourselves and become subjects of community, which
in this instance, though not all instances for Thoreau, is a synonym
for conformity. Later in the same paragraph in which he urged deliberate building, he writes:

> I never in all my walks came across a man engaged in so
> simple and natural an occupation as building his house. We
> belong to the community. It is not the tailor alone who is the
> ninth part of a man; it is as much the preacher, and the mer-
> chant, and the farmer. Where is this division of labor to
> end? And what object does it finally serve? No doubt an-
> other *may* also think for me; but it is not therefore desirable
> that he should do so to the exclusion of my thinking for my-
> self. (I, 65)

Thoreau seems to be echoing Emerson here, who writes:

> Man is not a farmer, or a professor, or an engineer, but he is
> all. Man is priest, and scholar, and statesman, and producer,
> and soldier. In the *divided*, or social state, these functions are
> parceled out to individuals. . . . The state of society is one in
> which the members have suffered amputation from the trunk,
> and strut about as so many walking monsters—a good finger,
> a neck, a stomach, but never a man.
>
> Man is thus metamorphosed into a thing, into many
> things.[18]

For Emerson, in this divided state, there is still a role for the scholar.
"In the right state [the scholar is] *Man Thinking*." Emerson's thinker
is very much like Thoreau's independent thinking man. She is
someone who studies nature, who reads books only in idle times
(though the ideal scholar has lots of idle time available to her), and
appreciates the common, the low, the familiar, the present, as well-
springs of understanding. And as the "designated intellect" in this
division of man, as Emerson's scholar seems as well to be akin to
the deliberate thinker. She is one who is free and brave, compre-
hending her limits only by a self-understanding based on the realization of self-trust, as he puts it, one whose only limitations derive
from her own constitution.[19]

And yet there is something about the designated intellect that
doesn't quite rhyme with Thoreau's house builder. Scholars, for all
their virtues in the divided state where we find ourselves, are not
yet builders. The house builder is more than a scholar: he is a poet,
a creator, a deliberator, a man who shuns the ongoing division of
labor and the splitting apart of a self into parts, a dismembered
member, no matter how elevated the scholar's admirers may believe
the value of his part to be.

Thoreau tells us early on in *Walden* that he is writing his book for poor students (I, 4). By this he does not mean impoverished only in a pecuniary sense. He also means students who are not good at being students, whose qualities as scholars will expand beyond the role of learning from teachers, who in the beginning and in the end will think for themselves. Thoreau's democratic turn is to urge us all to think, to think for ourselves, yes, to trust ourselves, but also to trust ourselves as more than scholars, or as something other than scholars, and instead as fully realized, robustly acting human beings. In Emerson's parlance, he wants us to re-member ourselves as much as we possibly can. When we do this, it will mean that we will have built our houses deliberately.

In building deliberately, we will not be building an airtight container but a breathing thing, something we will *inhabit,* an indwelling, a material result of our imagination's work. While he occupies his house from July 4 on, Thoreau only begins to inhabit his house when it becomes too cold to stay outside, the point of the year when he begins "to use it for warmth as well as shelter" (XIII, 6). Even then he is entering an uncompleted habitation. But this pleases him enormously. The chinks between boards of the rafters create a draft that helps the chimney carry away the smoke. Eventually he plasters his interior walls, though he is wistful about doing so. He writes: "My house never pleased my eye so much after it was plastered, though I was obliged to confess that it was more comfortable. Should not every apartment in which man dwells be lofty enough to create some obscurity overhead, where flickering shadows may play at evening about the rafters? These forms are more agreeable to the fancy and imagination than fresco paintings or the most expensive furniture" (XIII, 6). Here his house seems to be a variation on the cave that Plato writes of in *The Republic,* only Thoreau takes the side of the poets and sees, by watching the shadows flickering on the walls, all sorts of spurs to the poetic imagination. Practicality demands that we plaster our walls and ceilings, but our dreams require that we be allowed our obscurities as well.

Frescoes are images painted on the surface of wet plaster, and the pigments bind to the surface as they dry, lending depth to the images but also changing the colors slightly. The best techniques of fresco painting have been those that change the colors the least as the plaster dries. It is a painstaking process. Perhaps the greatest fresco, certainly the most famous, is Michelangelo's on the ceiling of the Sistine Chapel. While there are various scenes depicted in that fresco, the central panel on the ceiling depicts God's creation of Adam. Could it be that Thoreau was implicitly comparing his house—his sacred text—to that of Christianity's greatest house, the home of its most sacred relics?

In the very next paragraph Thoreau tells of a dream he has had: "I sometimes dream of a larger and more populous house, standing in a golden age, of enduring materials, and without gingerbread work, which shall still consist of only one room, a vast, rude, substantial, primitive hall, without ceiling or plastering, with bare rafters and purlins supporting a sort of lower heaven over one's head" (XIII, 7). He seems to be presenting a negative image of a great house, a house with its fancy painting and furniture. Thoreau's dream house is well appointed in the necessities of life, "containing all of the essentials of a house, and nothing for housekeeping" (XIII, 7). It is a house of freedom: "A house whose inside is as open and manifest as a bird's nest, and you cannot go in at the front door without seeing some of its inhabitants; where to be a guest is to be presented with the greatest freedom of the house, and not to be carefully excluded from seven eighths of it, shut up in a particular cell, and told to make yourself at home there—in solitary confinement" (XIII, 7). The first "great houses" of medieval lords in Europe contained only a single room, a great hall not unlike the one Thoreau describes.[20] But his dream seems to suggest a counternarrative to the aristocracy, the possibility of an open house available to all sojourners. Moreover, the closeness to each other of the functional parts of the house—the kitchen, the parlor, the workshop—suggests for him the possibility of richer metaphors and tropes, our symbols now too far from each other to be anything but "farfetched." "The dinner," he writes, "is only the parable of the dinner, commonly" (XIII, 8). This impoverished parable is a consequence of the degeneracy of our language. The parlor is so far from the kitchen and the workshop, we are so far from nature, that we are beginning to lack words. He asks, "How can the scholar, who dwells away in the Northwest Territory or the Isle of Man, tell what is parliamentary in the kitchen?" (XVIII, 8).

Thoreau's dream is a great counterargument to the idea of him as an opponent of sociality. He mentions companions in his great house. He hopes to socialize, perhaps to engage in meaningful conversation. His worry is as much for the continued richness of our tropes and metaphors properly to speak to each other, and these can only be protected if we tear down the walls that separate us from each other so that we may fetch our symbols back from the great distance we have established between each other, and lend a hand in the building of a greater house. This dream house is the culmination of his deep wish for publicity, for the openness of a life that he aspires to build, and does build, on the only scale available to him. It is his house of open doors, all entry, democratic. It is a dream house he refers to again in the conclusion of *Walden* when he writes, "I learned this at least by my experiment: that if one advances confidently in the direction of his dreams, and endeavors to live the life which he has imagined, he will meet with success unexpected in common hours" (XVIII, 5).

Home Alone

As much a democrat as Thoreau may have been—more so than Emerson, perhaps less so than Walt Whitman, though I doubt it—the question we must ask, now that we may have a good suspicion of how he thinks he has found a way to be at home, is whether it is a good way home, whether the path he takes is one that others, perhaps some of the rest of us, can and should take.

Most students of my acquaintance, when they first encounter Thoreau—by reading either *Walden* or his essay "Resistance to Civil Government," better known as "Civil Disobedience"—ask, as if in a first and final refutation, "But what if everybody behaved like Thoreau?" Speaking from our common condition as consumers in what is perhaps the greatest consumer society that has ever existed, we tend to think of Thoreau as being in possession of an unreal understanding of life, or at least an understanding not available to us who live in the Now, a life that could only be underwritten by the tolerance and generosity of others (qualities seemingly in short supply). After all, they say, he built on ground that was not his own, with a borrowed ax, and went back to town after a while, having other lives to live, as he put it, or, as more cynical observers have noted, often stopping by his mother's house for a meal or at least a piece of pie. Even in that simpler era of capitalism, he depended on others. And now we have realized again, as we enter into the disastrous era of the Anthropocene, the complexity of the interdependent network of relations that constitute our late modern neoliberal economy.

When students ask this question, they seem to be asking something that goes beyond pragmatic concerns about their place in neoliberal capitalist society. While explicitly they are suggesting that if everybody acted like Thoreau, society would fall apart, no one would take responsibility for others, implicitly, I believe, they are wondering about, and fearing, something else. The question, What if *everybody* behaved like Thoreau? hides another one: What if *I* were to behave like Thoreau? This is a more disturbing question, I think. Were any of these students to behave like Thoreau, it would mean that they would need at least in part to resist him, but their weapons against him can only be the ones he offers them, his terms of friend-ship and resistance, the conditions of thinking and experiencing that he insists upon. For if we are to meet him from a distant place that we have discovered and from which we can give sincere and honest account, we will have to be quite different from him even if we become, in the end, his fellow sojourners. The consequences of such internal reflection are enormous for anyone who is a serious person. So to imagine behaving like Thoreau is no more and no less than to take him seriously, and hence the question is as good a start as any. This is how Thoreau himself can become an exemplar for those who are desirous of change, those who want to find themselves at home.

In his philosophical memoir, *Little Did I Know,* Cavell ponders the question of seriousness. He wonders about the accusation "You take yourself too seriously." He asks, "If I am not to take myself se-riously, who is?" Seriousness is little in demand, it seems, and, as funny as he is—perhaps he inspires less laughter than he should, but nobody's perfect—as obtuse as he is, as frustrating as he is, Tho-reau is nothing if not serious. And his work invites, perhaps even demands, seriousness on the part of those for whom he writes.

Earlier in this chapter, when writing about Thoreau's sense that we need to sit in order to find a site, I suggested that for readers who are unable to sit still, *Walden* is a boring book, and that perhaps the extent to which we nowadays feel bored is a good measure of how far away from Thoreau's experience of home we have gone, and a sign of how far we have to travel to go back, should we even want to. We are restless, and he would suggest we should rest. We have buried ourselves, and he suggests that we might try to dig ourselves out from our graves.

Thoreau concludes *Walden* with a wild story that he says everyone in New England had heard about. It seems that a beautiful bug emerged one day from the dry leaf of an applewood table that was estimated to be sixty-three years old. The table had been close to a fireplace and was warmed, apparently stirring the bug from its deep slumber. This story cheers Thoreau considerably. He writes:

> Who knows what beautiful and winged life, whose egg has been buried for ages under many concentric layers of wood-enness in the dead dry life of society, deposited first in the alburnum of the green and living tree, which has been gradually converted into the semblance of its well-seasoned tomb— heard perchance gnawing out now for years by the astonished family of man, as they sat around the festive board—may unexpectedly come forth from amidst society's most trivial and hand-selled furniture, to enjoy its perfect summer life at last! (XVIII, 17)

The alburnum of the tree adjoins the liber, the inner bark. It is the soft white wood inside the tree that remains moist, eventually growing outward but remaining within the growing tree, turning into hard wood, as new layers of alburnum grow farther within. This insect egg is a gift, after so many years of turning inward, awakening to the vital heat and gnawing its way outward, re-marking on the inner bark, reminding us of the concrete and living things that just might lie buried within the words, within the woods. Is that insect not as astonished as we are for seeing its emergence from the table?

Could we gnaw our way outward? We may or may not be able to do so, but the fact of that insect's existence can be a source of wonder for all of us.

Thoreau's way home is largely achieved alone, but only by degrees. Not all of us can do what he did in the life he lived for himself. But so what? We should not be afraid to take him seriously, to understand that his way home is one among others, and perhaps one to celebrate and to imitate, if not fully, at least to an extent. Persisting in the writing of our own selves may be all we can and should do in order to plot our own ways. This may not be enough, but is it not at least a requirement? That is, as an alternative to failing to think, perhaps thinking—building deliberately, appreciating the obscurity overhead, turning wood into words, and words into wood—may at least make the journey more rewarding. As we go along, we might keep in mind that house on Walden Pond, even as we imagine other ways home.

Laura Ingalls Wilder's Little Houses

Eat or be eaten.

—LAURA INGALLS WILDER

Frontiers

Thomas Jefferson's home was defined by slavery, and what went with it, including a secret at its heart, a secret that he kept close, one that enabled him to fool himself into believing he was the father of American freedom. Thoreau's home, in contrast, was defined by freedom, what he would call liberty, and while he had secrets, as he put it, they were secrets not willingly kept. He knew how much he did not know about himself, and realized that this was a beginning of wisdom. Thoreau's freedom required that he resist the conventions of the society within which he lived. One might even say that Thoreau was able to be free to the extent that he was able to resist, that, in contrast to Jefferson's desire for fatherhood, he aspired to be an uncle. But what of other family members?

Alexis de Tocqueville, as he did with so many other American institutions, noted a paradox at the heart of the democratic family. In *Democracy in America,* he noted:

> Americans, who have allowed the inferiority of woman to subsist in society, have therefore elevated her with all their power to the level of man in the intellectual and moral world; and in this they appear to me to have admirably understood the true notion of democratic progress.
>
> As for me, I shall not hesitate to say it: although in the United States the woman scarcely leaves the domestic circle and is in certain respects very dependent within it, nowhere does her position seem higher to me. . . . [I]f one asked me to what do I think one must principally attribute this singular prosperity and growing force of this people, I would answer that it is to the superiority of its women.[1]

For Tocqueville, the democratic wife was also the democratic daughter, exerting power within the domestic sphere while adhering to the mores of patriarchy in society at large.

But the pioneer wife (and the pioneer daughter), facing the brutal facts of life on the edge of the frontier, helping her husband in the tasks of survival—butchering the animals he shot and trapped, participating in the hard labor of subsistence farming, as well as almost exclusively performing the household chores usually associated with "traditional" wives—of necessity had to engage in a more complex balancing act than did the wives of the more settled families of the East. Remaining within Tocqueville's domestic circle when the domestic was everything, when there were few or no public spaces, meant that the wife had immense practical power within the household. On the edge of the frontier, husbands were as dependent on their wives as wives were on their husbands. But this mutual dependence did not suggest an equality of rights. Women remained unequal under law, and in the eventual reassertion of the public sphere they would find themselves again confined to the home. Nevertheless, the frontier experience would contribute to a peculiar valorization of married women, and especially mothers.

Laura Ingalls Wilder is widely known as the author of one of most successful series of children's books in the history the United States, the Little House series.[2] Composed of nine novels tracing Laura's life from early childhood through her first years of marriage to Almanzo Wilder, it is widely considered to be a masterpiece of children's literature, her narrative providing almost anthropological details of the everyday lives of pioneers, giving insight into the workings of an ordinary nineteenth-century family while providing an epic tale of the precarious lives of those who settled the West. Three of the novels are included in the top 100 list of the *School Library Journal* 2012 national survey of best children's novels.[3] Since the initial publication of *Little House in the Big Woods* in 1932, the series has sold more than 60 million copies, and yet another new edition of the series was released late in 2016. Although the books are novels, they are of the genre of the roman à clef, closely following the true-life narrative of Laura's upbringing in the frontier regions of Wisconsin, Kansas, Minnesota, and the Dakotas in the 1870s and 1880s.

Wilder quite correctly understood the books to be up to something much larger than the story of her family. In a speech at a book fair in Detroit in 1937, while reflecting on how she came to imagine the writing of these books, she noted that eventually "I understood that in my own life I represented an entire era in American history."[4] But what was that era? How was it shaped, and what was so iconic about her experience that led her to make such an audacious claim? How was that claim translated into the books she wrote? And to what extent did the legend supersede the facts of her life?

The answers may be found in the stories she told, but one step removed from her actual childhood and adolescence, that enabled her to provide a wider scope on the pioneer experience within which her family's collective life unfolded. Wilder's way of illuminating the era was to present a quasi-historical narrative that would focus on how her family made their home. On the American frontier, with the ancient divide between *oikos* and *polis* practically nonexistent, the task of settlers was to re-create that division with whatever meager resources, both material and cultural, were available to them. The material resources that were needed are obvious: within the territorial frame, the labor of staking a claim to the land, bringing in the railroads to connect isolated farmers with the rest of the country, establishing government.

But Wilder's focus was on the mundane details of the everyday lives underlying those more eventful days. She wrote of the intercalated days not noted by appointment or public occasion as opposed to the calendar days of historical events. Her approach to the ordinary was to give us a sense of the affective dimension of the lives being lived. She was able to capture a sense of the nonmaterial resources depleted and regenerated across a range of experiences. What makes understanding her seemingly simple narrative so complicated is that among those affective resources are the very myths surrounding the pioneer experience that these settlers were to produce.

One question unasked by Wilder goes to the heart of her enterprise: *Whose* era was it? The subalterns whom representative pioneers encountered—Native Americans and recently freed African Americans who moved west following Reconstruction—play strangely marginal, and hence silently central, roles in the book series. The actual encounters with Indians were largely genocidal, though not completely so, while the encounters with the freed slaves were more part of the continued segregation, enforced invisibility, and pseudoslavery of chattel labor, after the formal freedom granted them by the Civil War amendments. Though, again not completely so. The violence of these encounters was to help shape the pioneer understanding of home. The decimation of Indians gave rise to the myth of the warrior; the violence of chattel slavery gave rise to the imagined African American absence from the West.[5] Both enabled the emergence of other forms of white cultural appropriation that would enable both ethnic bonding and division among the various immigrant settlers, whether they were from other countries or merely from the East.

It is important to note that the settlement of the West was not consistent with the recalled experience of the Ingalls family, at least as memorialized in the Little House books and the various writings connected to them. The series instead clings quite closely to stereotypes that developed within the popular culture of the United States through much of the twentieth century, and that have persisted into the twenty-first. But that is precisely the point. In Wilder's fictional reconstruction of her childhood, she significantly contributed to that culture. Her retroactive narrative exclusions and careful framings of the family's encounters with Indians and African Americans not only present us with adventures and dramas but also provide evidence of an implicit violence brought about by the constitutive exclusion and the active repression of other memories, memories of these other Others.[6]

Wilder's self-awareness about her role in representing an era may be thought of in another way. We can think of her work as contributing to what Alison Landsberg has referred to as "prosthetic memory." Landsberg has suggested that the personal construction of identity in modern mass societies is deeply dependent on the affective attachments people create between their personal selves and larger historical narratives, those created through films, television, novels, and other media, as much as through unmediated experience.[7] Wilder's series of books could be considered an example par excellence of prosthetic memory at play, helping to constitute a sense of rugged pioneer self-reliance through the suturing of one's identity to that of the experiences of the Ingalls family.

The novels emerged from an unpublished memoir by Wilder that covered the entirety of her childhood, a memoir she wrote with the encouragement of her daughter, Rose Wilder. Rose herself was a successful novelist and freelance writer. She edited her mother's memoir and served as her de facto agent but was unable to convince any contemporary publishers to grant her mother a contract. So, with Rose's encouragement, Laura rewrote the early part of the memoir as a children's book, *Little House in the Big Woods,* which was to be the foundational novel for the series.[8] (The memoir, *Pioneer Girl,* was finally published in 2014 by the South Dakota Historical Society Press.[9] In its first year, it sold 140,000 copies, which, considering that it was a large and relatively expensive hardback volume, with extensive annotations and an elaborate academic apparatus, is remarkable.)

In conjunction with the book series, the memoir presents us with puzzles regarding Wilder's own understanding of who she was, what she imagined her quest for a home to be, and indeed, what she repressed from herself and what she hid from her devoted readers, the millions of children her books eventually would reach. My hope is that the intercalated days and weeks that are present in either the memoir or the novels may provide us with a glimpse into how she remembered her past and what she thought of it. But how we remember is always fraught, our memories always shaped by degrees of ambivalence.

The most famous of the novels, *Little House on the Prairie,* describes a long journey from the Big Woods of Wisconsin to Kansas, where the family homesteaded on the Osage tribe's reserve. Laura would have been too young to recall the family's initial journey from Wisconsin to Missouri, made when she was only two years old. Her remembrance of the Big Woods that shaped the first novel, *Little House in the Big Woods,* was actually based on the Ingallses' return to Wisconsin after their experience in Missouri and Kansas—by then, Laura was a five-year-old. This manipulation of the chronology, and even of the starting point of the journey (because the Ingalls family moved to Kansas from Missouri, not directly from Wisconsin), for the sake of narrative flow was to mark the entire series. But it is particularly striking in the two early books. The editors of *Pioneer Girl* remark on this self-conscious manipulation of narrative in an annotation to Laura's (incorrect) mention of her age at the time they left Wisconsin for Minnesota: "Throughout *Pioneer Girl,* Wilder recorded her memories without using dates, marking the time principally in seasons and birthdays, rather than years. The fictionalized version of the Ingallses' sojourn in Wisconsin from May of 1871 to February of 1874 compounded the problem: the action of *Little House in the Big Woods* takes place roughly within one year, combining and compressing Wilder's Wisconsin memories into a single twelve-month cycle of activities" (PG, 59–60n2). This use of compressed time is not dissimilar to the technique Thoreau used in writing *Walden.* But Wilder's purpose is different. First, in the novels she wants to use whatever memories she has of the past. Because of the tenuousness of the memories of a child between the ages of two and five, they need to be supplemented by details remembered from later times, when she had reached the point in life when she could more accurately recall events and their sequence. So the trip to Indian Territory, as depicted in *Little House on the*

Prairie, borrows its details from the later trip that the Ingallses made from Wisconsin to Minnesota after the family had returned to Wisconsin from their first excursion to the west. That latter trip didn't occur until Laura was almost seven years old (PG, 54n89).

And so it goes in these novels, the rough and unvarnished memories of the memoir softened and polished for the young audience. For instance, the domestic abuse that Laura witnessed when she was hired out to sew shirts, depicted in *Pioneer Girl* in all its violence, is not mentioned in *Little Town on the Prairie.* The disturbing portrayal in *Pioneer Girl* of one of her uncles, a Civil War veteran— apparently suffering from what we would now recognize as posttraumatic stress disorder—is not included in *Little House in the Big Woods,* even as he appears there in the guise of Uncle George, blowing a bugle and dancing with young Laura at a party hosted by her grandmother (on her father's side) (LHBW, 144–147). While it is obvious that some of the more adult themes and sorrows from the memoir would be dropped from novels written for young readers, another way to think of the novels would be to consider what Wilder thought was acceptable to include in those books—vivid descriptions of animal slaughter, explicitly racist references to Native Americans and African Americans, sharp depictions of the rapaciousness of the railroad companies, and horrifying details about the extreme living conditions that almost resulted in mass starvation in the Dakota Territory town of De Smet during the long winter of 1880–1881. These inclusions matter for our understanding of the Ingalls family's quest for home because they present Laura as she would wish to be presented—not as the heroine of her own life but as a representative of the generation that settled the American frontier.

Laura's memories of the Ingalls family's experience give us the material to reconstruct her sense of home. Indeed, there is too much material to explore. Thus, I will only present several scenes from the Ingalls family's saga, ones that I hope will be representative of a larger truth. What we will find is not a bucolic resting place but a constantly contested and often violently defended arena of American life, in which the absence of a meaningful distinction between the public and private spheres and the deployment of a metaphysics of racial hatred undergird an image of home that is anything but peaceful and calm.

Eating Animals

"Every morning as soon as she was awake Laura ran to look out of the window, and one morning she saw in each of the big trees a dead deer hanging from a branch" (LHBW, 4). This passage introduces a major topic in *Little House in the Big Woods*—food, both in the descriptions of fruits and vegetables and, more vividly, in the detailed discussions of animals and how they are turned into meat. How to get food, how to process food, and how to cook and eat it are central topics throughout the series. Food and the effects of gathering, cultivating, killing, and preserving it are of foremost concern for the Ingalls family. The accounts of food's loss, through plagues of grasshoppers, severe storms, and winter weather, provide some of the most memorable events in the chronicle of their lives. But it is the passages that concern killing and preserving the kills that most clearly mark the turning of the seasons, especially from fall to winter.

Perhaps it is because the connection between killing animals and avoiding being killed by them is so closely noted in these passages, if only implicitly, that the descriptions of processing meat are so vivid. The first of these, early in the book, of the dead deer hanging from trees is preceded by young Laura's description of howling wolves, with Wilder observing, "It was a scary sound. Laura knew that wolves would eat little girls" (LHBW, 3). A bear is shot with a pig in its clutches (LHBW, 25–26). A story within the story tells of Grandpa being chased by a panther that "screams like a woman" and deriving from this experience the lesson to never go into the Big Woods without his rifle (LHBW, 41–44). Ma has a dangerous encounter with a bear in the barnyard (LHBW, 104–106). Aunt Eliza is saved from a panther by the family dog (LHBW, 68–72). Pa's play with Laura and Mary has him acting out the role of a mad dog, coming to get them. Pa himself is susceptible to the fear of death at the hands of a bear, so much so that when he is walking home from the nearby trading post one spring evening, he imagines in the shadowy gloom that a tree stump is a bear blocking his path and fears for his life (having left his rifle at home) (LHBW, 109–115).

Hunting for and preserving meat—stocking up for the winter when bears hibernate, deer lose weight, and birds disappear—is described in loving detail in this volume. There is the production of smoked meat, salted meat, and salted fish (the last caught by Pa from Lake Pepin). Animals also play a secondary role in the production of other foods, such as cheese, for which the stomach of a calf is important for producing the rennet necessary for separating curds and whey (LHBW, 186–187).

A long passage is completely devoted to the day the extended family gathers to slaughter a hog, the roast that follows, and the detailed description of the various parts and how they are preserved. It is a major project. Uncle Henry comes to help butcher, equipped, as are Ma and Pa, with his family's knife, freshly sharpened for the occasion. Every bit of the pig (like most of the other animals) is saved: not only hams, shoulders, side meats, and spare ribs, but tongue, liver, and the head (for headcheese). Scraps are saved for making sausage. The skin would be made into leather. The tail is given to the girls to roast over hot coals. Even the animal's bladder serves a purpose: it is blown up into a balloon-like ball for the children to play with (LHBW, 13–18).

The excitement of the children, their appetites, their fears and thrills that Wilder conveys throughout the novel are softened by their sentimental attachment to their own animals. When it is time to kill a calf to get rennet for the making of cheese, the calf of the Ingalls family is spared: the calf that is sacrificed belongs to an uncle. But there is a thrill in the danger of loss: "Laura was afraid Pa must kill one of the little calves in the barn. They were so sweet. One was fawn-colored and one was red, and their hair was so soft and their large eyes so wondering. Laura's heart beat fast when Ma talked to Pa about making cheese" (LHBW, 186). This fear for the innocent calves is not exactly a sympathy for the slaughtered. It is not as though Laura has no sensitivity for the lives of the animals, or the pain they suffer at the moment of slaughter, but the youth of the calf, its loss of life for the making of cheese, connects its death to food in a more complex way. The moment is brief, and the anticipation of what is to come—the killing itself—overcomes the worries that Laura and the other children have, both for the calf and then for the hog.

The hog killing is a more visceral experience, but also more direct in its depiction of Laura's coping strategy:

> When the water was boiling they went to kill the hog. Then Laura ran and hid her head on the bed and stopped her ears with her fingers so she could not hear the hog squeal.
>
> "It doesn't hurt him, Laura," Pa said. "We do it so quickly." But she did not want to hear him squeal.
>
> In a minute she took one finger cautiously out of an ear, and listened. The hog had stopped squealing. After that, Butchering Time was great fun. (LHBW, 13)

In both of these instances—for the pig and for the calf—the killing of the animal is not avoided, but the emotional cost is deflected. In the slaughter of the pig, this deflection occurs by way of Pa's lie of a painless death; in the sparing of the family calf, through the literal distancing of the death to an animal that does not belong to Laura's immediate family. To be sure, distancing still is the most common way that meat eaters avoid the emotional costs associated with killing other animals. But what is interesting here is that the fear of death at the hands of animals, and the companion deflection of the emotional costs of killing are themes that carry over into the encounters with Indians in *Little House on the Prairie*.

The Metaphysics of Indian-Hating

That the Ingalls family was constantly seeking a home but also constantly moving could be considered ironic on several levels. One irony is that they wittingly followed the same path that was a fatal one for so many of the Indian tribes in the nineteenth century, a trail succinctly outlined by Andrew Jackson several decades before the Ingalls family began their sojourn to the prairie. Michael Rogin, in his brilliant analysis of some of the psychopathologies expressive of the eliminationist bent of American liberal society, cites at length Jackson's second annual message to Congress, delivered on December 6, 1830. Jackson writes:

> Doubtless it will be painful to leave the graves of their fathers; but what do they more than our ancestors did or than our children are now doing? To better their condition in an unknown land our forefathers left all that was dear in earthly objects. Our children by thousands yearly leave the land of their

birth to seek new homes in distant regions. Does Humanity weep at these painful separations from every thing, animate and inanimate, with which the young heart has become entwined? Far from it. It is rather a source of joy that our country affords scope where our young population may range unconstrained in body or in mind, developing the power and faculties of man in their highest perfection.

These remove hundreds and almost thousands of miles at their own expense, purchase the lands they occupy, and support themselves at their new homes from the moment of their arrival. Can it be cruel in this Government when, by events which it can not control, the Indian is made discontented in his ancient home to purchase his lands, to give him a new and extensive territory, to pay the expense of his removal, and support him a year in his new abode? How many thousands of our own people would gladly embrace the opportunity of removing to the West on such conditions! If the offers made to the Indians were extended to them, they would be hailed with gratitude and joy.[10]

Jackson's comparison omits one crucial detail, namely, that the Indians did not willingly move but were forced to move. The claim that the treaties were being honored was a lie, of course, and the betrayal of the Cherokee, Sioux, and Osage—to name three tribes that touch upon the later experience of the Ingalls family—proceeded apace as they were pushed farther and farther west.

Nonetheless, the comparison of pioneer to Indian is worth lingering over because Jackson succinctly presents what would later be fulfilled as a promise, not to the Indians but to white settlers (and to some free black settlers) in the form of the Homestead Act, signed into law by Abraham Lincoln in 1862. That act was in the long tradition of pioneer settlement, encouraging the pioneer movement of which the Ingalls family was to be a part. I have already have noted how, in her books, Wilder self-consciously was attempting to serve as a representative of the pioneer experience, perhaps especially in her depiction of the pioneer encounter with an Osage tribe. But there was an earlier narrative than hers, one fixed as much on the Indian-pioneer experience, that seems to have resisted this desire to represent the interactions of settlers with Native Americans so benignly in its fierce opposition to narrative smoothness, all along framing the encounter of pioneer and indigenous people in ways that call into question the Jacksonian frame.

In the very middle of what is probably his least read novel, *The Confidence-Man,* Herman Melville presents a story about what he calls the metaphysics of Indian-hating.[11] This chapter departs from the other masquerades that constitute the bulk of the novel, establishing a character who had a "real" existence. The Indian-hater of Melville's account is not a confidence man. He is a supposedly heroic figure, Colonel John Moredock, an actual historical person who had previously been portrayed in writing by James Hall, who penned several books about the American frontier in the 1830s and 1840s. Chapter 26 of Melville's novel—the full title of which is "Containing the Metaphysics of Indian-Hating, According to the Views of One Evidently Not So Prepossessed as Rousseau in Favor of Savages"—discusses the character of the American Indian and explains why backwoodsmen hate him with such virulence. Chapter 27, "Some Account of a Man of Questionable Morality, but Who, Nevertheless, Would Seem Entitled to the Esteem of That Eminent English Moralist Who Said He Liked a Good Hater," is specifically Melville's retelling of Hall's discussion of Moredock, initially presented in an 1835 book of sketches Hall wrote about the American West.

Hall's essay is not just a portrait of Moredock. It is an attempt to explain Moredock's hatred within the context of the pioneer culture of the time. Hall writes of the relative enlightenment of the

nineteenth-century pioneer in comparison to that of the age of initial settlement. "America," he writes, "was settled in an age when
certain rights, called those of discovery and conquest, were universally acknowledged; and when the possession of a country was
readily conceded to the strongest."[12] But even as the civilization advanced and more moral understandings of right and wrong prevailed, pioneers, living as they did away from the sources of civilization, were only slightly affected by these changes. Living close to
Indians, they "form[ed] a barrier between savage and civilized men."
The pioneer does not believe "that an Indian, or any other man has
a right to monopolize the hunting grounds, which he considers free
to all. When the Indian disputes the propriety of this invasion upon
his ancient heritage, the white man feels himself injured, and stands,
as the southern folks say, upon his reserved rights." Moreover, every
pioneer child is raised with tales of the conflict between his or her
parents and the Indians. Everyone grows up with stories of scalping
and massacres: "The impressions which we have described are
handed down from generation to generation, and remain in full force
long after all danger from the savages has ceased, and all intercourse
with them has been discontinued." Hall is here describing precisely
the experience of Abraham Lincoln, whose father would likely have
handed down to him the tale of the death of his grandfather.

Hall then turns to the life and times of Moredock himself. Moredock's entire family was slaughtered by Indians when he was still a
child. He vowed then that he would hunt down all who killed them,
and eventually, after completing the slaughter of all of those Indians
responsible, simply continued to kill. According to Hall, Moredock
"resolved never to spare an Indian, and though he made no boast
of this determination, and seldom avowed it, it became the ruling
passion of his life." Hall warns us not to infer "that Colonel Moredock
was unsocial, ferocious, or by nature cruel. On the contrary, he was

a man of warm feelings, and excellent disposition." In that sense, Moredock represents what we would now call the normalization of the Indian killer, a man whose killing doesn't define him as being excluded from proper society.

In placing Moredock firmly within the narrative of his novel, Melville uses the words of Hall himself. That is, the Indian-hating chapter is composed of a speech that is a secondhand account of someone who heard Hall himself discussing Moredock. This double distancing is indeed part of the larger masquerade Melville presents throughout the novel. Moredock's hatred is thus taken by Melville to be witnessed by multiple others, providing ambiguous voices telling an almost mythical tale of the frontier. That he allegorizes the Indians as disciples of the Devil is fairly well accepted by most Melville scholars. Yet Melville's attitude about "savages" was in real life much more sympathetic. Of course, the relationship of Melville to the question of good versus evil is much more complex than to allow any simple conclusion concerning his attitudes. To make Indians into demons is not to relieve the other masqueraders of their bad behavior. Indeed, if anything, Melville blurs the distinctions between the various deceivers, gullible victims of con men, and the more directly evil demons, perhaps we could even say, the more honestly evil characters who also are floating down the Mississippi on the riverboat *Fédele*.

One of the frustrating qualities of *The Confidence-Man* is its impossibly complicated plot, made more so by the multiple voices that serially inhabit the tale. In this instance, the narrative lines can be especially confusing. Moredock's story is told to the cosmopolitan by a stranger. In an earlier chapter (chapter 25), the cosmopolitan had had an argument with a misanthrope. The stranger begins the conversation by explaining to the cosmopolitan that he had observed the cosmopolitan's argument with the misanthrope, and suggests

that the misanthrope reminds him of Colonel John Moredock. The
stranger seeks to distinguish Moredock from the misanthrope,
noting that Moredock's hatred wasn't directed at the human race
generally but instead at Indians specifically. Moredock was attractive
to most of humanity, except for Indians, and they were repulsed by
him as much as he by them. Moredock was "silky bearded and curled
headed, and to all but Indians juicy as a peach. But Indians—how
the late John Moredock, Indian-hater of Illinois, hated Indians, to
be sure!" (990). After introducing the subject, the stranger goes
on to suggest that he tell the story of Moredock as it had been told
by James Hall, a friend of his father.

Here we have the telling of a telling of a telling of a story. Hall's
nonfictional rendering of Moredock becomes fictionalized by way
of proxy. Who knows who the stranger is? Perhaps he is the biggest
liar of all, who, to fool us even more, decides to tell the truth. Perhaps even more telling, his truth may not be true, even for himself.
An epistemological quandary turns into a metaphysical conundrum.
Who are we? Who are they? The American mystery deepens as we
drift down the river.

According to the stranger, the way Hall explains the logic
of Indian-hating is straightforward, practically a syllogism. Even
though not all Indians are bad, because you can never know for sure,
you must assume that any Indian you deal with may be bad. Part of
the proof Melville adduces, in the words of Hall, is as follows:

> At any rate, it has been observed that when an Indian becomes
> a genuine proselyte of Christianity (such cases, however, not
> being very many; though, indeed, entire tribes are sometimes
> brought to the true light), he will not in that case conceal his
> enlightened conviction, that his race's portion by nature is
> total depravity; and, in that way, as much as admits that the

backwoodsman's worst idea of it is not very far from true; while, on the other hand, those red men who are the greatest sticklers for the theory of Indian virtue, and Indian loving-kindness, are sometimes the arrantest horse-thieves and tomahawkers among them. So, at least, avers the backwoodsman. And though, knowing the Indian nature, as he thinks he does, he fancies he is not ignorant that an Indian may in some points deceive himself almost as effectually as in bush-tactics he can another, yet his theory and his practice as above contrasted seem to involve an inconsistency so extreme, that when a toma-hawking red-man advances the notion of the benignity of the red race, it is but part and parcel with that subtle strategy which he finds so useful in war, in hunting, and the general conduct of life. (997)

For the Indian, then, there is no winning for losing. If he converts to Christianity, a sign of his conversion is his enlightened under-standing of his depraved past. If he fails to convert, then no matter how good he may claim to be, he is mistaken. He is either lying to the white man or, in an especially depraved sense, lying to both the white man and himself. In this sense, only someone who behaves as brutally as the Devil, in effect acting in response to the Devil, is capable of resisting and overcoming the Indian's cunning. Demon matches demon. There is no end to illusion, but it is not as Emerson would have it, in our dreams. For Melville it is our waking nightmare.

The paradigmatic Indian Judge Hall tells of is a chief named Moc-mohoc, who for many years harassed a colony of settlers composed of the extended families of seven cousins, the Wrights and the Weavers. Eventually reduced to five cousins due to the ongoing at-tacks of Mocmohoc and his tribe, the settlers finally succeeded in making a treaty with him. The chief not only treated with them but seemed genuinely pleased to become their friends. But, still suspicious, the five agreed never to enter Mocmohoc's wigwam together, so that if he was insincere, the remaining cousins could wreak their vengeance. Nonetheless, over time, Mocmohoc won them over and invited them all to a feast of bear's meat. He then killed them all. Many years later, when reproached for this act of treachery by a hunter he was holding captive, Mocmohoc responded, "Treachery? Pale face! 'Twas they who broke their covenant first, in coming all together; they that broke it first, in trusting Mocmohoc" (999).

The effect that such depravity has on those who observe the Indian is considerable. Not all backwoodsmen are victims, but they all know someone or know of someone who has been victimized. "What avails, then, that some one Indian, or some two or three, treat a backswoodsman friendly-like? He fears me, he thinks. Take my rifle from me, give him motive, and what will come? Or if not so, how know I what involuntary preparations may be going on in him for things as unbeknown in present time to him as me—a sort of chemical preparation in the soul for malice, a chemical preparation in the body for malady" (999–1000).

These lines say much. A chemical preparation in the soul, involuntary preparations, in the face of free will there is a compulsion on the part of the Indian that, even though he resists with all his will, may overcome him. And what may be even worse, should the Indian achieve a measure of success in resisting his inner self, there is no way that he will be trusted anyway. Despite this thorough examination of the soul of the Indian, the settler cannot know him, and even more astonishing, the Indian cannot know himself. The settler may be ignorant, but his quandary is no different than that of anyone else who has realized that no one can know the pain of others. But Judge Hall seems to suggest something more, that the Indian cannot even know his own pain, and his self-ignorance will lead to self-destruction, even if that self-destruction is at the hands of the settler.

In fighting against his own savage nature, the Indian cannot help but become a coward. To resist your own nature requires not bravery but submission to the superior culture of the white man, his Christianity, which leads the judge to his final observation concerning the Indian: "A coward friend, he makes a ruthless enemy" (1000).

At this point, Judge Hall discusses the Indian-hater par excellence. Of the type, he argues, the purest is he who leaves his kin, goes deep into the forest primeval, and acts out "a calm and cloistered scheme of strategical, implacable and lonesome vengeance" (1000). The emphasis might be on the word *cloistered,* for the Indian-hater par excellence is one whose biography can never be told, who lives in intense solitude. Such a man is almost a parody of Emerson's self-reliant individual. (It may even be the case that this was at least a part of Melville's intent.) It is here that Melville has the judge turn more specifically to the story of John Moredock. The judge emphasizes how the perfection of self-reliant distance from others is not the case for Moredock. While Moredock was an Indian-hater, he had a heart, something that is curiously true of almost all real Indian-haters, who live through a contradiction, "namely, that nearly all Indian-haters, have at bottom, loving hearts; at any rate, more generous than the average" (1005). He had a wife and children and even was considered to be a potential candidate for governor of Illinois, but he declined, knowing that the pomp of high office would interfere with his ability to kill more Indians, distracting him from his solitary task.

What are we to make of this tale? It would seem that the metaphysics of Indian-hating involves some deep contradictions. Loving yet hateful, suspicious yet open-hearted, the Indian-hater can only hate Indians on the condition that he be a lover of Christian mankind. He also, though, must be the sort of Christian who places suspicion above faith. But there is also the issue of grievance. Indian-haters must assume what William James was later to call "vicious naivety," that is, an innocence that is not so innocent, that cloaks aggressive hatred in a sense of moral superiority and just vengeance.

In using the Indians in this way, in making them into an entire race of confidence men, Melville is adding another chapter to his critique of the practicability of Christianity. That the Indian-hater is someone Melville uses to illustrate the unrealistic view of the world that a weak-minded Christian confidence might hold, presenting the Indian-hater as realistic in comparison, is but one dimension of his critique of American confidence. Another dimension of Melville's critique of confidence has to do with its total complicity with genocidal evil, an evil that wraps itself in the cloak of Christian love.

As long as Christianity persists, Melville seems to be saying, so will this metaphysics. And so it does The continued presence of such metaphysics in the United States, even after the almost total decimation of the Indian tribes, suggests that, like other forms of hatred, it is able to outlast its original object. But this persistence is also transmogrified over time, as substitute objects of hatred and the hidden expression of other desires come into play. In that, Indian-hating either parallels Christianity, which responds to the world with its own powers, on its own terms, so to speak, and constantly finds new objects, or is one of the forms that Christianity assumes in a frontier society.

Along with hatred and repulsion, the metaphysics of Indian-hating is driven by fear and desire. Indeed, fear and desire are the twins of hatred and repulsion. It is a bit like the story of the bear hunter, who kills a bear, is mauled by another bear avenging the first, heals, seeks revenge, and so the next year kills the bear that mauled him. But then he is mauled by another bear. He eventually kills that bear and is mauled again by yet another bear. This theater of pain and death goes on for a number of bears over the course of a number of years. Eventually, after he kills yet another bear, the hunter is tapped on the shoulder, and the biggest bear of all says to him, "You don't really come here for the hunting, do you?" This is the sort of dark comedy that Herman Melville is able to extract from his relating of the tale of Moredock. It is a desire that turns absurd. That which is forbidden exerts this sort of psychic power, in that we always seem to want most that which we are denied, no matter how much harm it causes us, or perhaps because of the harm it causes us. Melville's Indian-hater enjoys hating Indians, but the terrible price he pays is that there is no escaping this pleasure, and hence it becomes a pleasure that is no longer a pleasure.

Indian Territory

What does all of this have to do with the Ingalls family? If nothing else, the complex contradictions of the Indian-hater appear in the guise of a father who tries to reconcile his love of his family with his ongoing placing of them at risk, in the name of a freedom that can only be achieved by the denial of those who occupy the space that he will occupy and then abandon. As settlers closed in on his family living in the woods of Wisconsin, Charles Ingalls concluded that it would be good to move to the western country. "In the West the land was level, and there were no trees. The grass grew thick and high. There the wild animals wandered and fed as though they were in a pasture that stretched much farther than a man could see. And there were no settlers."[13] Wilder immediately explains, "Only Indians lived there" (LHOP, 2).

As is made clear in the conclusion of the story, Charles Ingalls had decided, apparently in a mistaken faith in politicians who had said that the Indian Territory of Oklahoma was about to be opened to settlement, to jump the gun and get there first. His working assumption, like that of others who squatted on the lands of Indian Territory, was that the Indians had no serious right to inhabit the land despite the treaties that had been made, and that if settlers like Ingalls would stake claims, eventually the government of the United States would be compelled to protect them from the Indians. But Ingalls's timing was off. At the end of *Little House on the Prairie,* the Ingalls family has left their house and are moving on, northward toward Minnesota.

But the arc of this narrative is effectively framed not so much by Pa Ingalls's restlessness as by little Laura Ingalls's desire. This desire is planted in her by her father:

> Pa promised that when they came to the West, Laura should see a papoose.
> "What is a papoose?" she asked him, and he said, "A papoose is a little, brown, Indian baby." (LHOP, 6)

Laura's curiosity about papooses grows throughout the book and is coupled with more general, vague discussions of Indians. The expression of unconscious desire embedded in these discussions is remarkable. Consider this exchange between Laura and her mother as they are eating supper while spending their first night on the land they were settling on the prairie:

> "Where is a papoose, Ma?" Laura asked.
> "Don't speak with your mouth full, Laura," said Ma.
> So Laura chewed and swallowed, and she said, "I want to see a papoose."

"Mercy on us!" Ma said. "Whatever makes you want to see Indians? We will see enough of them. More than we want to, I wouldn't wonder."

"They wouldn't hurt us, would they?" Mary asked. Mary was always good; she never spoke with her mouth full.

"No!" Ma said. "Don't get such an idea into your head."

"Why don't you like Indians, Ma?" Laura asked, and she caught a drip of molasses with her tongue.

"I just don't like them; and don't lick your fingers, Laura," said Ma.

"This is Indian country, isn't it?" Laura said. "What did we come to their country for, if you don't like them?"

Ma said she didn't know whether this was Indian country or not. She didn't know where the Kansas line was. But whether or no, the Indians would not be here long. Pa had word from a man in Washington that the Indian Territory would be open to settlement soon. It might already be open to settlement. They could not know, because Washington was so far away. (LHOP, 46–47)

In *The History of Manners,* Norbert Elias notes a dynamic in the emergence of manners as a civilizing process in European culture on the cusp of the modern era. Manners initially were developed by members of the late medieval nobility in order to distinguish themselves positively from the very highest classes of royalty. With less wealth, they invented other forms of distinction. Those of the highest rank took note, revised their behavior accordingly, and manners penetrated to the upper classes. Manners were even further refined by the nobility in an attempt to retain their distinction. While the back-and-forth of codes of etiquette was chaotic in the early going, Elias suggests that over time certain lines of development emerged. "These include," he writes, "for example, what may be described as an advance of the threshold of embarrassment and shame, as 'refinement,' or as 'civilization.'"[14] This internalization of distinctions crossing ranks bound medieval society together.

The carrying of manners to the frontier, it would seem, involved precisely a raising of the threshold of shame. Even within the limited frame of the Ingalls family, Laura is less civilized than Mary; Mary is older, of course, and also more refined. So the questioning about Indians comes from Laura, who is less ashamed, less embarrassed to ask. Her mother is the teacher of her children, and of her husband (for she was born and bred in the East). She is the teacher of shame, and of its eventual internalization as guilt. Having absorbed the lesson of manners far more completely, Ma is unwilling to explain her reasons for hating Indians to the girls. But hate them she does.

But there is also a coupling of the desire to *see* with the act of *eating*. Laura shifts from asking what a papoose is to wanting to see one, immediately after swallowing her food, without yet being given an explanation as to where a papoose is by her mother. Her father had already told her that a papoose is a little, brown, Indian baby, but here she wants to learn from her mother something more, namely where they are. And her mother resists, as if implicitly realizing the danger of Laura's desire. Ma focuses instead on Laura's manners—no chewing with your mouth open, don't lick your fingers. But rthe persistence of Laura's inquiry, which eventually elicits a longer response from Ma, communicates a deep familial nervousness regarding the boundaries they are crossing. The entire conversation is framed by questions concerning territorial lines. Laura wants to know whether they are in Indian country or not, and her mother tells her that she doesn't know, that it perhaps doesn't matter anyway.

The next major discussion of Indians occurs when two Indians invade the house while Pa is away hunting. Ma feeds them cornbread after they sign her to do so, and they take Pa's tobacco with them when they leave. When Pa comes home, he explains that Ma did the right thing to feed them. But Laura, whom Pa had warned not to let the dog Jack off the leash, inadvertently lets Pa know she had thought to do just that. Pa is angry when he speaks to Laura and Mary:

> "Do you know what would have happened if you had turned Jack loose?" Pa asked.
> "No, Pa," they whispered.
> "He would have bitten those Indians," said Pa. "Then there would have been trouble. Bad trouble. Do you understand?"
> "Yes, Pa," they said. But they did not understand.
> "Would they have killed Jack?" Laura asked.
> "Yes. And that's not all. You girls remember this: You do as you're told, no matter what happens." . . .
> "Do as you're told," said Pa, "and no harm will come to you." (LHOP, 146)

The need for absolute obedience in a situation of potential danger is his lesson to the girls. There is an echo here of Jefferson's advice to his daughter, with his admonition to always keep him in mind when she considers what she is to do. Of course, there is more going on here than even the possibility of a confrontation over the dog (though such a confrontation is to occur later in the narrative).

One of the distinctive features of the Indians who come to the house is that they smell strongly. When Laura goes into the house she smells them first, before seeing them. "Laura ran toward Ma, but just as she reached the hearth, she smelled a horribly bad smell, and she looked up at the Indians" (LHOP, 137). Laura soon realizes why they smell so bad: "Around their waists each of the Indians wore a leather thong, and the furry skin of a small animal hung down in front. The fur was striped black and white, and now Laura knew what made that smell. The skins were fresh skunk skins" (LHOP, 138).

Aside from the obvious use of skunk skins as codpieces, there is another symbolic role played by the presence of the skins. Many Native American tribes tell tales of how the skunk was a monster that was brought down to size by one hero or another, sometimes being a symbol of evil.[15] That the skunk skins are worn as codpieces indicates a threat of evil that has undertones of sexual violence. Pa seems aware of this fact. At one point during the evening after the Indians came to the house he says, "The main thing is to be on good terms with the Indians. We don't want to wake up some night with a band of the screeching dev—." At this point, Ma shushes him, presumably so that he won't frighten the girls (LHOP, 144). But the association of the Indians with demons is completely consistent with Melville's depiction of the rationale for Indian-hating. For the Indian-hater it is impossible to be on good terms with the Indians. The tension that comes from trying to do so while knowing that they might turn into devils at any moment is unbearable.

One wonders what Pa is thinking. Despite the obvious signs of danger, he continues to make excursions away from the house. He goes to Independence, Missouri, some forty miles away, to trade in furs for supplies and farming tools. Those trips also keep him informed of the latest developments concerning the status of the Indian Territory. The tensions with the Osage continue to build. Indeed, in the winter months preceding the planting season, two more Indians appear while Pa is away, and they almost make off with the furs Pa had been gathering to trade for farming supplies. (The Indian who was intent on seizing the furs was stopped by his companion, the implication being that to take the furs was to cross some line that should not be crossed. Apparently, the Indians had good reason for tracing a delicate path as much as the settlers did [LHOP, 233–234].)

When Pa comes home and is informed of this incident, he "looked sober." That evening he plays a song on his fiddle about an Indian maid named Alfarata, which contains the lines "Fleeting years have borne away / The voice of Alfarata." Laura asks where the voice went. "Oh I suppose she went west," Ma answered. "That's what the Indians do." This leads Laura to ask more questions about the Indians, eventually resulting in Pa providing a fuller explanation, though not quite a complete one:

> "When white settlers come into a country, the Indians have to move on. The government is going to move these Indians farther west, any time now. That's why we're here, Laura. White people are going to settle all this country, and we get the best land because we get here first and take our pick. Now do you understand?"
>
> "Yes, Pa," Laura said. "But, Pa, I thought this was Indian Territory. Won't it make the Indians mad to have to—"
>
> "No more questions, Laura," Pa said, firmly. "Go to sleep." (LHOP, 236–237)

This question, however, lingers throughout the rest of the book.

Desire and Possession

Eventually, the Indians do get mad and threaten to go on the war-path. Only the intervention of a leader of the Osage tribe, named Soldat du Chêne, prevents a war from breaking out, with the strong likelihood of the Ingalls family being massacred.[16] Two days after the war party breaks up, a procession of Osage Indians passes the Ingalls homestead. The procession stretches as far as the eye can see, and it takes all day for them to depart. Eventually, Laura gets her wish and sees a papoose, riding in a basket on the side of a pony with its mother. She looks deep into the baby's black eyes.

> "Pa," she said, "get me that little Indian baby!"
>
> "Hush, Laura!" Pa told her sternly.
>
> The little baby was going by. Its head turned and its eyes kept looking into Laura's eyes.
>
> "Oh, I want it! I want it!" Laura begged. The baby was going farther and farther away. but it did not stop looking back at Laura. "It wants to stay with me," Laura begged. "Please, Pa, please!" (LHOP, 308)

Fear has quickly transformed into desire. Laura persists, even in her shame, and begins to cry.

> Ma said she had never heard of such a thing. "For shame, Laura," she said, but Laura could not stop crying. "Why on earth do you want an Indian baby, of all things!" Ma asked her.
>
> "Its eyes are so black," Laura sobbed. She could not say what she meant.
>
> "Why, Laura," Ma said, "you don't want another baby. We have a baby, our own baby."
>
> "I want the other one, too!" Laura sobbed, loudly. (LHOP, 309–310)

Laura cannot say what she means, which is to say she cannot say why she wants what she wants. But want that baby she does. This desire to *have* that which she has been wanting to *see,* to *see* that which she originally wanted to *know,* a desire to know that is incited by her father's comments, conflates knowledge, scopophilia, and possession into a single urge.

Laura would add that baby to her collection—baby Carrie, and the papoose, the "other one, too." It is a hunger she feels, a deep desire to possess, a desire that will only be satisfied temporarily, and will require further fulfillment as time passes. (Throughout these volumes, baby dolls appear as contested objects of desire, substitute versions of the papooses, with their own class hierarchies [Nelly, the prosperous child rival of Laura, has china dolls, while Laura's more humble rag doll sometimes doesn't even have button eyes.])

Laura is not an Indian-hater in Melville's sense. But she is a member of a family of Indian-haters. It is apparent that she seems to be attempting to break with the family through the vehicle of desiring to possess the baby. Perhaps the desire to possess is not so far from the desire to destroy. But the generational shift is clear. Take the baby. Eat that baby, and move on. It is not surprising, then, that Laura is indifferent to the baby's mother. This indifference is remarkable only if we think that she is seeing these Indians as fellow humans. She is not. They have become things to her. But then again, so is her own little sister, further down the internal civilizational order of her family.

That evening, as the long procession finally comes to an end, the family seem to realize that they have been witnesses (at least) to something very wrong, and an uneasiness not associated with danger descends upon them as they watch:

> Then the very last pony went by. But Pa and Ma and Laura and Mary still stayed in the doorway, looking, till that long line of Indians slowly pulled itself over the western edge of the world. And nothing was left but silence and emptiness. All the world seemed very quiet and lonely. . . .
>
> [Laura] sat a long time on the doorstep, looking into the empty west where the Indians had gone. (LHOP, 311)

The quiet that the Ingalls now sense is not a relief to them. Tellingly, none of them are hungry. Their desire disappears. They all feel, as

Ma says, "let down" (LHOP, 311). This is what loneliness is about, the loneliness of being absent in presence.[17] Everyone here is alone. Yet they are alone together.

Why are they let down? Let down by whom? Ma and Pa are unable or unwilling to acknowledge their own complicity in this sad chapter. It is simply something that the Indians must bear. But they still feel their guilt, in the form of a loss of appetite.[18] The loss of appetite, as we know from *Little House in the Big Woods,* is no small matter.

The relevant Indians, the Osage people, were to return to a part of this land, in Oklahoma, and members of the Little Osage continue to live there.[19] They were one of the greatest of the Indian nations when French explorers—whom they called the big eyebrows, because of the uncouth way they refused to pluck their hairy faces—first encountered them in the seventeenth century, near the Missouri River. Their reach extended from what is now the Deep South of the United States to Wyoming, and among their offshoots are the Sioux Nation and the Apaches, with whom they were to fight. Most of the little Osage sided with the Confederacy during the Civil War, not seeing a meaningful distinction between the horrors of the slavery of the South and the brutality with which they and other tribes were treated by the North, hopeful that a Southern victory might ease the pressures on them.

Through the period from the first encounter with Europeans to the mid-nineteenth century, the Osage ranged widely in the west, from the headwaters of the Missouri River in what is now Wyoming, to what became Indian Territory, and eventually to Oklahoma. At the time that the Ingallses were squatting, the Osage were still nomadic.

None of this guilt is resolved. Instead, the next chapter begins, "After the Indians had gone, a great peace settled on the prairie"

(LHOP, 312). The page is turned, spring arrives, the burnt-over prairie turns green as if overnight, and a period of bucolic planting and caring for plants begins. "Pretty soon they would all begin to live like kings" (LHOP, 315). Only they won't. Within a few months they will be on their way again, ordered out of Indian Territory by the US government. Pa, hearing the news, will immediately make the decision to have the family leave the little house and homestead where they had spent the year. They take off the next day, but before they leave, he expresses his outrage: "'I'll not stay here to be taken away by the soldiers like an outlaw! If some blasted politicians in Washington hadn't sent out word it would be all right to settle here, I'd never have been three miles over the line into Indian Territory. But I'll not wait for the soldiers to take us out. We're going now!'" (LHOP, 316). The sense of betrayal that Pa expresses conveniently ignores the fact that he knew, when he entered Indian Territory, that he was squatting there. His own sense of the inevitability of the Indians' fate, his confidence in the government's bad faith, and his reliance on the politicians' willingness to break promises to the Indians remained unquestioned. So when those politicians, in a rare gesture, keep their promise (for a while) to the Osage tribes in the Indian Territory, *he* feels betrayed. This sense of betrayal can easily be transferred to the Indians themselves. Here in miniature we see the workings of the metaphysics of Indian-hating in Charles Ingalls.

They leave. But there is one last peculiarity embedded in the final chapter of *Little House on the Prairie.* As the family settles in for their first night back on the plain, again on the move, Pa breaks out his fiddle. He begins by playing "Oh! Susanna," Stephen Foster's song of the gold rush. Of course, the gold rush was that great leap that inspired so many to go west. But the next two songs that Pa chooses to play are most telling. First he plays "Dixie," a song that

originated in black minstrelsy of the 1850s and then became the un-
official anthem of the Confederacy. Then he plays "Battle Cry of
Freedom," an 1862 patriotic song of the Union. It is as though he is
enacting the tableau of race and reunion so powerfully explained
by David Blight in his historical masterpiece of the same name.[20]
Blight shows how the reconciliation of Southern and Northern
Americans in the post–Civil War era entailed a dramatic and drastic
revision of the reasons for and the outcome of the war, one that sub-
ordinated the emancipation narrative for one of "brother against
brother" quarrels concerning autonomy versus unity. What happened by way of this forgetting of the reason for the war was the
repression of liberated African Americans. If the war was fought
over differences that were exclusively between white Americans,
then the reconciliation of North and South, it follows, would involve
only them. Of course, that involvement would only entail the oppression of those who were the very reason for the war.

What might this strategic forgetting have to do with the metaphysics of Indian-hating? It turns out, everything. In the essay that
concludes the first volume of *Democracy in America,* Alexis de
Tocqueville writes about "the three races that inhabit the United
States."[21] For Tocqueville, "the Negro" and "white man," however
unhappily, are destined to be with each other even when and if
slavery is abolished. And even if the Negro remains servile, he will
nonetheless survive. But the Indian is destined to be destroyed.
Tocqueville writes at length of the process by which the penetration
of the wilderness by European settlers disturbed the game on which
the Indians depend; the settlements are made on territories ill secured by the tribes, since they possess those lands collectively, if at
all. According to Tocqueville, "The Indians, who had lived until
then in a sort of abundance, find it difficult to subsist, and have still
more difficulty in procuring the objects of exchange that they need.

By making their game flee, it is almost as if one had made the fields of our farmers sterile. Soon the means of existence is almost entirely lacking in them."[22] Tocqueville remarks on these matters sorrowfully, as though a natural calamity was occurring. (It is in a vein similar to the language used by investment bankers when the markets crashed as a consequence of their fraudulent practices, referring to the crash as a financial tsunami, something no one could have predicted, a sort of act of God.)

William Connolly has commented that Tocqueville's posture enabled the destruction of Indians to proceed under the guise of the civilizing process. He notes:

> Tocqueville registers, then, in carefully crafted language, the construction of "America," a civi-territorial complex in which the crucial dimensions of territory and civilization reinforce each other until they accumulate enough force together to propel the "triumphal progress of civilization across the wilderness." What of those wandering nomads who are, well, not dispossessed of territory they never possessed but displaced from a wilderness upon which they wandered? Tocqueville disposes of them sadly and regretfully, for they are dead to civilization even before the advance of civilization progressively kills them off.[23]

Connolly's description of Tocqueville's sorrow could be transferred completely and clearly to the Ingalls family, who feel empty and lonely when the Indians leave, knowing, without acknowledging, that their role in the civilizing process entailed driving the Indians away. Yet by the end of the next, and final, chapter, they are cheered by the songs of the Civil War, not the war that was fought but the fictive war between quarreling brothers, in which the ever-present bodies of black Americans are ignored in the name of national harmony.

Coda: Strange Weather

The Little House series is marked by catastrophic events. There is extreme weather. Drought, flood, blizzard—an entire volume is devoted to the long winter, a tale of the bare survival of the inhabitants of De Smet, who are cut off from the rest of the world by seven months of extreme weather. There is the loss of crops in consecutive years by plagues of locusts. There are prairie fires that scorch the earth. In the books these are presented as though they are acts of God. But in her recent Pulitzer Prize–winning biography of Wilder, Caroline Fraser notes that these events are all associated with the human interventions that constituted the settling of the Plains. She writes, discussing the move away from the Dakotas that Laura and her husband, Almanzo, were making in 1889, that "the drought was in large part created by the settlers themselves. The Dakota Boom had upended an ecosystem with dramatic and near immediate results. After the rapid removal of bison and the interruption of a fire regime eons in the making, more than two and a half million acres of native grasses had been abruptly cleared and plowed within a decade. This stripped out organic matter available to crops, and had profound effects on temperature and climate."[24] Cultivation of prairie land caused the temperature to rise dramatically, and the planting of wheat, which drinks large amounts of water, coupled with the destruction of the protective prairie grasses, exposed the soil to "intense heat, evaporation, and drying winds. . . . A few lucky farmers managed a few good harvests, but it could not last. They had changed the climate, the ecology, and the land itself."[25]

If one reframes the narrative of the pioneer experience on the Plains to account for the environmental disaster that the Ingalls and Wilder families participated in, a different account of home becomes visible: home as a quest for destruction, for the insatiable appetites of supposedly shrewd and knowledgeable settlers familiar with the flora and fauna of a hostile environment that they have come to tame. Wilder's representative story, then, becomes a cautionary tale, an American nightmare from which we have not yet, even now, awoken.

Other narratives, other stories, other ways of trying to be at home under extreme circumstances, may tell us more. I return, for a while, to Amherst, to ask what Emily Dickinson might have to offer us, what sort of heat she generated and, perhaps, even controlled, while building a house of possibility.

Emily Dickinson's House of Possibility

They put me in the closet.

—EMILY DICKINSON

Silhouettes of Being

How can one be at home when one is confined to the outside? This is a paradox we are presented with in the person of Emily Dickinson, someone we may fairly think of as having been confined to her house for much of her lifetime, yet whose art was to escape such confinement by simply refusing it. Dickinson was no pioneer in the sense that Wilder was, but it is also clear that she was much more an explorer. Wilder built on conventions. Dickinson destroyed them. Wilder was a popular novelist. Dickinson was an obscure poet. But even as Wilder's reputation has recently grown beyond her confines as a popular children's author to that of being a major American writer, she nonetheless is vastly overshadowed by Dickinson.

Anyone who has written of Dickinson with responsibility realizes the sheer ridiculousness of the quest to understand the heart of her being, what Jerome Charyn has called "that impossible plunder of capturing whoever she was."[1] We do not, we cannot know Dickinson. Of course, this is the dilemma we *all* share with each other, that we can never truly and completely know each other, any more than we can know ourselves, even as that remains the human quest. Dickinson may be thought of as the explicit reminder and patron saint of this deep unknowability.

Unknowability—the essential mysteriousness of each one of us to each other—is not a theme so much as it is a red thread running through the 1,800 or so of Dickinson's surviving poems and gorgeous nothings. But while we cannot see with her eyes, we nonetheless share in her language of the visual. And while we cannot hear with her ears—her poems come to us as letters from other worlds, uncovered communications from an alien being—we nonetheless share with each other the words she scrawled on scraps of paper, in hopes of getting a glimpse of something otherwise.

Dickinson has somehow become monumental. In that sense, her reputation is now fixed, even as we cannot say what the substance of that reputation is. Her outsider status has become a trap for some of us who want to understand her, and who see her monumental status as a barrier to that understanding. We want to know her still, without resort to her reputation, free of illusions of monumentality. In one sense, she has become a cliché in her radicalness. "Thinking outside the box is the new box," is the most recent, if ironic, conventional wisdom. And so with her. Or perhaps I am too attuned to the zeitgeist as it appears on the platform of ordinary life.

To explain. Dickinson's poetic legacy is unavoidable to me, both as a living force and also in the more banal sense for her having been a largely unspoken presence to me through much of my adult life. I have been employed for more than thirty years at the same New England college her family helped to found in 1821, before she was even born, and lived in the heart of Amherst for most of that period. My office is in an eighteenth-century house just a short stroll from the Dickinson Homestead. She haunts me, as she haunts the college and the town, and not necessarily as a benign presence. She was fierce, and her ferocity still scorches, burns in her poems. Confined to the outside, living within a house, she burned, and was not consumed in the burning. That she was not consumed in the burning for so long makes her a sort of secular saint, or at least an exemplar for a way of being a poet. She is the most famous poet in a town that has become famous for cultivating famous poets—home or school to Robert Frost, Robert Merrill, Richard Wilbur, James Tate, Dara Weir, Tess Taylor, and others.

She composed her poems as she lived, in the heart of a domestic life recognizable to us as not so different from ours. Although the Dickinsons were a prominent Amherst family, Emily's life was circumscribed by the claims made on young unbetrothed women in her time and place, not dissimilar to the circumstances of Laura Ingalls Wilder. She baked, she cared for her ailing mother and her sometimes brutal father, and her illnesses, variously speculated on in the biographical literature, enabled her to withdraw from the social life of the town and region. But these were not conditions imposed upon her so much as they were the conditions in which she negotiated the practical terms through which she could exercise her artistic vision.

As Adrienne Rich once put it, "I have come to imagine her as somehow too strong for her environment, a figure of powerful will, not at all frail and breathless, someone whose personal dimensions would be felt in a household."[2] And in another meditation on Dickinson, Rich implicitly compares her to Thoreau: "[She] chose her seclusion, knowing she was exceptional and knowing what she needed—She carefully selected her society and controlled the disposal of her time . . . neither eccentric nor quaint; she was determined to survive, to use her powers, to practice necessary economics."[3] "Necessary economics" is but a two-word condensation of Thoreau's philosophy of home.

The household in which Rich imagined Dickinson being a powerful and charismatic presence has been well documented as being a far from quiet and placid place. The sexual liaisons, the political world come to parlor, the Homestead and the Evergreens next door—her brother Austin's home—being a New England salon, the posthumous struggle over her poems by family and lovers, all of this composed a secondary crossroads of contemporary American intellectual life, right there in Amherst. She often listened from the top of the stairs to the whispered confidences and louder conflicts unfolding below, occasionally emerging with a flower to devastate a visitor.[4]

Many years ago, a professor friend, commenting on the peculiar academic institution of the invited lecturer, came up with a potent aphorism. "A genius," he said, "is someone from out of town." What he meant was, first, that someone who is worth inviting to travel to a college or university to give a lecture is someone the inviters assume will be able to provide a perspective or specific knowledge that otherwise would not be available to them, someone who would know something that we in the existing community of knowledge don't already know. As a corollary, though, I believe he was also suggesting that in our own locality we academics are not seen as geniuses by each other, simply because we *are* local. No matter how many times we may be invited to speak elsewhere, when we return home, with our exhausted heads and dirty laundry, we are, metaphorically speaking, without honor in our own country. This idea is a variation on another, better-known, and perhaps more apt aphorism: familiarity breeds contempt. It is only when *we* become the invited guests of others that our own genius is recognized. Until then, we assume the guise of the ordinary, and we miss the extraordinary as it lies before us in the form of our colleagues and our own selves.

Such has been my experience of Dickinson. She is the genius who never left town, and hence for too long I have failed to recognize her. Her posthumous fame has served to provide the requisite distance for some, but many of us who have lived in Amherst, especially among the academics who dominate this community, often have seen her primarily as a backdrop, just another local tourist attraction, though perhaps our most prominent one. More than most people, I should have known better, as I have long insisted that the ordinary is itself a repository of the extraordinary. So, I begin this chapter, on Emily Dickinson's creation of another understanding of home, chagrined, abashed, a foolish latecomer to her genius. Better late than never, the saying goes. But I wonder if that saying is always so wise.

My path to Dickinson, moreover, is not only a result of the happy coincidence of geographic proximity. Once upon a time there was to be a chapter in this book not simply about Dickinson but about some other New England maidens who stayed enclosed within their father's house. These women lived not in Amherst but in Beverley, Massachusetts, one generation succeeding Dickinson. These were the Barnet sisters, Eva and Jeannette, older siblings to the artist Will Barnet, who devoted a series of paintings to their domestic life. But that chapter became something else, another book, a different meditation, a companion to this one, perhaps, with its own reflections on loss and family.[5]

Interestingly, Barnet devoted an entire sketchbook to Dickinson, and one poem that he focused on in that book seems to be an early harbinger of that later series of paintings. That is, the paintings, col-

lectively called *My Father's House,* juxtapose members of the
Barnet family in the past and the present, enabling the viewer to *see*
the memories of the paintings' subjects. They span generations, as
old members of the family and younger versions of the adult Barnet
children are represented in the imaginations of the next generation.
Similarly, his drawing accompanying "We do not play on Graves"
portrays a young version of himself, holding a baseball glove, looking
upon Emily Dickinson as she stands in a graveyard.[6] We may
imagine that young Will is waiting for her to leave the cemetery so
that he can, in fact, play on graves. But she has already provided a
caution to the baseball players:

> We do not play on Graves—
> Because there is'nt Room—
> Besides—it is'nt even—it slants
> And People come—
>
> And put a Flower on it—
> And hang their faces so—
> We're fearing that their Hearts will drop—
> And crush our pretty play—
>
> And so we move as far
> As Enemies—away—
> Just looking round to see how far
> It is—Occasionally—
> [599][7]

We do not play on graves because they have no room for play,
because they slant. "Tell all the truth but tell it slant—," she writes
in a more well-known poem [1263]. That famous poem refers more
directly to children than does the grave poem. There she suggests
that we all need a certain protection from the Truth, because it dazzles. While we all need a certain protection from blinding Truth, it

is children who are the analogues for her: "As Lightning to the
Children eased / With explanation kind / The Truth must dazzle
gradually / Or every man be blind." What is the greatest Truth that
we need to face? Perhaps it is that of the death of those we love. And
burial slants the Truth of their absence, rolls it downhill.

There is a claim here as well that the truth blinds. This is an old
observation, at least as old as the allegory of the cave. But Dickinson
may have been thinking not so much of Socrates as of Thoreau, and
his insistence that only by being fully *awake* may we have a chance
to see the truth. Thoreau knew how truth dazzles, and yet he needed
that dazzle to live. We may recall what he writes in *Walden:* "To be
awake is to be alive. I have never yet met a man who was quite awake.
How could I have looked him in the face?" (II, 14).[8] Is this what
Dickinson is suggesting? Are we for the most part nothing more than
somnambulant? Are we the walking dead? Is she?

The slant of truth reflects the slant of the sun in autumn or in
spring, when the shadows of dusk and dawn heighten our awareness of time. But the grave is always slant. What could that possibly
mean? The truth of the grave is one of memory, of people placing
objects that memorialize, with their hanging faces and crushing play.
But Dickinson is nothing if not playful. Hence, the exclusion of play
on the grave may be Dickinson signaling something about the relationship or lack of relationship of play to death itself. Could we say
that her death poems are not playful, but fatal? We move away from
the grave when we are able, and measure our lives by the distance
from what turns out, in this poem, to be our enemy. We look back
at "It" only occasionally. Inert, simply a plot of land, how can the
grave have such power over us? The answer should be clear: it is
the power of finitude, the grave, our long home.

Yet another poem associates the word *slant* with death. Here the
light of winter afternoons oppresses:

There's a certain slant of Light,
Winter Afternoons—
That oppresses, like the Heft
Of Cathedral Tunes—

Heavenly Hurt, it gives us—
We can find no scar,
But internal difference,
Where the Meanings, are—

None may teach it—Any—
'Tis the Seal Despair—
An imperial affliction
Sent us of the Air

When it comes, the Landscape listens—
Shadows—hold their breath—
When it goes, 'tis like the Distance
On the look of Death—
[320]

New Englanders know the fading light of a winter afternoon. But so do all of those who inhabit the farther northern and farther southern reaches of the Earth. They are more aware of the slant than are those from the equatorial regions, and hence potentially more aware of the curvature of the Earth. Does this slant translate into a heightened awareness of death?

"Shadows—hold their breath—." Helen Vendler, whose commentary constitutes my primary tutelage on Dickinson's poems, suggests that the Shadows depend on the slanting light for their very existence, that they hold their breath, awaiting their own disappearance, for the moment suspended.[9] Another way of thinking about the shadows, a complementary way, is to think of them as shades, that is to say, as ghosts, the dead who are suspended, hanging, no longer inspirited, or inspired. Between inspiration (breathe in) and expiration (breathe out) there is the holding of breath, a waiting for the sun to fall and obliterate the shadows, for the shadows to properly die, in their dance for the ghosts to retire, to fade into . . . light? Twilight is the time of ghostliness, the moment of day moving farthest away from morning. This slant of light, this winter twilight is "the Seal Despair." Despair is the end point of winter light, night is coming, the landscape listens. "When it goes, 'tis like the Distance / On the look of Death—." Despair is an end point, and Vendler points out that in an older Christian theology it is one of two sins of attitude, rather than of action, that can prevent salvation (the other being the Presumption of already being saved).[10] Hence the Seal Despair is an ending, and winter, always most experienced in the farther northern and southern regions of the Earth, is an end of life.

Of course, there is a spring as well, for later, for rebirth. And the cycles are important for Dickinson, for in each cycle there is the possibility of new light and new shadow. But it is the twilight that is Dickinson's deepest concern here. Twilight is when there is suspension and hence suspense, when a fullness of being may be paused over, when what most matters is clearest to us, revealed in the way that silhouettes reveal, as in contrast, not in detail. It is the time of day of haunting, of the uncanny.

"We can find no scar. . . ." Dickinson, as a reader of Emerson, may have been thinking of a passage early on in his essay "Experience." When comparing the death of his son, Waldo, to the loss of an estate, Emerson tried to show by analogy the numbness he felt, the distance from the tragedy of his loss. He writes, "So it is with this calamity; it does not touch me; something which I fancied was a part of me, which could not be torn away without tearing me nor enlarged without enriching me, falls off from me and leaves no scar. It was caducous." *Caducous* is an amazing word, referring to the lack of a mark left behind, say, when a leaf falls from the branch of a tree. (Stanley Cavell remarks that *caducous* can also refer to the birth of a child, or another animal, that supposedly leaves no visible mark on the mother.)[11] This scarless state, a hurt borne internally, invisibly, may allow us to pass through our days unnoticed, but nonetheless oppressed by loss. The tree will be bare, naked in the cold of winter. This is bleak, indeed. This is the state of mourning. But is it also the moment of morning, of a dawning within?

If we explore the etymology of the word we may find another link. The *Oxford English Dictionary* tells us that *caducous* is derived from the Latin *cadacus,* which is derived from the word *cadere,* "to fall." The word was coined in the seventeenth century to describe the state of being epileptic, to experience the falling sickness. One of the rumors concerning Dickinson herself is that she retreated into solitude because she suffered from epilepsy. And her command of language was such that her self-understanding could well have included a deep appreciation for the death she carried around inside herself, the fall she felt, the fall she knew, what Emerson called "the Fall of Man."

Dickinson's poems that are most explicitly about homes and graves, or homes as graves, show her familiarity with home as a place and expression of the finitude we most closely associate with death. The Dickinson way of thinking about being at home, it seems, is a crystallization of home as the uncanny, the home as a haunted place. The poems trace a path toward death not as an end but as continuous with a passion for life. This is a poet Vico would have endorsed. Of course, Dickinson is a part of everything—cats, and spiders, lovers and fields, changes in weather, the grief of loss extending farther than even death. But it is in her poems of home and death that she seems to me to be, well, most at home. And given how home is a long home in the end, her way of being at home with death may prove instructive.

If I suggest that there is something impossibly quixotic in attempting to write biographically about Dickinson, because Dickinson highlights the unknowability of other people, I acknowledge that what I want to explore instead is something probably equally impossible, but nonetheless worth essaying: to try to show how she creates silhouettes of being, a residue of home in her living death. As Thoreau provides us with an example of auto-biography, as the writing of the bios by the body in question, an art variously considered to be an attempt to confess, with all partiality, the datum of the life as experienced by that self, Dickinson gives us her shadows, her uncanny, her ghostly presence. Admitting from the start the impossibility of the task of receiving this gift, we still turn to her poetry for its possibilities beyond what our familiar prose can offer.

Prose versus Possibility

Dickinson's most famous poem on home equates dwelling with poetry, poetically rendered as Possibility. And Possibility is a counterpoint to death.

> I dwell in Possibility—
> A fairer House than Prose—
> More numerous of Windows—
> Superior—for Doors—
>
> Of Chambers as the Cedars—
> Impregnable of Eye—
> And for an Everlasting Roof
> The Gambrels of the Sky—

Of Visitors—the fairest—
For Occupation—This—
The spreading wide my narrow Hands
To gather Paradise—
[466]

Dickinson's dwelling, her attempt at living, is Possibility. If despair and presumption are sins, Possibility would seem to be their opposite, a virtue, an indeterminate opening to the future, an orientation forward but not foreordained, as is presumption, nor stuck in misery, as is despair. What is possible? Everything, anything, all things, even nothing, is possible. Why is possibility "a fairer House than Prose"?

Vendler suggests that what Dickinson means by possibility is actually poetry itself, that poetry stands in comparison to prose, and prose is found lacking in comparison. This equation of poetry with possibility is fair, if fairly obvious. But this equation is also the opposite of what is usually imagined to be the capacity of prose, with its immense multitude of words, sentences, and paragraphs that supposedly can create or re-create worlds through representation. Yet another way of thinking of this comparison is that the extended metaphor of the house—windows, doors, chambers, roof, gambrels—and the comparison of poetry to prose render the essay form, and the novel as well, as inferior, or at least the lesser of the powers we should associate with imagination. The reason this is so is because prose's economy is poor; it requires more words to do less. We could imagine how each metaphor Dickinson uses here advances the case for poetry as the home for our words. More windows could mean more vantage points on the world. And doors? Entry and exit are easier in poems than in prose, which have more words and require more work to enter and to leave. Cedar, as opposed to pine, is everlasting (like the Cedars of Lebanon). Gambrels and roof, open to sky, oppose the narrow and steep, enclosed roofs of old New England.[12]

It is helpful here to think of Dickinson as a reader and admirer of Thoreau. Take, for instance, her roof that is open to the sky. As I mentioned earlier, in a chapter in *Walden,* fittingly entitled "House-warming," Thoreau writes about the ceiling over his head, while the rafters were still exposed, his wish for there to be some "obscurity overhead" (XIII, 6).[13] Thoreau's "obscurity overhead" conceptually rhymes with Dickinson's "Gambrels of the Sky." Though they are not the same, they *do* complement each other. Her view is to the infinite beyond our mortal lives, his to the images of obscurity, the indefinite open. He too is referencing the allegory of the cave, in which men can only see the images that flicker before them, and never see the true and ideal forms of blinding daylight. This is similar to Dickinson's understanding of how Truth is so brilliant as to blind us.

And what of Dickinson's gathering hands? Here we may think along with Emerson, again from "Experience." In a passage on the grief he has expressed over his loss of Waldo, he writes, "I take this evanescence and lubricity of all objects, which lets them slip through our fingers then when we clutch hardest, to be the most unhandsome part of our condition. Nature does not like to be observed, and likes that we should be her fools and playmates." Emerson here is playing with the idea of *hands* and their relationship to thinking, as well as our inability to "master" nature by dint of possessing It. For him, thinking is receptivity, and its opposite is clutching, closing a hand into a fist, perhaps, grasping. Our un*hand*some condition comes about when we fail to use our hands as hands should be used. To hold, but to hold openly; to hold as one holds a child in one's arms; to receive, as a gift, that which comes to us. This is that aspect of the human—that we have hands to receive—that allows us to think in a human way. (Cavell is responsible for making this connection, in a book called *Conditions Handsome and Unhandsome*. There he also notes that this idea of Emerson's can be traced forward as well, having decisively influenced Martin Heidegger, who came to name thinking as being a "handicraft.") Dickinson's narrow hands are not clutching, but gathering, and they are gathering that which can only receive us, Paradise, the long home of death.

Vendler reads the final stanza of "I Dwell in Possibility," where Dickinson drops the comparison to prose, as her gesture of prayer. I would agree, but again would push on further. "The spreading wide my narrow Hands / To gather Paradise—," this, her Occupation, is also her way of thinking poetically. Gathering by spreading—there is undeniably an erotic figuring here—and Paradise? What is being gathered? Aside from death, and aside from the parallel ecstasy of sexual fulfillment (the "little death"), one might think of this gathering as Dickinson's version of moral perfectionism, that is, what is imagined by Cavell as an attempt to be "present in the present," to focus one's moral attention on the immediate possibilities of *becoming*, unfolding one's self, one's life, in such a way as to be more acutely aware of the gravity and ecstasy of life itself.

But all is not ecstasy. There is another, darker vision of prose that Dickinson presents in an earlier poem, one that seems to suggest more directly her consciousness of a politics of poetry that underwrites her moral perfectionism:

> They shut me up in prose—
> As when a little Girl—
> They put me in the Closet—
> Because they liked me "still"

Still! They could themselves have peeped—
And seen my Brain—go round—
They might as well have lodged a Bird
For Treason—in a Pound—

Himself has but to will
And easy as a Star
Look down upon Captivity—
And laugh—No more have I—
[445]

Here we may imagine Dickinson as an unruly child, confined to a closet to shut her up. We could think about a brilliant and socially straitjacketed child with her incessant questioning, her tantrums, her unhappiness, her frustration with the limitations of the language made available to her, her confinement inside the prison house of language, her retrospective comparison of a confinement to the closet as a child with a confinement to prose, both as means of silencing—"They shut me up"—directly suggesting that They, whoever They are, are silencing her as a means of controlling her. But she is not to be confined, any more than a bird may be confined for treason. As a bird cannot commit treason by dint of the fact that birds are constant migrants, ignorant of boundaries and frontiers, so too the poet cannot be confined by prose because the boundaries of sentences and frontiers of paragraphs do not apply to poetry.

And yet They tried. Had They only peeped and seen her brain go round, They may have realized the futility of closeting her. Who are They? In the first instance, it would seem They are the parents who confined her, but the word also encompasses any and all of those who shut her up in prose. Prose here is not a house but a closet, not simply a place that is not as fair a house as possibility, but a dark place of confinement within another house altogether. It is solitary confinement, this prose form of language, but a futile means of correction. Why should They look at her Brain, and not perceive her mind? Dickinson seems to be suggesting that They must be made to see concretely, in their imaginative lack. In referencing her brain she is emphasizing the materiality of her struggle, her own concrete resistance to the demands of convention, the dynamic of her movement as opposed to the stillness imposed upon her because They *liked* her still as opposed to moving.

This poem resolves itself ambiguously. Himself is introduced, willingly looking down from the perspective of a Star upon Captivity, and He laughs. Captivity seems to play with the Christian scene of the Nativity. From the perspective of the Star, God (?) looks down upon this family scene, only it is a scene of Captivity, closing up the possibilities that had at some point been opened up in a new birth. He laughs because He realizes just how futile the attempt to close down the poet in prose may be. "No more have I" may suggest that the poet has the same will as God, the same insistence on natality and new beginning over the confinement of captivity. Or, given the ambiguity of its placement, after another dash, it may mean that the poet does not have the will of God but her own will, an ungodly will, and hence is left to her own devices, outside of prose, turning toward possibility.

We return again to the contrast of natality with captivity, a subject broached by Hannah Arendt in *The Human Condition,* where she suggests that every new birth contains the possibility that a potential thing—an action, a work of art—that has not previously existed has an always latent possibility of coming into existence. But when Arendt suggests that every birth is a gift from nowhere, secularly speaking, she is divorcing birth from motherhood, in an act that enables both the freeing of a woman and the disabling of mothers in the same movement. This is an understanding that Dickinson seems to anticipate, the freedom from motherhood as linked to the freedom to create. Arendt does not employ the charged term *captivity* but instead refers to the repetitive and uncreative activity of labor as simple reproduction.

As Patchen Markel has observed, there is greater ambiguity in Arendt's own category of "work," which culminates in an appreciation of art as the highest form of expression that work takes, on the boundary of "speech" and "action." Markel also provides a reading of Arendt on Bertolt Brecht that suggests an acute understanding of the role that poetry may play in politics: "Joining poetry to politics by holding both at a distance from philosophy, Arendt assigned poetry the vocation of disruptive faithfulness to factual reality, which allowed her to praise Brecht on political grounds and to leverage forbearance for his political 'sins.'"

Like Arendt, like Brecht, Dickinson realizes that the role of poetry is not to philosophize but indeed to provide a "disruptive faithfulness to factual reality." The question for her becomes one of living poetically. And what is required for Dickinson to do so brings us back to what Adrienne Rich called her "necessary economics." It is as rigorous an economy as may be imagined, impossible in execution, and yet it is her practice, as her brain—goes round—as the soul unfolds itself materially. It is a brain, after all, not a mind, that she is exercising.

Self-Immolation

How does anyone sustain herself in pursuit of such creative powers? Dickinson seems to realize that life in the village of souls involves certain practices that, mundane in and of themselves, may in their very hard reality allow the extraordinary to unfold within ordinary life. Such, for example, in the practice of the blacksmith:

> Dare you see a Soul at the "White Heat"?
> Then crouch within the door—
> Red—is the Fire's common tint—
> But when the vivid Ore
>
> Has vanquished Flame's conditions—
> It quivers from the Forge
> Without a color, but the Light
> Of unanointed Blaze—
>
> Least Village, boasts its Blacksmith—
> Whose Anvil's even ring
> Stands symbol for the finer Forge
> That soundless tugs—within—
>
> Refining these impatient Ones
> With Hammer, and with Blaze
> Until the designated Light
> Repudiate the Forge—
> [401]

This poem appears to be about a dare. "Dare you see a soul transformed from fire into light?" would be a more direct way of reading the first two verses. Dare you look? Can you stand the heat? Dare you watch the red become without color (white)? What does Dickinson suggest we are seeing here, and why does it require one to take up a dare?

The Ore in the forge is transformed by the fire's heat but also by the hammer of the blacksmith. Removed from fire it is without color—red hot becomes white heat, the light of "unanointed Blaze," something unholy, yet holy still. Vendler sees this as a trip through purgatory, or the process of becoming saved, or reborn, through (im)patient suffering. She emphasizes the suffering of the Ore as it is refined by the process of the anvil and the hammer, and the surprising repudiation of the forge in the end.[14] But there is also a question of a dare: one's presence as a witness. The vanquishing of the flame is an implicit quenching of the metal with water, re-formed, shining the light of a blaze, a baptism of sorts.

When Dickinson reminds us that every village has its blacksmith, and has the blacksmith's anvil's even ring stand as symbol, the parallel with church—every village has a church—seems clear. By being so explicit about the standing symbol of the "Anvil's even ring," with the silent but tugging inner conscience of the soul, she sets up a moral struggle between the unanointed, that is to say, the poetical, and the church. True redemption for her is a repudiation of the Forge. Her Protestantism is deeply personal in that it will acknowledge the power of the church as a hostile but shaping force. But her understanding of the power of the White Heat is also profoundly ordinary, a process of suffering so familiar that it is easily compared to being shaped by a hammer, and ubiquitous, a part of everyday life. This is another instance of the extraordinary ordinary uncovered by poetry. It is a holocaust, in the sense bequeathed to us, and then lost as a consequence of that word's appropriation as a symbol for a different, twentieth-century, catastrophe. Heat transforms and annihilates, destroys in order to create. In it is a moment akin to twilight, a vestibule of being.

Is being at home even possible for a soul at the White Heat? Or is Dickinson giving us instructions in arson? In what may be her most scientific poem she provides us with further insight into fire:

> Ashes denote that Fire was—
> Revere the Grayest Pile
> For the Departed Creature's sake
> That hovered there awhile—

> Fire exists the first in light
> And then consolidates
> Only the Chemist can disclose
> Into what Carbonates
> [1097]

Vendler understands Dickinson in this poem to be presenting us with a way to understand how she herself saw her poems as "the cryptic residue of her incandescent emotional and intellectual fires."[15] She also provides us with the references contemporary to Dickinson's time that elaborate on the meaning of ashes. She points to a reference by Richard Sewall in his *Life of Emily Dickinson* to the Amherst College geologist, professor, and eventual president Edward Hitchcock, who wrote a volume entitled *The Religion of Geology,* in which he explained that nothing is annihilated by fire, an observation that has profound theological, but also practical, consequences. Hitchcock writes, "But chemistry informs us, that no case of combustion, how fiercely soever the fire may rage, annihilates the least particle of matter; and that fire only changes the form of substances. Nay, there is no reason to suppose that one particle of matter has been annihilated since the world began."[16]

Among other things, Dickinson may see this observation as providing some sort of strange reassurance. There is an earlier, slighter poem, referenced by Sewall and referred to by Vendler, that suggests as much:

> The Chemical conviction
> That Nought be lost
> Enable in Disaster
> My fractured Trust
>
> The Faces of the Atoms
> If I shall see

> How more the Finished Creatures
> Departed Me!
> [1070]

If all matter is preserved, eternity for all is assured, whether it be in heaven or in hell. Fractured trust is enabled at the moment of disaster, since that which disaster suggests, the destruction of a world, is not destroyed after all. Our atomic immortality is assured in this cosmology. (One wonders what Dickinson could have done with quantum theory.) But one's personal finitude is also assured.

"Ashes denote" is almost two separate poems. The first stanza may immediately be seen as a reflection on the cremated remains of someone. The fire that was is the life that is consumed, and the ashes are the memory of the creature that hovered there that we are to revere. A creature hovered—is it hovering still, in the slant of the shadow of twilight? But the remains are ashes, after all. And fire, as the second stanza tells us, exists first in light and then consolidates, which suggests that as the fire goes out, as life leaves, only the Chemist will be able to tell us of what the residue is composed. Is this the only memory, that which can be disclosed by the Chemist? Who is the Chemist? Carbonates are the chemical basis of living creatures, and their remains are a concentration of their living being. Is the Chemist the judge of what has been a living creature?

The possibility that there may be a judgment made concerning the *remains* of a creature is exceedingly strange, unless one is thinking from the perspective of the creature itself. That is, if Vendler is correct, and this is Dickinson describing her poetic process, then the Chemist is the reader of her poems. But the connection between the poetry and the life is so close. An ultimate judgment of a life can only occur after the lights have gone out. How is one to control for that? Only by taking control of when one dies. Dickinson may be thought of as seeking to die at the right time, each and every time she writes a poem. (Nietzsche has Zarathustra preach this doctrine. "Many die too late, and some die too early. Yet strange soundeth the precept: 'Die at the right time!' Die at the right time: so teacheth Zarathustra.")

Combining the judgment of the Chemist with the quest to write poetry—that is close to being a perfect distillate of life as may be possible. It also suggests a self-immolating impulse, not simply the cremating of the remains of a Creature. Self-immolation is usually a form of suicide protest, an inherently political act. What Dickinson offers is a politics of self-immolation that constantly renews itself. She is continuously in the process of burning down the house. Home economics for her involves the always ongoing cleansing by fire, its transformation into light, and then into ash. But to what purpose?

The politics of the ordinary entails the diurnal repetitions of mundane activities—baking, cleaning house, emptying bedpans, sweeping floors, toiletry, weeding gardens, picking flowers, walking, observing the flora and fauna that surround one as one lives another day of life. For Dickinson, to reveal the extraordinary that lives within the ordinary requires a cleansing fire that can only occur as a sacrament of writing. That fire must constantly be renewed—by whatever mysterious means she was to will it so—but eventually that fire will burn out nonetheless. Dedicating herself to the fire, Dickinson burned for a long time.

Living at the End of the World

"Called back," reads her tombstone in West Cemetery in Amherst. This is the long home, the home she imagined reaching toward all her life. It is in her return to Earth that Dickinson provides us with a certain comfort. One need not believe in a god to embrace that return. One need not even be a poet, though it helps. As does reading.

Dickinson offers us a way to imagine home otherwise than as home. In her persistent uncanniness—the ringing of the anvil—she offers an alien view of the silence that awaits us all. It is an ecstatic perspective, but it is available to us, not distant. She imagines this as gathering paradise. And she is aware that her poetic vision depends upon a constant striving to reach for paradise—even if one never, in this mortal life, arrives there. Authors and artists, poets, painters, musicians reach for this perfection (Emerson called it "the flying Perfect"), whatever the mode and even whatever the substantive focus of expression—be it figurative, abstract, realist, grotesque, Gothic, suffused with piety or evil, even embracing representations of the worst we may imagine, even embracing representations of nothing, almost always it seems, even risking ridicule for the striving itself. As do they, so must we, if we are to have any hope of home.

We are living through a period in our human habitation of this Earth when we have risked forgetting this Truth of our lives together. Smallness of desire, reduction of desire to consumption, and a clutching when we most need an open hand put us at risk of losing our humanity, at least. The metastasis of hatred that currently has a seeming upper hand in the politics of the United States of America as I write in 2019 would seem to be encouraging an antipoetry, a guttural house of prose—call it Trump Tower.

But this is a mood, a distorted reflection of our most unhandsome condition. We must fight it as citizens, with a greater awareness that even hatred can die. In other words, we can both understand the urgency of living at the end of the world, and still seek and sometimes find the comfort of home. Dickinson says to me, let us burn down the house, but let us be careful to keep the flame alive, and pay due respect to the ash we leave behind. While that is not enough, it is something, a trouble, and a comfort.

SIX

Herman Wallace's Dream House

My dreams are but a reflection of the man that I am.

—HERMAN WALLACE

Longing for Home

The Louisiana State Penitentiary is commonly known as Angola. It is so named after the plantation that originally existed on its grounds, said plantation having been established in 1835. It is claimed that the plantation was named after the region in Africa where most of the slaves who labored on the plantation when it was founded had originated. To state the obvious, the history of this plantation/prison cannot be told without reference to the history of chattel slavery in the United States and its aftermath. Indeed, in an uncanny linkage, Angola, the region of Africa, is depicted on the one map of Africa that can be found in the entry hall of Jefferson's Monticello. It is also the case that this particular entanglement of punishment with slavery is not exceptional but is instead typical of the history of southern prisons.

As has been more than amply documented, beginning with W. E. B. DuBois's history of Reconstruction and down to the present, in the post-Reconstruction era a de facto reestablishment of chattel slavery occurred in the defeated South largely through the instrument of the penal system. (Scholars often note this language from the Thirteenth Amendment: "Neither slavery nor involuntary servitude, *except as a punishment for crime whereof the party shall have been duly convicted,* shall exist within the United States, or any place subject to their jurisdiction" [emphasis added].) As happened in so many other southern penal systems, at Angola, freed slaves became reenslaved through the means of the criminal justice system: black men were made into convicted felons, convicts were hired out as enslaved laborers, and involuntary servitude—not simply imprisonment—rebuilt the planation economy as a de facto rather than de jure system of slave labor, complementing the work of the alternative form of involuntary labor, peonage, after Reconstruction. Eventually the Angola facility became a complex facility containing both maximum-security and multi-security prisons, with its own peculiar history still mired in the mores and folkways of slavery, but one that nevertheless gave lip service to the model of the penitentiaries in the North.

While it may rightly be claimed that every American prison has its own particular history of misery, it is also probably true that no prison has had as miserable a history as Angola. It has sometimes been the largest single prison in the United States, peaking with nearly 6,000 inmates in the late twentieth century. As of 2009 a majority of the imprisoned were serving life sentences. (The average prison sentence in 2007 at Angola was an astonishing eighty-eight years.) The original cemetery at Angola had to be supplemented by a second one late in the twentieth century when the older one reached its capacity: because so many prisoners were sentenced to life imprisonment, the rate of death of inmates at Angola was higher than any other prison anywhere else in the United States. Hard labor on the farm has remained the primary occupation of the vast majority of prisoners throughout Angola's history. And behind these harsh facts of prison labor is an almost mythic history of cruelty—sexual slavery internal to the prison population, hundreds of unaccounted for buried inmates, terrific abuse and torture of prisoners, a brutal system of solitary confinement, corruption of officials that leads to the denial of some of the basic necessities of life for those under the charge of the state—food, health care, security of body—all of which resulted more generally in a continuation of the de facto slavery that has marked the post-Reconstruction era of the American South well into the twenty-first century.

Angola is a place that is large enough to have its own newspaper, the *Angolite,* which for many years was edited by a lifer named Wilbert Rideau, a gifted writer and memoirist. Here is a description he gave of his habitat:

> This is my reality. Solitude. Four walls, graygreen, drab, and foreboding. Three of steel and one of bars, held together by 358 rivets. Seven feet wide, nine feet long. About the size of an average bathroom or—and my mind leaps at this—the size of four tombs, only taller. I, the living dead, have need of a few essentials that the physically dead no longer require—commode, shower, face bowl, bunk. A sleazy old mattress, worn to thinness. On the floor in a corner, a cardboard box that contains all my worldly possessions—a writing tablet, a pen, and two changes of underwear. The mattress, the box, and I are the only things not bolted down, except the cockroaches that come and go from the drain in the floor and scurry around in the shower. This is my life, every minute of the year. I'm buried alive.[1]

This experience of living death is common for prisoners, who more banally find themselves while incarcerated to have attained the legal status of civil death, of being physically alive but without the human rights that are supposedly the accompaniment of life itself. Rideau gives weight to being alive, but also being buried, being the living dead, as he puts it. His description is exemplary, only in that it distills what so many have claimed about the experience of confinement in a maximum-security prison throughout the decades. To be in prison is to experience life as a dead person.

In *Homo Sacer,* Giorgio Agamben writes:

> Today a law that seeks to transform itself wholly into life is more and more confronted with a life that has been deadened and mortified into judicial rule. Every attempt to rethink the political space of the West must begin with the clear awareness that we no longer know anything of the classical distinction between *zoē* and *bios,* between private life and political existence, between man as a simple living being at home in the house and man's political existence in the city.[2]

Agamben suggests that we are living in an era of the ascendance of the *nomos* of the camp, when the very possibility of being at home has been lost for us. Is that the case? We are living in an era of mass refugees, of deep displacement, but also of a more ordinary set of economic dislocations. But have the very conditions of life reached the point that home has actually ceased to be the central way we think of our world?

Even if it is not the case that we have reached Agamben's new *nomos,* does Angola constitute an example of the *nomos* of the camp, as he has presented it? Is Angola exemplary of "the hidden matrix and *nomos* of the political space in which we are still living"?[3] Perhaps the role of chattel slavery, overlooked by Agamben in favor of a genealogy of colonial law (to the extent that the law of slavery can be so separated), offers another way to thinking about this disastrous turn in modernity. How disastrous is this turn?

Similarly, we may ask: Is the life that is lived in Angola an example of precarious life, as Judith Butler has elaborated it?[4] Refugee populations, the living embodiment of the contemporary crisis of homelessness, are exemplars of precarious life. Does the civil death suffered by those caught in the carceral system operate in such a way as to render the lives of those so categorized unworthy of grieving as well? Mass incarceration in twenty-first-century America, then, with its focus on black men as the primary target, might be seen as an exemplar of this way of being. Rather than simply a new version of Jim Crow segregation, it would be understood to presage the most extreme, eliminationist political strategy of power, what some political theorists have, for the past decade, been calling thanatopolitics or necropolitics.[5] Angola, then, would be an example of Agamben's camp.

The camp may be thought of as an extremity of modernity, a form of power when power is at wit's end. But it is also the case that the very absolute character of the critique that Agamben presents leaves those who still seek degrees of freedom and the possibilities of being at home that are a part of being free with little in the way of resources. A radical passivity, a withdrawal from the politics of the ordinary, a retreat into solipsism—all are results of such a form of political despair.

A common approach by critics of Foucault and others who have been influenced by him has been to assert something similar, that there is just such an absolutism at work in the logic of the claims he makes concerning disciplinary society, that the *practices* of such institutions and the modern carceral constitute less a totalizing power than he seemed to suggest. But Foucault offered a more nuanced understanding of the practices of freedom that emerged from discipline than those critics will admit.[6] In his work (as well as that of Gilles Deleuze, for instance), freedom is not constituted by movement in abstract space but by the shaping of particular ways of living within and through, and engaging in partial transformations of or mutations of the spaces that are pregiven to oneself and others. The key to being free, then, is to reach an understanding of freedom as an ongoing practice of *becoming* within and through the constraints that always already exist as a precondition of one's existence.[7]

The space of the prison, within which Herman Wallace lived most of his life, reflects the difficulties but also the possibilities of being free even within the confines of something that looks very much like the *nomos* of the camp. Lest I be misunderstood, I reiterate: the *nomos* of the camp is not confined to specific institutions but is a more general experiential condition of those societies that have embraced a particular exercise of sovereign power. So Wallace's exercise of imagination may be thought of as a source of a counterfreedom, operating in resistance to that more general power even as it is confined within its horizon. Wallace's life in prison follows the usual scripts of extreme deprivation and loss. But his practical exercise of imaginative thinking demonstrates that even the most absolute subjection contains an element of being free.

Moreover, it is through the exercise of imaginative thinking that Wallace's project serves as an exemplar for ongoing efforts to achieve a sense of home, not only within a political world in which the *nomos* of the camp has become less a hyperbolic phrase and closer to an ontological condition, but also in the epoch of the Anthropocene, which could be said to come close to reflecting Agamben's worst fear concerning the *nomos* of modernity itself. The fact that Wallace developed his project with the aid of an artist—Jackie Sumell—and a support system outside of Angola serves as an indicator of the degree to which power and resistance emerge from the same root, to paraphrase Foucault. So when these thinkers describe the confinements, the constitutive exclusions, the exposed bodies that are rendered coherent within prison, they are also describing the circumstances under which (un)bare life of a kind that evades, if not escapes, the current paradox of modern power is made possible.

Despite the skepticism with which we might view Agamben's claim concerning bare life, the modern American prison is becoming an exemplary site of the struggle for being at home in a world in which home is an increasingly rare place of being and becoming. Agamben writes, "If the essence of the camp consists in the materialization of the state of exception and in the subsequent creation of a space in which bare life and the juridical rule enter into a threshold of indistinction, then we must admit that we find ourselves virtually in the presence of a camp every time such a structure is created, independent of the kinds of crime that are committed there and whatever its denomination and specific topography."[8] To what extent is it possible to render distinctive from each other the experiences of those who live within the confines of the camp? What difference may that distinction make for our understanding of the possibilities of being at home in the emergent epoch of the Anthropocene, an era that seems to be so deeply imbricated with the *nomos* of the camp?

Primo Levi understood the camp to be suffused with a longing for home. In *If This Be a Man* (also known as *Survival at Auschwitz*), he wrote, "When one works, one suffers and there is no time to think: home is less than a memory. But here the time is ours despite the prohibition, we exchange visits from bunk to bunk, and we talk and talk. The wooden barrack, crammed with suffering humanity, is full of words, of memories, and of another pain. *Heinweh,* the Germans call this pain; it's a beautiful word that means 'longing for home.'"[9] This other pain, this longing, entails for those who suffer it alone, in solitary confinement, a madness that can only be relieved by imagining that there is someone there, out there, with whom one can talk and who can share the suffering. To come home may only mean to imagine what home might be.

The Angola Three

Herman Wallace first entered Angola prison in 1967 after having been convicted of armed robbery.[10] In 1971, four years into his sentence, he joined with two other activists for prisoner rights, Albert Woodfox and Robert King, to found a chapter of the Black Panther Party. Their focus was on working within the prison to assert prisoners' rights and to break up the practices of sexual slavery and abuse being propagated by both gangs within the prison and prison guards. As Rideau noted, the system of rape and subjugation was a keystone element of the informal system power at work, linking trusties and guards in a hierarchy of terror.[11] Wallace, along with Albert Woodfox, was convicted of the stabbing murder of a prison guard named Brent Miller in April 1972. Robert King, though never charged with the killing, was placed in solitary confinement immediately following Miller's murder, as were Wallace and Woodfox, lending plausibility to the argument that Wallace and Woodfox were framed for the murder, and that they *all* were sent to solitary because of their activism, especially because of their membership in the Black Panthers (a membership none of them ever repudiated).

What did it mean to be a member of the Black Panther Party during this time? Historically, it was a period of confrontation with police within what were then called ghettos, a period of self-help within black communities, and an enormous amount of harassment for those who espoused the ideology of the Panthers. Wallace was to remain committed to revolutionary change throughout his life. But what did that mean? The demands in the Black Panther Party Ten Point Platform from 1972 (included as an appendix to HHB), are both straightforward and depressingly contemporary in character. They include economic equality, free health care for all, full employment, decent standards of housing, an end to wars of aggression, and access to technology for all. The platform also includes two points that are depressingly anticipatory of the contemporary condition: "7. We want an immediate end to police brutality and murder of black people, other people of color, all oppressed people inside the United States of America. . . . 9. We want freedom for all black and oppressed people now held in the US Federal, state, county, city and military prisons and jails. We want trials by a jury of peers for all persons charged with so-called crimes under the law of this country" (HHB). The Black Panther Party Platform of 1972 thus anticipates the development of mass incarceration that had begun with the Nixon administration's commitment of new funds to drug interdiction, the opening salvo in the War on Drugs, and was to take off with the Reagan administration's enormous commitment to the militarization of policing and its more overt racial demonology, that contributed so powerfully to the new Jim Crow.

None of these three prisoners left solitary confinement until King was released from prison in February 2001. The other two continued to serve in solitary until Wallace was released—by order of a federal judge, with state authorities being threatened with contempt of court—three days before his death of liver cancer in 2013. (Wallace was briefly released from solitary and into the general population of the prison during 2011 but then returned to solitary after eight months for reasons unspecified in the return order. He had, claimed the prison authorities, violated Rule 30-c, which penalizes "general prohibitive behaviors" [HH].) Woodfox was finally released in February 2016. In short, these three men spent twenty-nine years, forty-one years and ten months, and forty-three years and ten months, respectively, in solitary confinement, records not matched anywhere else in the world.

It was during this long period before King's 2001 release from prison—which was to have profound consequences for Wallace—that Wallace first developed the imaginative practices he would later deploy in their collaboration on his dream house. One finds only indirect testimony concerning Wallace during this period. It comes in the form of testimony by a young convict who encountered him at Camp J, the site of the solitary cages employed by Angola for its most intransigent inmates. That convict, Michael Musser, was sent to Angola at the age of fifteen to serve a twelve-year sentence for robbery. He found Wallace to be "a calm old guy," who provided him with both practical and philosophical advice on how to get through prison life without giving up his humanity. Wallace, he said, became his "companion in a new way of being" (HH). Musser spent a total of seven years in Camp J. He remained in touch with Wallace after his release from prison and credits Wallace with having saving his life, as well as his soul.

Herman's House

After his release from Angola in 2001, Robert King went on a speaking tour to publicize the conditions of solitary confinement at Angola. It was while he was speaking in San Francisco that Jackie Sumell, at the time an MFA student attending Stanford University, first learned of the plight of Wallace and Woodfox. During the question-and-answer session at King's public talk, she asked him what she could do to help the remaining prisoners. He urged her to write to them. She did, and thus began a relationship with Wallace that lasted until his death, three days after his release from prison, in 2014.

Sumell's work as an artist was activist and conceptual in character, even before she met Wallace. Earlier in 2001, as part of a national protest against the new Bush administration's reinstatement of the Mexico City protocols prohibiting international health NGOs that received monies from the US government from discussing abortion as a means of prenatal care, she put together a project called "Shame on Bush" (alternate title, "No Bush—It's Not Yours, It's Mine"), which involved about a thousand women shaving their pubic hair and saving it in plastic bags, which Sumell then displayed at a demonstration of feminists against Bush on the National Mall. (The idea was that the women had nothing to hide, and so they were giving Bush their bushes, so to speak, in order for him to hide his shame.)

In Sumell's first letters to Wallace and Woodfox, she included twenty-three individual photos, which she had taken once on the hour, as an attempt to show them her life from her subjective perspective. Wallace seemed to understand better than Woodfox what Sumell was trying to communicate by sending the pictures—she was exposing herself to him, trying to make herself vulnerable, but also noting her freedom versus his confinement. If he had a camera, all twenty-three of his photos would have depicted essentially the same view. This exchange marked the beginning of their friendship.

About eight months after she began corresponding with Wallace, and through her exposure to his experience having become an advocate for prison reform, Sumell "was given an assignment which required that I speak with the professor of my choice about spatial relationships and indulgent dream houses" (HHB, introduction). Finding the assignment to be absurd in comparison to what she had learned about Wallace's intensely limited spatial relationship to his six-by-nine-foot cell, she decided that rather than speak with a professor, she would speak with Wallace. As Sumell later explained, "I struggled to balance the futility of this assignment with the reality of Herman's condition. Communicating with a person who is suffering so greatly is a complicated emotional experience to navigate. So, with the support of both Herman's lawyer and his personal advocate, I asked Herman Wallace a very simple question: *'What kind of house does a man who has lived his life in a six-foot-by-nine-foot cell for over 30 years dream of?'*" (HHB, introduction). What emerged from her posing this question and Wallace's response was a multiyear collaboration between Wallace and Sumell that ended only with his death. By 2012, *Herman's House,* a multimedia exhibit, had appeared in twelve different galleries in five countries (HH). (The exhibit continues to be shown to this day.) It is to that collaboration that I now turn.

Sumell's appeal to Wallace was initially met with skepticism on his part. He wrote, "To be truthful, I never dream of a house—not one to live in. You forget, my dreams are but a reflection of the man I am" (HHB, November 11, 2002, 1 [this citation refers to the date and page of the letter; there is no regular pagination in this self-published book]). Wallace thought of himself as a freedom fighter, living in dangerous, enemy territory. He had remained a Black Panther throughout his life in prison. Yet the challenge of Sumell's question led him to begin to rethink his position. He wrote, "We really can't focus too much upon what is on my mind because I really never gave that any thought. I never thought it was necessary because I've always thought of myself in the bush; in the hills of Mexico—on the battle field. But I guess 35 years in prison and 30 of that in solitary tells me I would not be able to carry out such extreme dreams/plans. Nonetheless, my objectives are intact" (HHB, November 11, 2002). Wallace's correspondence is peppered with references to himself as a political actor and a political prisoner, as well as references to the miserable living conditions under which he suffered. As their friendship deepened, Wallace revealed more of himself, and Sumell of herself, as is common in personal correspondences, perhaps especially in jailhouse letters. But, at least for the letters chosen for the self-published book, there is more focus on the house itself and less on the efforts being made to free the Angola Three.

As can be seen throughout the correspondence, though, Wallace, while deeply aware of his own status, was also, as someone who has been confined in solitary for so long, out of touch with the details of life outside of prison. This lack is reflected in many of his comments concerning his dream house. But it is also quite telling that his initial response to Sumell reveals his self-understanding as one who does not have a home, that is, as the revolutionary he would in the bush or on the battlefield, a guerrilla fighter living off the land. This romantic vision of revolution seems to be easier to sustain when one is living a life of severe confinement.

Shortly after she sent her letter, Sumell mailed Wallace some pictures of famous modern houses, primarily from the Los Angeles area—Neutra VDL, the Stahl House (with a panoramic view of the city), the futuristic Lautner Chemosphere (a round house, built on a single pile, perched precariously on a hillside), and others—in an effort to inspire Wallace. But he was having none of it. "Those sample houses you sent to me suck! Where did you find those ugly places from? Those are dream houses? Embarrassing!" (HHB, November 11, 2002, 3). Instead, he listed components of the house he wanted built:

1. First, a swimming pool with a green bottom and a Panther in the center.
2. Flower gardens surrounding the house.
3. A garage for two cars.
4. A large tree in the backyard, where his patio would be, made of marble brick.
5. Kitchen with wall and base cabinets, racks for pots, pans, utensils, tile floors and several microwaves.
6. A. 3 bedrooms, all with thick carpet, king size beds; one bedroom with lots of mirrors, mirrored ceiling, crystal furniture; African art, mahogany furniture, soft blue light; in third room consisting of different cultures, with white birch furniture and white carpet. B. A very large conference room with portraits of political prisoners and prisoners of war all around.
7. Beside the conference room, his library.
8. Office with computer, files and large picture of his Hero.
9. Two bathrooms. One with counter, mirror, and a large bathtub, the other with a shower and thick glass casing.
10. A large dining room with a video wall screen for whatever occasion.
11. A. A guest house with 4 rooms to accommodate out of state activists, with sliding glass doors to accommodate those who may be suffering from claustrophobia. B. An underground bunker with and escape tunnel from his bedroom, made of strong cement and equipped with military essentials "—that reminds me the house is to be made of wood."
12. A workshop.
13. A large fireplace. (HHB, November 11, 2002, 2–3)

This list was to remain largely consistent through the various iterations of the house as it was drawn and redrawn. Though the guest house was eventually placed in the background, only gestured at in the various architectural drawings developed by Sumell and various volunteer architects, it remained a part of Wallace's vision, especially as an asylum for others.

It is not difficult to see how the first items in the list reflect an idealized American middle-class set of desires: pool, garden, garage, kitchen, patio, three bedrooms. Even in this, though, the time spent in prison is reflected in a few telling details. For instance, Wallace suggests that, in a mock-up of the house, Sumell should use pipe cleaners to construct a TV antenna, though by this time TV antennas were becoming obsolete. And the color he wants the kitchen painted—a bright yellow—was a popular choice in the early 1970s.

But, gradually, other components are revealed that suggest this will be a very unusual house. Details of the earlier rooms reflect atypical, even seemingly eccentric, wishes. These included a conference room with portraits of famous political prisoners, themes in the furnishing of the various rooms reflective of different cultures, the eventual master bedroom (it is only a bedroom at first but becomes the master bedroom in a later iteration, decorated with African art). A guest house of four rooms with sliding doors for activists (with the assumption that some of them will suffer from claustrophobia). A dining room that would also serve as a screening room, which would also have a gallery of portraits of revolutionary heroes—Gabriel Prosser, Denmark Vesey, Nat Turner, John Brown, and Harriet Tubman. A bunker and an escape tunnel, the entrance of which is a trapdoor placed in a corner of a fireplace in the master bedroom of the main house.

Perhaps the oddest comment he makes concerns the escape tunnel and bunker. Why does it remind him that the house should be constructed of wood? In a later letter, Wallace explains:

> Look, we can leave the underground bunker out of the project as it would only make the project too complicated—we could

even leave the swimming pool out—but in reality that is what I would build because of my thinking. I prefer the house made of wood, not because of beauty but to easily set afire—and escape to the tunnel and bunker to safety in case of a serious attack. It's the idea that counts, no? (HHB, December 9, 2002)

Wallace is convinced of the need for escape routes because his practical wisdom was such that he understood there to be a conspiracy of power designed to oppress black Americans, and to crush all those, such as the Black Panthers, who would try to foment revolution. As Mahile Rahim, a former convict, member of the Panthers, and contractor who was enlisted to try to bring the house into material existence, said, "His spirit is a threat" (HH).

What eventually became the exhibit *The House That Herman Built* was composed of a set of blueprints, a set of drawings produced by computer-aided design (CAD), a balsa wood model of the house, and an exhibit prepared by Sumell that included a full-size recreation of Wallace's six-by-nine-foot cell, as well as various representations of the dream house and copies of their correspondence. Also included in the exhibit was the catalog/book that presents the history of Wallace and Sumell's correspondence and dialogue. Throughout the exhibition's history, it has been transformed from a work of activist art into a component of an anti–solitary confinement, anti–mass incarceration activist movement, spearheaded by Sumell.

Herman's House has, as of this date, not been built. But as a refiguring of the meaning of home in the twenty-first century, its emergence from the radical precarity of the prison and its refiguring of bodies enlist the powers of imagination and memory in ways that give us new insight into a very old human process, the memory palace as a pneumonic device, an aid to the creative powers otherwise constrained by walls. So my focus in what follows is not on the immediate politics of Herman's House but on the processes by which the affective power of Herman's House came into being.

Embodiment and Geography

The floor plan of Herman's house reveals another element of the imagination Wallace cultivated while in confinement. One prison architect, Jeff Goodale, upon observing the plan, remarked on how the house reflected the experience of being in solitary confinement. There was no free-flowing space, no windows or openings from which one could observe the rising or setting sun. The focal point of the house was an interior room—the expansive kitchen, which was very much akin to a day room in a prison, only with amenities. "If I were in solitary," Goodale said, "I'd want a home of all glass" (HH). But Goodale had *not* experienced solitary confinement. And that was Wallace's point. "This house is built in an order and manner to demonstrate and illustrate what I've been through," he said. "You look at the house, you're looking at me" (HH). It would, in fact, be impossible to experience what Wallace experienced without going through it yourself.

The brilliance of Jackie Sumell's intervention was that she made no assumptions concerning what Wallace would want. Her suggestions to him were only that. And to the extent that he rejected her advice, she readily acceded to his wishes. In part this may have been because of Sumell's own life experience. She grew up on Long Island, and during her childhood her parents experienced deep conflict, much of which expressed itself in emotional abuse by her father. She was an unusual young woman, with diverse interests. She was a participant in beauty pageants as a teenager, but she also was the first young woman on Long Island to participate in varsity high school football, playing safety for her school team. Throughout her interactions with Wallace, she came to be a surrogate daughter to him and embraced that role fully. When Sumell's mother was diagnosed with cancer, Wallace had to persuade her to put the Herman's House project on hold to care for her. Sumell's determination, even after Wallace's death, to continue with the project of building the house demonstrates a deep commitment that could be considered a sympathetic response to the sense of embodied isolation that Wallace felt. In all representations, Sumell's personal life beyond her participation in this project is only hinted at, and then only occasionally. When she moved to New Orleans to more fully pursue the project of building Herman's House, she opened up her home to the children of the neighborhood (HH). Paradoxically, through her work on the exhibit and her activism on Wallace's behalf, she allowed outside observers to appreciate the experience of Wallace's isolation, his loneliness, even as she herself maintained a modicum of privacy.

Sumell served as a sort of surrogate for Wallace, not simply as his representative. She presented her work with him as an embodied experience, emphasizing the emotional connection and love that existed between the two of them. Hence Wallace emerges not as a representative of an abstract experience of isolation as imagined by those who first brought the practice of isolate punishment into being.[12] Instead, he becomes an exemplar of how solitary confinement works on the body, how it shapes the self in ways that may be difficult to understand fully.

This is not to say that Wallace was unable to share his experiences. He is eloquent in his descriptions, especially thoughtful concerning the unconscious effects that solitary confinement has on the body. For several months, he was removed from solitary confinement.

Here is his description of the contrast between being in the general prison population and being confined:

> Being in a cage for such an extended period of time—it has its downfalls. You may not just feel it, you may not know it, you may think that you're okay and you're just perfunctorily moving about. However, when you was removed from out of that type of situation and placed in an open environment where you're even breathing that oxygen and it's getting into your lungs and you're feeling something growing within you. You begin to develop a different mode within your body. I even watched my body. I looked in the mirror, and I seen muscles and shit begin to pop out. I began to run even faster. . . . And I'm saying whoa, what the hell is going on here? Much was preserved. (HH)

These words emphasize the quotidian—even in solitary confinement there is a mundane, everyday quality to the experience that one fails to recognize in its extremity until one is relieved of the burden of living within its confines. It is when one leaves the cell that one notices how the cell itself has shaped one's body, from the inside out. The body performs its circumstances, and the most basic of those circumstances has to do with the space one is able to inhabit. That the release from solitary, not into freedom but merely into the general population, results in a transfiguration of the body is evidence, if more is needed, of the fluidity of bodily existence and identity.[13] One puts on the walls of the cell; one takes them off. Are they Wallace's liber, his true bark? I think his exercise of freedom was even more complicated.

After eight months of enjoying the experience of living in the general population, Wallace was returned to isolation. Here is how he described that experience: "But then I got locked up again, after eight months, and, being locked up like that the whole body just got confused" (HH). This confusion is wrenching, the development of the body is arrested, and a new turn inward occurs. His body is confused, re-amalgamated, condensed into a new form.

In this sense, from the perspective afforded by Wallace's expansion and contraction of the body, the organization and arrangement of rooms within his dream house make enormous sense. The interior walls are extensions of the shell Wallace's body has been accreting throughout his time served. The abruptness of the return to solitary heightens the destructive power of the experience of the shell's softening. Wallace's body both expands and contracts within the confines of Angola. It is psychic torture, yet, but it manifests itself materially, as do all elements of the psychic life of power.

How Wallace overcame this contracted space is the essence of how he came to make his home in prison. Much of the process involved desensitization, across the senses. He says, "When you stay in a pile of shit for such a long time, you get to the point where you don't even smell it. That's not to say it's not there" (HH). It is akin to the fishes in water, famously allegorized by David Foster Wallace in a graduation address. The young fish are mystified by the old fish, which suggests to them that the water is good today. "What is water?" asks the one fish to the other.

Wallace's Memory Palace

One remarkable aspect of prison life generally is the ingenuity with which prisoners figure out ways to communicate not only with each other but also with the outside world. Usually those linkages are prosaic, focused on the immediacy of need, politics of the most local sort, those required to survive in the immediate circumstances in which prisoners find themselves. What happened between Wallace and Sumell had a different character altogether. The link that Sumell provided him enabled Wallace to communicate through that barrier, rather than be reduced to madness and / or silence. As Wallace wrote of the project as a whole: "[This project] helps me to maintain what little sanity I have left, to maintain my humanity and dignity. It is probably the best move that I've ever made in my life" (hermanhouse.org).

But we might see something more specific going on in regard to the task that Sumell first presented to Wallace as a question / challenge. Whether wittingly or not, Sumell's question, *"What kind of house does a man who has lived his life in a six-foot-by-nine-foot cell for over 30 years dream of?"* could be understood as the first step Wallace might take in creating a memory palace. The memory palace, also known as the "method of loci," is a mnemonic device that was first developed in antiquity. The person using it creates an imaginary building within which he or she places specific memories, of objects, words, number, events, and so forth, and then imagines the room within the palace where that specific memory has been stored. (Contemporary neuroscientists have found that when people use the memory palace technique, it activates the area of the hypothalamus that is associated with spatial memory.)[14] This device has a long and illustrious history, but it seems to have fallen by the wayside in the modern era, possibly because the art of memorization has become less in demand in education and also because external memory has so vastly expanded, first with the invention of movable print and, most recently and most radically, with the rise of digital memory.[15]

In fact, in his commentary on Herman's House, Jean-Baptiste Joly, the director of Akademie Schloss Solitude (the German art foundation that sponsored Sumell as a fellow and underwrote the cost of the book), refers directly to Cicero's ancient texts on mnemonics and goes on to suggest, referring to Paul Virilio's text *La machine de vision,* that in the contemporary world "nothing more than the actual phenomenon of visualization can be seen. . . . Those who no longer see are also no longer capable of fantasizing images and whoever is no longer able to fantasize images can no longer spatially orient himself. And whoever cannot orient himself is lost, physically as well as mentally" (HHB, appendix). For Joly, the project of Herman's House is no more and no less than an exercise in "seeing."

One of the worst forms of punishment while in prison, beyond the brute fact of solitary confinement itself, is solitary confinement while being deprived of all reading and writing materials. At Angola, it is called the Dungeon. Sumell describes it in this way:

> Solitary confinement at Angola, or *closed cell restriction* (CCR), consists of a minimum 23 hours a day in a 6-foot-by-9-foot cell (2 meter × 3 meter) & seven days a week. When I began writing Herman, he was in Camp J, what Angola calls the "Dungeon." It is the most punitive area of the prison, where prisoners go to suffer. When the current warden of Angola describes Camps J he states, "even a Death Row inmate will find the Spartan quarters he once 'enjoyed' on Death Row plush compared to Camp J."
>
> Herman was kept in the dungeon for two years. Each time he was due to return to solitary prison officials found another absurd reason to keep him in. Imagine, relief would mean returning to solitary confinement. (HHB, preface)

It would be surprising if Wallace, confined to such an extremely sensory-derived space, would not experience something like madness. When he referred to "what little sanity I had left," this may be considered not as hyperbole but as an honest assessment of his state of being.

Wallace described in detail various iterations of the house. At least twice he wrote narratives for what was to be a guided tour of virtual versions of the house. To gain a sense of how detailed his understanding of the house was, one can review the following comment he made concerning the first floor of the house after reviewing drafts of some of the CAD mock-ups (see appendix A of HHB for several architectural drawings of the house):

> Let me get right to it. 2-car garage—instead of empty boxes you want to hang hose pipe on the wall—2 spare tires in both sides and the cars should be parked in them. Without the cars no one would figure it's a garage.—In the pantry, there should be *ONIONS, POTATOES, TABASCO,* various bottles of *WINE.* The hobby shop; yes, old typewriters, speakers. . . . I see you got a pot of beans under a fire. That is alright. Put a sprinkler in ceiling—you want to bring in refrigerator—what is a kitchen without a refrigerator? Let's dress the table with a plate of food by each chair—small basket of hot rolls. Put a skillet under a fire making shrimp and oyster gravy.—The conference room is the Bomb. I think we should lay a small notebook in every spot where someone should sit. (HHB, February 21, 2006, 1–2)

The point here is to note less the specific details than the fact of them—though it is interesting that Wallace was insisting on the preparation of traditional south Louisianan cuisine. It is also interesting that there remained enough of a political actor in him that he imagined being able to hold conferences. One wonders, with whom would he confer? Putting this question aside, for Wallace, such detailed interest indicates his familiarity with every room of the house.

We can also note this attention to detail in his descriptions that he prepared for the two versions of his audio tour of the house. A condensed version illustrates how he imagined his walk-through of the place. (This version is taken from his April 2003 written tour guide.) He begins with background on himself, beginning with his joining the Black Panthers in 1971, then briefly describes his time in solitary as a consequence of his membership. He mentions the beginning of his relationship with Sumell (though he gets one detail wrong, suggesting it started before his comrade King was released, although her involvement came about as a result of her hearing King speak in San Francisco). Wallace imagines the approach to the house: "The drive connects with flagstone and brick walkway to matching indoor walls and chimney." The house is built of wood and surrounded with plants because they provide food and oxygen (Wallace once had mentioned that it was impossible to grow anything within the steel and concrete environment that was his cell). The house has a wraparound porch. Viewers enter the first door, and on the right is a salon, the next room is a library, again in a room to the right, and visitors then proceed down a long hallway, passing yet another room on the right, a guest room. At the end of the hall to the right is a garage, but before that there is a pantry with two large storage areas. The back door of the pantry opens out onto a large patio, which is shaded by a very large oak tree (oak to withstand hurricane winds). Adjacent to the pantry is a hobby shop with various tools. To the southwest side of the shop is a spiral staircase leading to the second floor, but the shop also has another door that leads to a kitchen, which has yellow walls and contains a table for four people, sinks, built-in counters and cabinets, several microwave ovens, a double-door refrigerator, tile flooring, and all sorts of cooking implements. A swinging door from the kitchen leads to the dining/conference room, with a polished wooden floor, a wall for video screening, a table that seats sixteen, a wall with room for five large portraits of revolutionary heroes, and three large windows overlooking a flower garden. To the far west side is the living room, with an L-shaped sofa and an entertainment center. An opening leads to the west wing of the house, and the hallway has portraits in honor of prisoners of war and individuals missing in action. There is a bathroom with a shower, and at the end of the hall a guest room. Adjacent to this room, visitors find themselves at the base of a spiral staircase that opens up to a master bedroom, equipped with beautiful African-themed furniture, and a master bath that features a six-by-nine-foot bathtub (the same footprint as Wallace's cell in solitary). The bath is accessed privately by way of the master bedroom. There are sliding glass doors that lead to a rooftop garden for flowers and vegetables. The chimney is here as well (as Wallace had tellingly noted twice previously). The chimney actually is an escape route from the bedroom and from the pantry below, leading to a tunnel beneath the patio and under the swimming pool. Wallace is always thinking about escape. He writes, "Beneath the bottom of the pool's concrete floor is the bunker for safety measures. If attacked, seriously under attack, the house can be set afire to with more than enough time for you and your family to escape unharmed" (HHB, April 1, 2003, 3–5).

If we trace the path that Wallace asks us to follow, we find ourselves walking through something akin to a labyrinth. The two matching long hallways, the burrow-like rooms, the doors leading to doors, the enclosed spaces throughout the first floor all create a claustrophobic atmosphere, that is, they would do so for someone who had not spent the bulk of his life in solitary confinement. The relatively open second floor can only be reached by a spiral staircase contained in a corner of the pantry/hobby room. And, perhaps most important, the secret passage to an underground bunker implicitly summarizes the story of a man who is taking every precaution not to be sent back to prison ever again, even as he suspects there will always be forces that would seek him out so as to force such a return, or even worse.

That Herman's House is a fortress, a bunker, with long interior corridors, secret doors leading to a secret passage, a kitchen embedded deep within the house, yet with flower beds, bay windows, a rooftop greenhouse, a large social space—the conference room—as its central focal point, with guest rooms, and even a guest house, is of interest in and of itself.

But it is of great importance to note something more: Wallace may have believed that he would someday live in this house. He was insistent that Sumell keep working to find a site for the building, and he was absolutely focused on winning his freedom. But he had been in prison for more than thirty years when he met Sumell and most likely suspected that he would never live to walk through a real, rather than virtual, Herman's House. It is probably as important that he was presenting this house as a viable place to live for whoever may be interested in it, whoever that may be. He refers to "you and your family" in the audio tour transcript. Herman's dream house becomes a memory palace not simply of his utopian vision but of the practical politics of a lifelong revolutionary. Wallace knew that those who would be attracted to the exhibit would be of like mind to him, or at least sympathetic to his cause.

Home as Embodied Resistance

Herman's House remains an ongoing project and has as its primary end the creation of a community center based on the blueprints that were the product of Wallace and Sumell's collaboration. The project is, as it always was, also devoted to publicizing the problems associated with solitary confinement and mass incarceration in the United States. Sumell, who moved to New Orleans in 2005 in order to pursue the project, continues to present versions of the original exhibit, *The House That Herman Built*, which was first displayed in Stuttgart in 2007. She continues to work as an artist, a community organizer, and political activist.

As of ten years ago there were about 80,000 men, women, and children residing in solitary confinement cells throughout the United States. As of 2017, approximately 2.4 million people were imprisoned in the United States, and another 4.8 million were on probation or parole. Three percent of all black men in this country are currently incarcerated.[16] These staggering numbers, to which many of us have become inured, represent—what do they represent, after all? Many of those who advocate for an end to mass incarceration in the United States argue that there needs to be a direct confrontation with the history and subsequent presence of the racial caste system that continues to exist in the United States, a coming to terms with the central role of slavery in the history of this country.[17] Through this lens there is much that can be gained in the form of a more general comprehension of the current predicament of punishment and its political role here, a recognition of the foundations on which the homes of generations of Americans have been built, an enormous unpaid debt that lays bare the need for reparations, with the resulting incredible bad conscience of the white plurality leading it to intensify, in its denial, the harsh inequalities of the justice systems of this country, criminal and otherwise.

But in the story of Herman's House there is something more at work. This might be called Wallace's work of "embodied resistance." What might I mean by this phrase? It may be useful here to refer to a recent intervention into the ongoing Kulturkampf regarding race in America. In his celebrated book *Between the World and Me*, Ta-Nehisi Coates begins his letter to his son by citing yet another question posed to a black man in the United States. He writes, "Last Sunday the host of a popular new show asked me what it meant to lose my body."[18] For Coates, to lose one's body is simply to die. And it is under that constant threat of death that race, the child racism, is so effective in controlling those who do not call themselves white, because it abstracts the body into a concept, allowing those who name the race the privilege of allowing and disallowing the bodies of those so named their continued existence. In short, for Coates, disembodiment, that Cartesian pretense, holds the very specific terror of death. Toward the end of his epistle, he writes:

> [I] believe that when they shatter the body they shatter every-
> thing, and I knew that all of us—Christians, Muslims,
> atheists,—live in this fear of this truth. Disembodiment is a
> kind of terrorism, and the threat of it alters the orbit of all of
> our lives and, like terrorism, this distortion is intentional. Dis-
> embodiment. The dragon that compelled the boys I knew,
> way back, into extravagant theater of ownership. Disembodi-
> ment. The demon that push the middle-class black survivors
> into aggressive passivity, our conversation restrained in public
> quarters, our best manners on display, our hands never out of
> pockets, our whole manner ordered as if to say, "I make no
> sudden moves."[19]

For Coates, the terror of disembodiment is a predominant existen-
tial threat for those who do not call themselves white. Committed so deeply to his atheism, though, it may be that he is unequipped to understand that there is such a thing as living death, the death that comes about from the failure to see, a failure to perceive, a lack of vision that is deeply imbricated with disembodied thought and has as its symptom a peculiar commitment to a form of secularism that denies vision itself.[20] In a similar vein, Emerson, in describing the most unhandsome part of our condition, wrote, "Our life not so much threatened as our perception."[21] Wallace might have

responded to both Coates and Emerson by noting that the threat to our perception *is* a threat against our life.

The project of Herman's House might be called the secular resurrection of the body of a man who had undergone civil death, who was, until he was interpolated by Jackie Sumell, existing at the edge of existence, a disembodied ghost in his own life, experiencing the terror that is the fatal threat to all of those whose bodies are subject to elimination because of their very province of being. Wallace's growing sense of his body, and of its diminishment when he was returned to solitary confinement, constitutes a strange parable of modernity, no less bizarrely true than a fable by Kafka. For Wallace, holding onto the body meant resisting the terms of his imprisonment not by floating above it but by digging deeply into it, sustaining his imagination, avoiding complete madness—a madness that is no less than Descartes imagined it to be, an endless questioning as to whether one even exists—by thinking about the meals he would serve, the baths he would take, the books he would read, and the company he would keep in his dream home. This is the way Wallace sought to overcome his *Heinweh,* his longing for home, which was not so much a beautiful pain he was able to reflect upon in those rare moments when there was a pause from the terrible labor he would have suffered from the one extreme of camp life, as it was for Primo Levi, but from the opposite form that torture took for him, the forced idleness of solitary confinement.

Mom, Revisited

Trauma bleeds. Out of wounds and across boundaries.

—LESLIE JAMISON, *The Empathy Exams*

Denny, Buckets, and the Amazing Rescue

Once upon a time—actually, one day in early June 1961—Tommy, Terry, and Denny were playing in the sandbox in the backyard of their home at 2800 West Chestnut Avenue, in Altoona. It was late morning, around eleven o'clock, and a slightly overcast sky, as well as the shade of a big maple tree, were keeping it from getting too hot. Mommy was inside the kitchen, probably working on preparing lunch, or maybe taking her late morning coffee and cigarette break. The older children, Johnny, Katie Anne, Jamesy, Patty, and Mary Rita—everyone except for the oldest, Maureen, who was attending Altoona Catholic High School—were due home from our neighborhood parochial school, Our Lady of Lourdes, in just a little while. Mommy could look out the back window from her seat at the kitchen table to keep her eye on the younger kids, but she had explained to Tommy before they went

243

outside that he was the big boy in charge, and he had to make sure that Denny and Terry didn't fight with each other or run out of the yard. Tommy was five, going on six (he would start first grade in the fall). Terry was about to turn three, and Denny was about eighteen months old. Tommy was hard at play, building a road with his yellow plastic shovel so that his dump truck could roll across the sandbox, when Terry said, "Where's Denny?" Tommy looked up and saw Denny waddling (he still wore diapers) out of the backyard toward the alley behind the garage. Tommy immediately got up and started yelling, "Denny! Denny! Stop, Denny!" But Denny didn't stop. He kept going around the corner, and the next thing Tommy saw through the backyard fence was Denny chugging along as fast as he could up the alley. Tommy ran after him, but he also had been told many, many times that he was never to go off of the sidewalk without Mommy or Daddy or a bigger brother or sister holding his hand. So, he stood on the edge of the sidewalk and kept calling, "Denny, come back here! Denny, come back!" Suddenly, Denny *was* coming back down the alley. But that was not because he was listening to Tommy, but instead because a car had started coming down the alley and was headed toward him! He ran right past Tommy, out of the alley and into the middle of the street! "Come back here, Denny!" Tommy yelled, jumping up and down on the sidewalk. But Denny, who was very frightened by now, sat down in the middle of the street with a plop and started to cry. He would not get up, no matter how much Tommy yelled at him. And he was sitting right where the alley—between West Chestnut and Maple Avenues—crossed with Twenty-Eighth Street. Denny was sitting at a crossroads, in the middle of the intersection of the alley and the street. "Come back, Denny, come back!" Tommy shouted, waving his arms from the sidewalk and jumping up and down. But Denny just sat there, crying. The car coming down the alley came to a stop. Over the course of the next few minutes, which seemed to Tommy like forever, it was joined by three other cars, one from each direction—from the other alleyway and from the opposite sides of Twenty-Eighth Street. Strangely, no one got out of their car—perhaps each driver thought one of the other ones would. But one of them started honking his horn, which made Denny cry even louder. Just then, when it seemed like things couldn't get worse, Buckets showed up. Buckets was this old, scrofulous neighborhood mutt, a mixed-breed hound with black and white spots. He belonged to the Moyer family down the street, who let him wander the neighborhood. Tommy was especially frightened of Buckets. He thought the old dog would bite him if it could (even though, at that point of his life, Buckets had lost most of his teeth). Buckets came trotting up to Denny, sniffed at his crotch, and then sat down beside him and began to howl. So, there was Denny, crying, Buckets howling, a car honking, and Tommy calling out to Denny. It was crazy! But at that very moment, from out of the blue, Tommy and Denny's big brother Johnny came running down the middle of the street, shooed off Buckets, picked up Denny, and ran back to the house, where he took Denny through the kitchen screen door, which slammed shut behind them. Johnny, then an eighth grader at Our Lady of Lourdes, had been coming home for lunch after super-vising the patrol boys who guided the schoolchildren across the streets on their way home for lunch. And that is all that Tommy remembered about Denny, Buckets, and the amazing rescue.

Children's Stories

When my own children were young, about the same ages as Tommy and Terry, I would tell them this tale as a bedtime story, and at the moment in the telling when Buckets started to howl, we would all howl. Sometimes our dog, Fred, would join in. It was an often-requested story. We liked to howl.

In his famous study *The Uses of Enchantment,* Bruno Bettelheim argued that fairy tales enable children to confront the everyday troubles of their life by providing a frame for interpreting what is happening around them. Fairy tales tell compelling stories that often involve magical solutions to life-threatening dangers. They are filled with heroes and villains, larger than life but realistically enough drawn as to spur the imagination. They act as narratives that provide interpretive frames for children to make sense of their place in the world. Bettelheim writes, "[The child] needs ideas on how to bring his inner house into order, and on that basis then be able to create order in his life."[1] The darkness of fairy tales thrills the child, while simultaneously the "once upon a time" narrative puts the story at a safe psychological distance. The ordering of the inner house depends upon understanding the wildness of the world outside.

Like all "once upon a time" stories, there was, of course, a dark side to "Denny, Buckets, and the Amazing Rescue." What in the world was Mom thinking, to leave a five-year-old boy in charge of an almost three-year-old and a toddler? Where was she while this entire drama unfolded? What was going on with Mom? Once upon a time I thought I had a semblance of an answer to questions concerning her presence in my life, by way of another story of childhood, one that more directly concerned just Mom and me.[2] But there is more to tell, about Mom, and also about the burden of homemaking that she was charged with during her life, an impossible task involving the care and feeding not only of me but of eight other children.

I began this inquiry by reflecting on a journey to visit my father in his declining years, reflecting on the metempsychosis of his soul to mine; I want to end by thinking again about the role Mom had to play, the parallel metempsychosis of her soul to mine. Mom was a homemaker, a keeper of the flame of family, the everyday presence in the lives of all of her children as Dad worked such long hours to feed and shelter a large Catholic family. Mom provided an example of the larger role that so many moms in America were forced to play in the era of post–World War II prosperity. It is an old story, and the roots of modern American feminism are deeply entangled in some of the earliest resistances to the domestic prison so many women were forced into during this era.[3]

That the noontime of Mom's motherhood coincided with the beginnings of modern American feminism is a historical coincidence. But there is long history to the more general domestic politics that informed Mom's life. At the heart of mother love in America there has often been the operation of a powerfully reactionary ideology of the family. Michael Rogin, in some ways the most profound critic of the political culture of the Cold War era, once put it this way: "Confined to the home, [women] were promised substantial indirect power—the power to sacrifice their identities in service of others and live through the achievements of men. That solution did not free men from women, for the sons and husbands whose intimate needs women served felt dependent for their freedom on the women who attended them."[4] This basic dynamic of confinement and freedom is an enduring one in the United States; as we have seen, it informed the lives of the women in the pioneer family of Laura Ingalls Wilder.

But it also informed, if in a different register, the Cold War family of Mom and Dad. Rogin noted that, "since appearing on the American scene, the subversive has made the home into his or her central target," but he also emphasized that protecting a particular vision of motherhood during the Cold War era became a proxy for efforts throughout the culture to demonize civil rights movements as Communist in character. Motherhood became the private bastion of goodness, and efforts to move beyond private morality into public movements for equality and justice came to be seen as attacks on it.[5]

Of course, those who were excluded from this ideology of family during this era usually were poor, and often black. In his report on the status of the black family in America, Daniel Patrick Moynihan infamously argued (on the basis of no real evidence) that black men were emasculated by black women, who, he falsely claimed, earned more than they did. As Rosalind Rosenberg summarizes, "America was built, Moynihan insisted, on the foundations of the male-headed family. As long as black Americans lived in the more primitive matriarchal family form, they would never enter the mainstream."[6]

How this denigration of black women in the 1960s relates to my family is a complicated but quite relevant matter. During Altoona's history, the African American population has never been more than 5 percent of the city's total population, but the absence of black folk is in part the point here (and part of the story of the explicit racism to be found throughout central Pennsylvania, in part because the very absence of African Americans is an ongoing fact of life).

Mom and Dad grew up as Roman Catholics in a region where, as children in the 1920s, they witnessed the resurgence of the Ku Klux Klan.[7] Mom and Dad would tell stories of drive-by shootings at Grandpa Dumm's house in Newry and of an intimidating cross-burning at Grandpa O'Leary's farm in Altoona's Pleasant Valley. While eventually, like so many other ethnic and religious minorities in the United States, they came to achieve equal status with other white people, they did so in large part as a consequence of the continued oppression of blacks.[8]

As New Deal Democrats, and later Kennedy Democrats, in a town and region dominated by a Republican political establishment, my parents were sympathetic to the civil rights movement, though they also were products of the local culture, and we grew up with almost no African American friends or neighbors. Our local Catholic church was instructive as well, weighing in on the side of Martin Luther King Jr., and on the side of the War on Poverty, long before the church came to its right-wing turn under a Polish pontiff. We children were taught to respect all people and never to use denigrating language, even though it was standard among most of our peers.

(It was also during this era that some of the worst and most widespread sexual abuse of children was occurring in the Altoona/Johnstown diocese. While all of us brothers were altar boys at Our Lady of Lourdes, none of us was ever approached by a priest. My older brother and I have speculated that we were left alone because we come from a fairly prominent Catholic family—two of my uncles being local priests, one a monsignor.)

It was in this community that our family life unfolded. We, like so many other families during this turbulent era, fought on an intergenerational battleground as the fifties turned into the long decade of the sixties. Mom was caught between the evolving allegiances of her children and the culturally conservative leanings of a predominantly Republican town. Dad found himself outraged by what he saw as the disrespectful behavior of an entire generation of spoiled children. Both of them fretted and worried about what the children who had already left home were doing.

Maureen, the oldest child, against her father's wishes and in spite of his worries, volunteered as a nurse in an orphanage in Na Trang, (then South) Vietnam, almost losing her life during the first Tet Offensive in 1968. John, the oldest son, initially given over to a vocation as a priest—he left home at the tender age of thirteen to attend seminary—quit the seminary, finished his education at Seton Hall University, and as a conscientious objector became a Peace Corps volunteer in the Philippines. Perhaps most radically, James, a William F. Buckley fan and ROTC member, made a drastic turnaround, quit ROTC to join the Penn State chapter of Students for a Democratic Society, and helped take over Old Main, the university's administration building, during one of the protests against the Vietnam War. He eventually became a VISTA volunteer in South Carolina. Katie, Patty and Mary Rita, while less engaged in the politics of the era, still found their own ways to remind our parents of the generation gap, in the more usual ways that children annoy their parents.

I was too young to be directly caught up in this turmoil, though I did campaign for George McGovern in 1972 (I was not yet eligible to vote). I sometimes mark the generational shift in American society that occurred from the Vietnam generation to the post-Vietnam generation to that year. By the time I was eligible for the draft, for the 1974 lottery (my number that year was 142), there were no call-ups. The last call-ups had occurred on December 9, 1972. I believe that date marked the beginning of the post-Vietnam era, not for the Vietnamese, whose suffering continued, but for Americans, who by then were turning toward our usual way of coping with the horrible things done in our name, a practice of historical amnesia.

Mom was in the middle of this turmoil, and it hurt her a lot. Her sympathies seemed to be with her children, but the ongoing conflict between Dad—who eventually, to his everlasting regret, voted for Nixon in 1968, the only time in his life he voted for a Republican—and his older children took a toll on her. And we younger siblings still living at home felt the brunt of their conflict, since these older children were gone from the home, only reporting back to their parents their latest political, social, and (yes) sexual transgressions. This put Mom in a position of divided loyalties, and her instinct to protect her children was often overwhelmed by her wish to follow Dad, in his anger and frustration with the children in whom he had invested his greatest hopes and dreams, and who seemed to be betraying those hopes.

I mention all of this because it goes to the heart of the role that most moms play in making a home. We might generally say that mom is the negotiator of intergenerational guilt and shame, the one who gives us guilt as a gift, and who gives it under circumstances beyond her powers, though, paradoxically, with degrees of freedom that can be overlooked when we think of the confinements of home itself. Within the finitude of home, mom is the missing link, the negotiator for our freedom, who, in seeking her own ways of being free, may eventually both save us from home as it is and provide some leads on how we may move forward. What that means requires some unpacking.

Love and Hate

What do I owe Mom? How am I indebted to her? Growing up, that I was able to identify with Dad and not with her is an obvious truth from the perspective of classic psychoanalytic theory, but still, I inherited so much from her—my body, my depression, my musicality, my academic ambitions, my early and intense Catholicism (which contributed to my later, intense rejection of it), so many of the gestures that define me as her son. But inheritances can give shape to some misleading impressions, some serious mistakes. We might note that the desire to avoid our inheritances is often the source of tragedy. But what constitutes inheritance?

This has always been the key question underlying the arts and sciences of psychoanalysis. Unfortunately, it is also the case that mothers have not been served well by more orthodox forms of analysis. In the Oedipus complex, successful resolution entails a sacrifice on the part of the mother, a giving up and giving over to the child, a consistent nurturing in the face of the infant's hostility, an investment in the child that subordinates the mother's wishes for autonomy even as the child's identifications and desires will fall away from her, to the extent that the child is seen to successfully resolve his or her complex, to complete an identification. But to the extent that such a resolution is incomplete—and when is it ever complete?—the burden of responsibility falls not on the father but on the mother.

Jacqueline Rose has recently and systematically explored just how damaging such a view of mothers is. She asks what purpose is served by those versions of the role of the mother that insist upon her self-sacrifice. Indeed, she specifically notes how politically useful a mother's guilt can be for retaining a gendered status quo, critically citing an astonishing admission by Bruno Bettelheim himself, who, upon being asked to endorse a book by Elisabeth Badminter that critiques the idea of inborn maternal instinct, refused. He explained as follows:

> I've spent my whole life working with children whose lives have been destroyed because their mothers hated them. . . . Which demonstrates that there is no maternal instinct—of course there isn't. . . . This book will only serve to free women from their feelings of guilt, the only restraint that means that some children are saved from destruction, suicide, anorexia, etc. I don't want to give my name to suppressing the last buttress that protects a lot of unhappy children from destruction.[9]

Bettelheim demanded that the knowledge that there is no maternal instinct be suppressed in the name of *not* suppressing the operations of guilt, the guilt that prevents mothers from thinking about their relationship to their children in ways that he thinks will lead to the children's destruction. Rose notes that Bettelheim was driven by a deep desire to protect children from the hate of the mother: "Children must be saved from hatred at any price. And since he will not give his name to Badminter's book, even though he thinks she is right, the price includes repressing the truth. Hatred is therefore the guilty party (something of a tautology). What is being demanded of mothers—perhaps the demand behind all demands—is a hate-free world."[10]

Rose points out that even within the tradition of psychoanalysis this view concerning hate has been challenged in an illuminating way. She provides a reading of D. W. Winnicott's essay "Hate in the Counter-transference" (1949) in order to rebalance the scales, so to speak, giving hate its due as an important force in the relationship between mother and child. She focuses especially on the eighteen "reasons" Winnicott gives for "why a mother hates her baby, even a boy," from feeling the baby is not her own, to her frustrated excitement ("she mustn't eat him or trade in sex with him").[11] This focus makes sense for Rose's purposes, which is to demonstrate the ubiquity of hate in the love relationship between mother and baby. But it is also important to note that Winnicott's primary focus in his essay is not on mothers per se but on the role that hate and its repression play in the process of analysis *for the analyst.*

Winnicott is focused on the problem of countertransference, not only how the analyst understands the stages of the emotional development of the patient but how the analyst's self-understanding in relation to that patient affects the process of therapy. Such self-understanding entails "the identifications and tendencies belonging to an analyst's personal experiences and personal development which provide the positive setting for his analytic work and make his work different in quality from that of any other analyst."[12] Among these identifications and tendencies are those that incline the analyst to love and hate her patient. In this sense, the analyst is a mom. As Winnicott puts it, "An analyst has to display all the patience and tolerance and reliability of a mother devoted to her infant, has to recognize the patient's wishes as needs, has to put aside other interests in order to be available and to be punctual, and objective, and has to seem to want to give what is really only given because of the patient's needs."[13]

Rose provides a reading of Alison Bechdel's graphic novel *Are You My Mother?* to underline Winnicott's insight that hate is a part of love, and must be acknowledged and appreciated if there is to be a way forward in the relationship between mother and child. (At one point, Bechdel's fictional narrator states of Winnicott, "I want him to be my mother.")[14] This insight raises important questions. For instance, what is the best distribution of hate and love in a mother and child relationship? But, more important for my Mom, what is the best distribution of love and hate in the mother and child relationship when more than one child is involved with the mother?

Obviously, there is no single answer to such a question. To rephrase Tolstoy, no family is unhappy in the same way. For the family I grew up in, the compounding of maternal love and hate with nine children born across a sixteen-year period meant that there had to be a complex balancing act. If mothers are in the position of the analyst, as Winnicott suggests, then what insights into her own balancing of love and hate made my mother the mother she was? And how did she cope with her own guilt?

Just posing the question presents extraordinary difficulties. To answer it with any adequacy would require a full-length work, an auto-biography. Mom isn't here to do that. But I am. What follows is no more than a note toward how such a work might be attempted.

Memoir / Confession / Auto-biography

The paradox one faces when writing autobiographically is that to say too much may be to say too little. Moreover, to say too little may be to say too much. The biography of the self remains an open site not simply because of the indeterminacy of writing itself but also because for as long as the author lives, and even after death, the life under review remains contestable. Because of the open field on which it takes place, auto-biography itself is always partial and open. Moreover, within the history of the auto-biography, there are degrees of exposure. The memoir especially, which doesn't rely on anything more than the memory of the writer, can be especially vulnerable to accusations of being self-serving, self-deceiving.

Nonetheless, it is useful to mark the spot, to note the problem. It is especially useful here to reflect on the philosophical memoir of Stanley Cavell, who explicitly raised these issues even as he wrote. Cavell was a philosopher who himself claimed that Freud was a philosopher (albeit one who was in [Freudian] denial). As an extension of the spirit in which Winnicott compared analysts to mothers, it may be useful, following on Cavell, to think about the therapeutic role that writing an auto-biography might perform not only for the writer but also for the writer's readers. (This is a point that Leslie Jamison makes concerning her own personal essays, noting how the confessional form may encourage others to share their confessions. Whether that is an unambiguously good thing is not clear.)[15] Perhaps such a therapy, rather than encouraging us to be at home, would instead encourage us to overcome the costs associated with being at home. Such a therapy would need to consider who and what is in need of co mfort, and the conclusion we might reach would be in response to a mourning of the self-limitations of the kind of thinking that struggles to overcome our finitude, our own deaths as realized through the deaths of our parents.

As Cavell put it, "What interests me is to see how what Freud calls the detours on the human path to death—accidents avoided or embraced, strangers taken to heart or neglected, talents imposed or transfigured, malice sufficiently rebuked, love inadequately acknowledged—mark out for me recognizable efforts to achieve my own death."[16] The desire to complete a life, to achieve one's death, means for Cavell to work through a series of puzzles, to go back and forth in time, to compress and to ignore some of his story (say, the long period after he resettled as a full professor at Harvard) in favor of childhood stories; character sketches of friends, lovers, and colleagues; encounters with teachers, musicians, and others—always motivated by the desire to understand why the person who was then Stanley Cavell became the next one, and how that next one was, doubling back in time to another time, someone who was either prepared or unprepared to become that next Cavell. The trust in self that is involved in such a project entails a willingness to appreciate the repetitions of one's own stories, to notice that memory is fragmentary, incomplete.

This discussion of a philosopher's memoir may seem a digression. What does this have to do with Mom? Perhaps not much of anything, except that there is in every family story no unified narrative but a multiplicity of perspectives, partial in both senses—incomplete and subjective. To think about Mom is to enter into a treacherous terrain of uncertainty, in the case of my family, one multiplied by the simultaneous rememberings and forgettings of her nine children, her late husband, and her own haunting ancestors.

Mom's ghost has haunted the writing of this book in several ways, not only because she made our home, which made me, but less obviously, because the dissolution of our nuclear family, as we all went our own ways, was accelerated by my own earlier reflections on her memory. I have learned the hard way that when one biographs one's own self, the risk one undertakes is in making one's most inner thoughts outwardly visible. This can disturb the peace of others and the self who is writing. The exposure of family life—the interior of home—to the outside can render the private loves and hates of the members of the family matters of the most profound contestation.

I first reflected on my own childhood publicly in my book on loneliness to try to make a point similar to a point I hope to make here, concerning the varying capacities of the members of what I thought of as an exemplary lonely family—my own—to negotiate the sorrows of life, to try to make a home. I made several observations in that book concerning my upbringing that attracted considerable and mainly unhappy attention from several of my siblings. My younger brother Denis (of "Denny, Buckets, and the Amazing Rescue"), in particular, who to my knowledge had never before read anything I had written (and who apparently received the offending passages from one of my offended sisters), used the occasion of a family reunion in our hometown for the funeral of an elderly relative to tell me that he was disowning me. He informed me of this in the parking lot of the mortuary where my elderly aunt was being "shown for viewing," as we would say. (Steven's Mortuary was our family funeral home dating from before I was born. I recall going there for the wakes of well over a dozen aunts and uncles through the years of my youth. [Large Catholic families!] It also was where we held wakes for both Mom and Dad. Denis, it turned out, would not be there for Dad's wake.)

Denis had read the passages I had written about my mother—her depression, my desire for her love, and her inability to love me—and pronounced me guilty of being "sick and evil." Having never read Freud, he mistook what I had written as an explicit and perverted lusting for our mother. I was unable to convince him otherwise, to explain to him the power of the Oedipus complex (as I then understood it). I actually didn't get a chance to try, standing in the driveway of the mortuary where he yelled at me. Upon returning inside, he refused to speak to me any further.

He also took deep offense, I suspect, at something he *did* understand and that I believe he knew to be true. Here is the offending passage:

> Each of my siblings has a memory, and each of us must remember our childhood differently. While some of us look back in anger, and others with regret, I know, I swear I know, that none of us look back with joy. But it is also true that none of us can claim to tell the story of our separate childhoods, our individual traumas, our lonely family, with greater authority or a truth any more fundamental than the others. There are no experts when it comes to these questions of remembrance. We all recall from our own experience. We are separated by our common past.[17]

This is, admittedly, a complicated paragraph. I make a strong assertion, only to withdraw it. The idea is to try to convey the truth of my subjective experience, to emphasize the pathology of separated siblings, recalling and repressing, shaping our understandings of each other in ways that are bound to fail. In such a large family as ours there is bound to be a multiplication of misunderstanding. I remain convinced by my experience, but what does that tell us about anyone other than me?

Denis remained on nonspeaking terms with me until his death, an untimely death that occurred the summer after his confrontation with me. (He drowned while on a vacation in Ocean City, Maryland, brain-dead but lingering for a couple of days until he was removed from the machines that breathed for him and kept his heart pumping.) And here I am, writing again about what should not, from his perspective, be written about or, more accurately, should not be written for the world at large. This act marks me within the politics of my family as an outlaw of sorts, or at least an outlier, one who will not willingly keep family secrets, having found the holding of those secrets to be more damaging to me than the releasing of them might be harmful to them.

But to whom am I releasing secrets? And why? When I reflect on the matter, I ask if I am seeking some sort of vengeance on Mom, though it does not seem that way to me now. In my self-image, I am trying to understand what my own experience may contribute to understanding the pathos of a particular kind of self-possession, one that separates us from each other as much as it unites us in our mutual isolation. I hear Winnicott gently laughing here, my ongoing resistance to understanding how I am loving and hating. My sharing of this experience is only a part of my negotiation of my love and hate, not only of my mother but of my brothers and sisters and father, as well. This is, I imagine, a late act of fealty to Mom.

Sharing such experiences, however qualified and however self-consciously partial, requires the risk of being misunderstood, or being understood too well. But in such misunderstandings I am trying to locate a strange source of hope.

Misgivings

When I write about saying too much and saying too little, I have been thinking about a specific passage in Cavell's memoir. Turning, as he so often did, to one of his most important philosophical companions, he noted toward the end of the book:

> Wittgenstein's advance is to have discovered the everyday and
> its language themselves to be esoteric, strange to themselves,
> one could say, to be irreducibly philosophical, prompting us
> unpredictably to say too much or too little, as if we chronically
> fail to know what actually interests us. It is with our inheri-
> tance of language as Lacan says Freud holds of the Ego, that
> it continually misrecognizes or (mis)understands itself. In-
> stead of saying we are full of mistakes about what is closest to
> us, we might say of ourselves that we are filled, as Thoreau
> might say, with misgivings.[18]

Where there is mistaking, there is also misgiving. The compulsion
to write is born, in some events, certainly in this one, out of a deep
sense of giving, an anxiety about giving, the adequacy or inadequacy
of the gift one is offering, an ongoing worry about its acceptance and
rejection. We might even say that all gifts are misgiven, except of
course, for perfect gifts. But, pace Jesus Christ, there are no perfect
gifts.

Roberto Esposito comments on this idea of the gift in the context of his attempt to retrieve a deep sense of the meaning of the word
and phenomenon of *communitas*.[19] Esposito notes that the first
meaning of *communitas* is that which becomes meaningful in opposition to what is proper, that which begins where what is proper
ends (3). Such an opposition to what is proper extends to the acts
of those who give. There is an underestimated relation of *munus* to
domun, he suggests. "The *munus* in fact is to *donum* as 'species is
to genus,' because, yes, it means 'gift,' but a particular gift, 'distinguished by its obligatory character implied by its root *mei-,* which
denotes exchange" (4). Relying on Benveniste and Mauss, whose
earlier explorations into etymology led to their insights into the gift
and its exchange, Esposito goes on to assert, "Yet it is in this withdrawal from being forced into an obligation that lies the lesser in-

tensity of the *donum* with respect to the unrelenting compulsion [*co-genza*] of the *munus*. In short, this is the gift that one gives because one must give and because one *cannot not* give. . . . Although produced by a benefit that was previously received, the *munus* indicates only the gift that one gives, not what one receives" (5). This is, I believe, a version of what has been termed the Emersonian impersonal, the working through of a life that is open, incomplete, and subject to further mis-givings. It is impersonal in this sense—because, once given, it cannot be taken back. We cannot trace back everything we receive. Emerson suggests that the gift was overflowing from the start. We can only give, and all giving, in this sense, is misgiving.

Another way of putting the matter is to refer to what is perhaps the most philosophically consequential pun of all time, coined by Emerson: "I am thankful for small mercies." Cavell once noted that this is a literal translation of the French expression "Merci, beau coup." "I am thankful for giving thanks" would be another way to think of what Emerson is conveying through this pun. To give thanks by noting that thanks are a mercy, a plea for mercy, and maybe even a response to a plea for mercy, is yet one more indication of the asymmetry of all gifts. Perhaps that is the point. That is to say, the writing of the biography of the self is always a misgiving, the inheritance of the past is always too much, and as important as it is to recognize departures from it, obligations to it, and mistakes in the making of it, the living of it, it is also as important to recognize it as a gift.

Mom's gift to her children varied from child to child. I mistook her gift to me as an abandonment, a disappointment, a willingness to turn away from me when I felt I most needed her. But this was not all she did. She bore other children who helped to raise me (especially my sister Katie), she kept us all close to the home she made, no matter how far away we strayed, she forced us to go out into the world, for better or for worse, to create our own homes, to return to her as long as she would have us, which was until she finally gave up the ghost on that first day of a new millennium. Her gift, in her refusal, her self-sacrifice, her daily grind in the kitchen at 2800 West Chestnut Avenue, in her persistent stoicism through a lifelong depression, an addiction to tobacco, and possibly alcohol, in her unquestioning Catholic faith, and in her dark sense of humor, was a misgiving that I have inherited, in my own refusals and commitments, my own addictions, my own depression, my own stoicism and dark humor. That at times some of us did not always want to receive her gifts is but another part of the giving, our mistakes in the taking, and in the making of our own gifts to our own children. Is this what home is in the end? A mistaken gift?

The Book of Life

If we think of our individual lives as stories we are telling about ourselves, to ourselves and others, we may be better able to reimagine our relationship to finitude in ways that may allow us to understand what we are longing for when we long for home. We may proceed, in telling our stories, by comparison to other stories, by analogy. Kaja Silverman puts it this way:

> Analogies that are not of our making really do connect our lives to many others—to lives that are over, and to lives that have not yet begun, as well as to those proximate to us in time and space. Rather than a self-contained volume, authored by us, our history is only one chapter in an enormous and ever-expanding book, whose overall meaning and shape we cannot

even begin to grasp, let alone determine. But this does not mean there is another kind of author; no one stands outside the Book of Life, to whom it could be imputed. This volume is written from inside, through the analogies we acknowledge and those we refuse. Its production is also a collective process, in which everyone participates and everyone is implicated.[20]

Silverman echoes Emerson. The enormous intelligence cradling us in its lap is beyond us, but always close at hand, and we participate in its continuance whether we wish to or not. Thus, Silverman provides a fitting frame to end these ruminations. Life after home may broaden our senses of time and place, or may narrow them. But we cannot deny that in its very insatiability, our desire for home, our impossible home, spurs us on. The conditions and terms under which we proceed, the materials for our analogies, so to speak, will change, but the desire will remain.

Notes

Prologue

1. See Benedict Anderson, *Imagined Communities* (New York: Verso, 1983).
2. Avital Ronell, *Finitude's Score: Essay for the End of the Millennium* (Lincoln: University of Nebraska Press, 1994), 2.
3. See Stanley Cavell, "Aversive Thinking: Emersonian Representations in Heidegger and Nietzsche," in *Conditions Handsome and Unhandsome: The Constitution of Emersonian Perfectionism* (Chicago: University of Chicago Press, 1990), 33–63.
4. For a fascinating reading of one small part of this larger landscape, see Michael J. Shapiro, *Violent Cartographies: Mapping Cultures of War* (Minneapolis: University of Minnesota Press, 1997), prologue.
5. Ralph Waldo Emerson, "Self-Reliance," in *Essays: First Series,* in *Emerson: Essays and Lectures* (New York: Library of America, 1983), 277.
6. Friedrich Nietzsche, *The Gay Science: With a Prelude of Rhymes and an Appendix of Songs,* translated, with commentary, by Walter Kauffman (New York: Random House, 1974), 338.
7. Emerson, "Self-Reliance," 278.

8. Paul Gilroy, *The Black Atlantic: Modernity and Double Consciousness* (Cambridge, MA: Harvard University Press, 1993).

9. For a sustained reflection on this form of uncanniness, see Renée L. Bergland, *The National Uncanny: Indian Ghosts and American Subjects* (Hanover, NH: University Press of New England, 2000).

10. Gaston Bachelard, *The Poetics of Space,* trans. Maria Jolas (Boston: Beacon Press, 1969), 6. He also refers to the house as providing us with our "first universe, a real cosmos" (4).

1. Habitations of the Human

1. I was unaware of the existence of this clock until stumbling upon it while visiting Copenhagen's city hall while engaging in some casual tourism in December 2013 after helping conduct a seminar at the Copenhagen Business School. I am deeply grateful to Kaspar Villadsen of the faculty in Management, Politics, and Philosophy of CBS for both his invitation and his hospitality during this visit.

2. Don DeLillo, *White Noise* (New York: Viking Press, 1985).

3. Sigmund Freud, *The Uncanny,* trans. David McLintock (New York: Penguin, 2003).

4. See Thomas L. Dumm, "The Withdrawal of Consent from Above," *Theory and Event* 21, no. 1 (January 2017): 23–29.

5. See Thomas L. Dumm, "You Are Here: Laura Kurgan at the Storefront" *Newsline* 7, no. 1 (Summer, September, October 1994): 16.

6. See Hannah Arendt, *The Human Condition* (Chicago: University of Chicago Press, 1958).

7. Arendt seems to be effacing the role that mothers play in this process. We all emerge from the womb of a mother, so the nowhere from which we emerge is actually a rather important somewhere. I discuss the problem of the missing mother at length in *Loneliness as a Way of Life* (Cambridge, MA: Harvard University Press, 2008). I return to the question of mother in the epilogue of this book.

8. Arendt, *The Human Condition,* 1.

9. On Foucault and freedom, see Thomas L. Dumm, *Michel Foucault and the Politics of Freedom,* 2nd ed. (New York: Rowman and Littlefield, 2002).

10. The best meditation on the question of how to think about the past in relation to the present and future remains Friedrich Nietzsche, *On the Advantage and*

Disadvantage of History for Life, trans. Peter Preuss (Indianapolis: Hackett, 1980).

11. This issue is explored in depth in the opera *Death and the Powers: A Robot Pageant* (2010), music by Tod Machover, libretto by Robert Pinsky. See http://opera.media.mit.edu/projects/deathandthepowers/.

12. Quoted in Thomas L. Dumm, *A Politics of the Ordinary* (New York: NYU Press, 1999), 35. I bring this up again, even as I have written of it before, because I cannot get it away from me. To believe that the Earth is so bereft of life possibility for anyone is devastating. How are we to respond to such finality on the part of anyone who calls herself human?

13. Such a phenomenon has recently been subject to new examination. See David. B. Morris, *Eros and Illness* (Cambridge, MA: Harvard University Press, 2017).

14. For an explanation of the Mars One project, see http://www.marsone.com/mission/humankind-onmars#sthash.jqnwuD3f.dpuf. An even more optimistic view is held by Elon Musk, who is preparing a human trip to Mars for the year 2020. See https://futurism.com/elon.musk.has.a.new.timeline.for.humans.living.on.mars/.

15. The philosophical literature on the relationship of other animals to human beings is a rapidly expanding one. Many of us are continuously learning from the work of Cary Wolfe. And to take one exemplary study that focuses on twentieth-century philosophers, from Heidegger, to Levinas, to Agamben and then to Derrida, see Matthew Calarco, *Zoographies: The Question of the Animal from Heidegger to Derrida* (New York: Columbia University Press, 2008). Of course, this only scratches the surface of a large and important literature, much of which is increasingly focused on the problem of human exceptionalism and the crisis of the Anthropocene. The best statement I have read concerning this problem is William E. Connolly, *Facing the Planetary: Entangled Humanism and the Politics of Swarming* (Durham, NC: Duke University Press, 2017). Another course that resists this impulse and seeks to retain a more sharply defined distinction concerning the human is George Kateb, *Human Dignity* (Cambridge, MA: Belknap Press of Harvard University Press, 2011), which secularizes the Judeo-Christian understanding of the relationship of the human to the animal as one of human stewardship.

16. For this criticism, directed specifically at Immanuel Levinas, but meant as an example, see Paola Cavalieri, *The Death of the Animal: A Dialogue (with Matthew Calarco, John M. Coetzee, Harlan B. Miller, and Cary Wolfe)* (New York: Columbia University Press, 2009), 4. Veena Das presents an interesting critique of Wittgenstein that bears upon his understanding of the "verticality" of the

human in reference to the animal. See Das, *Life and Words: Violence and the Descent into the Ordinary* (Berkeley: University of California Press, 2006).

17. There is a growing literature in contemporary political theory that tries to take nonhuman actants into account when thinking about the dynamics of human actions. These theorists, called by some the "new materialists," include such thinkers as Jane Bennett, William E. Connolly, and Samantha Frost. See especially Jane Bennett, *Vibrant Matter: A Political Ecology of Things* (Durham, NC: Duke University Press, 2010).

18. Arendt, *Human Condition*, 2.

19. See the conclusion to Michel Foucault, *The History of Sexuality, Volume One* (New York: Pantheon Books, 1978). Also see Arendt, *Human Condition*, 3. Giorgio Agamben has written about the linkages between these two on this subject. See Agamben, *Homo Sacer: Sovereign Power and Bare Life,* trans. David Heller-Roazen (Stanford, CA: Stanford University Press, 1998).

20. For a systematic treatment of this theme, see Connolly, *Facing the Planetary.*

21. Walter Benjamin, "On Language as Such and the Language of Man," in *Reflections,* ed. Peter Demtz (New York: Harcourt, Brace Jovanovich, 1978), 314–332.

22. Robert Pogue Harrison, *The Dominion of the Dead* (Chicago: University of Chicago Press, 2003), 34.

23. Harrison, *Dominion of the Dead,* 34.

24. For a discussion of what Quentin Meillassoux calls "ancestrality," which focuses on the knowledge that humans have of what existed before there were humans, see Meillassoux, *After Finitude: An Essay on the Necessity of Contingency,* trans. Ray Brassier (New York: Continuum Press, 2008), esp. 13–18. I am grateful to Andrew Poe for his suggestive reading of Meillassoux.

25. Benjamin, *Reflections,* 332.

26. On this relationship in regard to Benjamin and Wittgenstein, see Stanley Cavell, "Benjamin and Wittgenstein: Signals and Affinities," *Critical Inquiry* 25 (Winter 1999): 235–246.

27. This paragraph is a close rephrasing of marginal comments on an earlier draft of this chapter by Adam Sitze. I am grateful for his permission to appropriate his notes here.

28. Martin Heidegger, "Building, Dwelling, Thinking," in *Basic Writings,* exp. ed., ed. David Farrell Krell (San Francisco: HarperCollins, 2008), 343–364. Subsequent page references to this work are provided in the text.

29. See Adam Sharr, *Heidegger's Hut* (Cambridge, MA: MIT Press, 2006).

30. Heidegger, "On the Essence of Truth," in *Basic Writings.*

31. Maurice Blanchot, *The Writing of the Disaster,* trans. Ann Smock (Lincoln: University of Nebraska Press, 1985).

32. Martin Heidegger, *Introduction to Philosophy—Thinking and Poetizing,* trans. Phillip Jacques Braunstein (Bloomington: University of Indiana Press, 2011), 24.

33. See Giambattista Vico, *The New Science of Giambattista Vico,* trans. from the third edition by Thomas G. Bergin and Max H. Fisch (Ithaca, NY: Cornell University Press, 1948).

34. Vico, 37. Bounded as he was by a pre-Darwinian sensibility, and as a man of Catholic faith, Vico offered a reconstruction of this world that relied heavily on an imaginative rereading of key religious/mythical texts, and not only in the Jewish and Christian traditions. The chronological table that he places at the beginning of book 1 is, as he says, "based on the three epochs of the time of the Egyptians, who said all the world before them passed through three ages: that of the gods, that of the heroes, and that of men."

35. See Robert Pogue Harrison, *Forests: The Shadow of Civilization* (Chicago: University of Chicago Press, 1992), esp. 3–13. In what follows I rely extensively on Harrison's extraordinary summary of Vico on the origins of the primary institutions. Subsequent page references to this work are provided in the text.

36. Vico, *New Science,* 38–40. Here Vico focuses on Greek mythology, from Prometheus to Hermes to Hellen.

37. See Ralph Waldo Emerson, "Experience" in *Essays: Second Series,* in *Emerson: Essays and Lectures* (New York: Library of America, 1983), 487.

38. Vico's insight concerning burial finds confirmation in the work of Denis Fustel de Coulanges, the great eighteenth-century historian of ancient Greece and Rome, especially in his descriptions of ancestor worship in the earliest days of both. See Fustel de Coulanges, *The Ancient City* (Baltimore: Johns Hopkins University Press, 1980), originally published in France as *La Cité antique* in 1864. His work is relied upon extensively by Hannah Arendt in *The Human Condition.*

39. Harrison, *Dominion of the Dead,* 27–38.

40. On the political consequences of blocked grief, see Judith Butler, *Precarious Life: The Powers of Mourning and Violence* (New York: Verso), 2004, and Dumm, *Loneliness as a Way of Life,* chap. 4, "Grieving."

41. For a perspective on the problem of rest in late neoliberal capitalism, see Jonathan Crary, *24/7* (New York: Verso, 2016).

42. Robert Frost, "The Death of the Hired Hand," in *Selected Poems,* introduction by Robert Graves (New York: Holt, Rinehart and Winston, 1963), 25–30.

43. *Unforgiven,* a film directed by Clint Eastwood, Malpaso Productions, Warner Brothers, 1992.
44. Philippe Ariès, *The Hour of Our Death,* trans. Helen Weaver (New York: Alfred A. Knopf, 1981), chap. 12, "Death Denied," 559–601.
45. Louis Hartz, *The Liberal Tradition in America* (New York: Harcourt, Brace, Jovanovich, 1955), 17.

2. Thomas Jefferson's Monticello

1. See *Thomas Jefferson's Monticello,* ed. Beth L. Cheuk, for the Thomas Jefferson Foundation (Chapel Hill: University of North Carolina Press, 2002).
2. My most recent visit to Monticello was on July 19, 2018, shortly after the opening of a new exhibit on the Hemings family. The docent explicitly integrated the story of slavery into the narrative telling of the story of Jefferson's home. This tour was in marked contrast to my first visit to Monticello, made in the summer of 2010.
3. Maira Kalman is quoted in the February 17, 2012, episode of Studio 360, "American Icons: Monticello," http://www.studio360.org/story/96253-american-icons-monticello/.
4. Henry Wiencek, *Master of the Mountain: Thomas Jefferson and His Slaves* (New York: Farrar, Straus and Giroux, 2012), 97–98.
5. On the central role of slavery in the economic development of the United States as a whole, see Edward E. Baptist, *The Half Has Never Been Told: Slavery and the Making of American Capitalism* (New York: Basic Books, 2014).
6. See Douglas A. Blackmon, *Slavery by Another Name: The Re-enslavement of Black Americans from the Civil War to World War II* (New York: Random House, 2008). Also see Michelle Alexander, *The New Jim Crow: Mass Incarceration in the Age of Colorblindness* (New York: New Press, 2012).
7. Annette Gordon-Reed and Peter S. Onuf, *"Most Blessed of the Patriarchs":* *Thomas Jefferson and the Empire of the Imagination* (New York: Liveright, 2017), xvi, citing *The Selected Prose of Fernando Pessoa,* ed. and trans. Richard Zenith (New York: Grove, 2001), 294. Interestingly, this understanding of persona closely parallels that developed by Gilles Deleuze and Felix Guattari, who begin the second volume of their work *A Thousand Plateaus: Capitalism and Schizophrenia* with the following observation: "The two of us wrote *Anti-Oedipus* together. Since each of us was several, there was already quite a crowd." See *A Thousand Plateaus: Capitalism and Schizophrenia,* trans. and

with an introduction by Brian Massumi (Minneapolis: University of Minnesota Press, 1987), 3.

8. Gordon-Reed and Onuf, *"Most Blessed of the Patriarchs,"* xx.

9. Thomas Jefferson, *Notes on the State of Virginia,* "Query xix," quoted in J. G. A. Pocock, *The Machiavellian Moment: Florentine Political Thought and the Atlantic Republican Tradition* (Princeton, NJ: Princeton University Press, 1975), 532–533.

10. See Fawn Brodie, *Thomas Jefferson: An Intimate History* (New York: W. W. Norton, 1974).

11. The most comprehensive treatment of the Hemings family to date is Annette Gordon-Reed, *The Hemingses of Monticello: An American Family* (New York: W. W. Norton, 2008). All contemporary scholars of the slaves who Jefferson considered his larger "family" are indebted to the work of Lucia Stanton. See especially Stanton, *"Those Who Labor for My Happiness": Slavery at Thomas Jefferson's Monticello* (Charlottesville: University of Virginia Press, 2012).

12. See Chapter 6, "Herman Wallace's Dream House."

13. See Michel Foucault, *Discipline and Punish: The Birth of the Prison,* trans. Alan Sheridan (New York: Pantheon Books, 1977), 31.

14. Barbara B. Oberg and J. Jefferson Looney, eds., *The Papers of Thomas Jefferson Digital Edition* (Charlottesville: University of Virginia Press, Rotunda, 2008), http://rotunda.upress.virginia.edu/founders/TSJN-01-06-02-0286.

15. This letter is not exceptional for Jefferson. His correspondence with his daughters more generally was harsh and judgmental and kept them at a distance. For more on his correspondence with Polly, see Joseph Ellis, *American Sphinx: The Character of Thomas Jefferson* (New York: Alfred A. Knopf, 1997), 108–109. Ellis's more general evaluation of Jefferson often reads as an apologia for his behavior, emphasizing what may be referred to, in short, as the "in the context of the times" argument. In particular, his evaluation of Jefferson as a slave owner is more sympathetic to the dilemmas Jefferson faced than may be warranted.

16. Even so, Jefferson seemed to establish a distance between himself and his daughters that was more than conventional for this period. When his daughters joined him in France, Patsy first, Polly later, he immediately sent them away to a convent for education rather than keeping them with him. And when his younger daughter, Polly, crossed the ocean, landing in England, he did not cross the Channel to greet her (she was staying with John and Abigail Adams) but delegated the task to one of his servants. (Abigail did not approve.) See Gordon-Reed and Onuf, *"Most Blessed of the Patriarchs,"* 116–117.

17. See Thomas Jefferson, *The Portable Thomas Jefferson,* ed. Merrill D. Peterson (New York: Penguin, 1975), 400–412. Subsequent page references to this work are provided in the text.

18. Ellis, *American Sphinx,* 112.

19. Ellis, 111. My recounting of Jefferson's period with Cosway relies heavily on Ellis's retelling of the sequence of events.

20. Ellis, 113.

21. Ellis, 115.

22. Gordon-Reed, *The Hemingses of Monticello,* 272. The original passages in *Notes on the State of Virginia* can be found in Jefferson, *The Portable Jefferson,* 184–193.

23. Ellis, *American Sphinx,* 345. Jefferson explicitly freed five of his Hemings children, anticipating that most of his remaining slaves would need to be sold at auction after his death in order to pay off debt. It should also be noted that while he didn't formally free Sally, she was practically given her freedom by Jefferson's heirs and lived the remainder of her life in Charlottesville. She was listed in the 1830 census as a free white woman. See Gordon-Reed and Onuf, *"Most Blessed of the Patriarchs,"* 315–317.

24. Cited in Wiencek, *Master of the Mountain,* 8. The citation of the letter is "Notes on Arthur Young's letter to George Washington," June 18, 1792, in *The Papers of Thomas Jefferson Digital Edition,* vol. 24. Original document: Thomas Jefferson to George Washington, June 18, 1792, "Notes on Mr. Young's Letter," General Correspondence, 1651–1827, Thomas Jefferson Papers, Series 1, image 734, Library of Congress, http://memory.loc.gov/ammen/collections/jefferson_papers/.

25. Wiencek, *Master of the Mountain,* 8. Wiencek notes that Jefferson went on to suggest to another acquaintance that purchasing slaves is a sound investment strategy, that if his friend had any cash left after a series of financial reversals, "every farthing of it [should be] laid out in land and negroes, which besides a present support bring a silent profit of from 5. to 10. per cent in this country in the increase in their value."

26. Wiencek, 9.

27. For all calculations of inflation in what follows, I have made use of the calculator at http://www.westegg.com/inflation/.

28. Weincek, *Master of the Mountain,* 92.

29. Weincek, 96–97.

30. Weincek, 97.

31. Weincek, 98.

32. President Thomas Jefferson to William Henry Harrison, Governor of the Indiana Territory, 1803, http://www.digitalhistory.uh.edu/active_learning /explorations/indian_removal/jefferson_to_harrison.cfm.

33. Maurizio Lazzarato, *The Making of the Indebted Man: An Essay on the Neoliberal Condition,* trans. Joshua David Jordan (Los Angeles: Semiotexte, 2012). Subsequent page citations to this work are provided in the text.

34. See C. B. MacPherson, *The Political Theory of Possessive Individualism: Hobbes to Locke* (Oxford: Oxford University Press, 1962).

35. For a close examination of this psychology, see John Wikse, *About Possession: The Self as Private Property* (University Park: Penn State University Press, 1977).

36. Stanton, *"Those Who Labor for My Happiness,"* 76.

37. Stanton, 77. For a critical genealogy of the origins of the American penitentiary, see Thomas L. Dumm, *Democracy and Punishment: Disciplinary Origins of the United States* (Madison: University of Wisconsin Press, 1987), esp. chap. 4, "Republican Machines."

38. Dumm, *Democracy and Punishment,* 109. An interview with a prisoner of Eastern State Penitentiary in Philadelphia: "Ques: Do you believe you could live without labour? Ans: Labour seems to me absolutely necessary for existence; I believe I should die without it."

39. Dumm, 91.

40. Stanton, "Those Who Labor for My Happiness," 77–80.

41. Stanton, 86.

42. Stanton, 41, citing Foucault, *Discipline and Punish,* 208.

43. Stanton, 85.

44. Terrence W. Epperson, "Panoptic Plantations: The Garden Sights of Thomas Jefferson and George Mason," in *Lines That Divide: Historical Archaeologies of Race, Class, and Gender,* ed. James A. Delle, Stephen A. Mrozowski, and Robert Paynter (Knoxville: University of Tennessee Press, 2000), 60.

45. Epperson, "Panoptic Plantations," 68.

46. Letter to James Madison Paris, September 6, 1789, http://www.let.rug.nl/usa /presidents/thomas-jefferson/letters-of-thomas-jefferson/jefl81.php.

47. Gordon-Reed and Onuf, *"Most Blessed of the Patriarchs,"* 280.

3. Henry David Thoreau's Walden

1. Because there are so many different editions of *Walden,* I have adopted the system of providing the chapter numbers in Roman numerals and the paragraph

numbers in Arabic. In this I follow the convention used by Stanley Cavell in his study of Thoreau. See Cavell, *The Senses of Walden: An Expanded Edition* (1981; Chicago: University of Chicago Press, 1992). The specific edition of *Walden* I have relied on for this book is Henry David Thoreau, *Walden,* with an introduction by Edward Hoagland (New York: Library of America, 1991). Here it is appropriate to acknowledge the profound influence that Cavell's understanding of Thoreau has had on my own.

2. It is worth noting that the association of property with wealth is a modern phenomenon. In fact, laws of entailment and primogeniture were not abolished in all states of the United States until the early nineteenth century. This is significant, because those laws prevented the commodification of property, precisely what Thoreau laments. On estate law's importance, see Alexis de Tocqueville, *Democracy in America,* trans. and ed. Harvey C. Mansfield and Delba Winthrop (Chicago: University of Chicago Press, 2000), vol. 1, pt. 1, chap. 3, esp. 46–48. More generally, Hannah Arendt notes the effects on the divide between public and private wrought by the confounding of wealth with property. See Arendt, *The Human Condition* (Chicago: University of Chicago Press, 1958), 66–67.

3. For a genealogy of this complex set of relationships, see Stanley Cavell, "Aversive Thinking," in *Emerson's Transcendental Etudes* (Stanford, CA: Stanford University Press, 2003), 146.

4. See Stanley Cavell, "Heidegger Thinks of Rivers, Thoreau Thinks of Ponds," in *Philosophy the Day after Tomorrow* (Cambridge, MA: Belknap Press of Harvard University Press, 2005), 134–157.

5. In a sense, Thoreau is closer to Arendt than he is to Locke or Marx. Arendt makes a strong distinction between *labor* and *work* throughout *The Human Condition,* but especially in chap. 3, "Labor."

6. I am referring here to the mechanical clock known as Jens Olsen's World Clock, discussed in Chapter 1.

7. In this sense, Thoreau anticipates more recent understandings of how economy produces subjectivities. See especially Maurizio Lazzarato, *The Making of the Indebted Man: An Essay on the Neoliberal Condition,* trans. Joshua David Jordon (New York: Semiotexte, 2011), chap. 2, "The Genealogy of Debt and the Debtor." Also see Judith Butler, *Giving an Account of Oneself* (New York: Fordham University Press, 2005).

8. Stanley Cavell, *Must We Mean What We Say?* (1969; Cambridge: Cambridge University Press, 1976), esp. 277–278.

9. Shannon Mariotti, *Thoreau's Democratic Withdrawal* (Madison: University of Wisconsin Press, 2010).

10. I give a fuller explanation of these two forms of resignation in Thomas L. Dumm, "Resignation," *Critical Inquiry* 25, no. 1 (Autumn 1998): 56–76.

11. Jane Bennett, *Thoreau's Nature: Ethics, Politics, and the Wild* (Thousand Oaks, CA: Sage, 1994), xxi.

12. Cavell, *Senses of Walden,* 14–15. Subsequent page references to this work are provided in the text.

13. For a telling reading of Jefferson's obsession with marking land, especially as expressed in the Northwest Ordinance, see Michael Shapiro, *Deforming American Political Thought* (Lexington: University Press of Kentucky, 2005), chap. 1. We might pause here to ask, what kind of writer is Jefferson? He is a naturalist like Thoreau in some respects. He meticulously records his accounts. But is he deliberate in Thoreau's sense of the term? One wonders about the person who continuously wrestles with controlling and overcoming the natural world, attempting to bend it in his direction, marking townships and counties and states in uniform units, overriding geologic formations in hopes of what Emerson might have called a foolish consistency.

14. Robert Pogue Harrison, *The Dominion of the Dead* (Chicago: University of Chicago Press, 2006).

15. Harrison, *The Dominion of the Dead,* 46.

16. John Locke, *Two Treatises of Government,* critical edition, with an introduction and notes by Peter Laslett (Cambridge: Cambridge University Press, 1960), 342 (Second Treatise, chap. 5, "Property," ¶ 46).

17. Cavell, "Heidegger Thinks of Rivers, Thoreau Thinks of Ponds," 141.

18. Emerson, "The American Scholar," 54.

19. Emerson, 65.

20. See Bill Bryson, *At Home: A Short History of Private Life* (New York: Doubleday, 2010), chap. 2, "The Hall."

4. Laura Ingalls Wilder's Little Houses

1. Alexis de Tocqueville, *Democracy in America,* trans., ed., and with an introduction by Harvey Mansfield and Delba Winthrop (1845–1840; Chicago: University of Chicago Press, 2000), 576.

2. The Little House series was published as a boxed set by Harper's Trophy, an imprint of HarperCollins, in 1994. All of these books were illustrated by Garth Williams (the first editions were illustrated by Helen Sewell) and include, in chronological order, *Little House in the Big Woods* (1932), *Farmer Boy* (1933),

Little House on the Prairie (1935), *On the Banks of Plum Creek* (1937), *By the Shores of Silver Lake* (1939), *The Long Winter* (1940), *Little Town on the Prairie* (1941), *These Happy Golden Years* (1943), and *The First Four Years* (1971). *The First Four Years* was published posthumously, from an unfinished draft. All subsequent page references to individual volumes will be found in the text, and references to specific volumes will condense the titles so that, for example, *Little House in the Big Woods* will appear as LHBW.

3. "Top 100 Children's Novels, 2012 Survey," *School Library Journal*, http://www .slj.com/wpcontent/uploads/2012/08/SLJ_Fuse8_Top100_Novels.pdf. This is but one of many top 100 lists that include the Little House volumes.

4. Quoted in Pamela Smith Hill, *Laura Ingalls Wilder: A Writer's Life* (Pierre: South Dakota Historical Society Press, 2007), 3.

5. This is not to say that there was no mass migration of African Americans to the West following the Civil War, especially after the end of Reconstruction. This migration was concentrated in Kansas, Oklahoma, and Texas, and a number of exclusively black towns were established, most famously Nicodemus, Kansas. By the turn of the twentieth century, 765,000 African Americans lived in the West. For a history of this migration, see Dan Moos, *Outside America: Race, Ethnicity, and the Role of the American West in National Belonging* (Hanover, NH: Dartmouth College Press, 2005). The Kansas settlement seems to have been part of the inspiration for Colin Whitehead's Pulitzer Prize–winning novel, *The Underground Railroad* (New York: Doubleday, 2016).

6. Gayatri Chakravorty Spivak, in her now classic essay "Can the Subaltern Speak?," argues that attempts to speak for subaltern groups are bound to perpetuate their oppression by reinscribing their experience as a named group, retrapping a diversity of experiences within a collective identity that only extends the cultural domination of the Western intellectuals who come to speak for those groups, unwittingly (or wittingly) reinscribing an ethnocentric Western logos onto the very subjects they wish to help, simply reinforcing the mythology of group identities. This is a structural problem as well as a political one. I cannot escape core contradictions concerning my culpability in perpetuating that myth, but only hope, by drawing more explicit attention to the mythical character of the Little House series, to mitigate it. See Spivak, "Can the Subaltern Speak?" in *Marxism and the Interpretation of Culture,* ed, Cary Nelson and Lawrence Grossberg (Urbana: University of Illinois Press, 1989), 271–313.

7. See Alison Landsberg, *Prosthetic Memory: The Transformation of American Remembrance in the Age of Mass Culture* (New York: Columbia University Press, 2004).

8. Laura and Rose's relationship was complex and in many ways unhappy. A thorough examination of it may be found in the most comprehensive of the biographies of Wilder, Caroline Fraser, *Prairie Fires: The American Dreams of Laura Ingalls Wilder* (New York: Metropolitan Books, 2017).

9. Laura Ingalls Wilder, *Pioneer Girl: The Annotated Autobiography,* ed. Pamela Smith Hill (Pierre: South Dakota Historical Society Press, 2014). Subsequent page references to this work are provided in the text, and the title is condensed as PG.

10. Michael Rogin, *Ronald Reagan, the Movie, and Other Episodes in American Political Demonology* (Berkeley: University of California Press, 1987), chap. 5, "Liberal Society and the Indian Question," 154–155. Rogin's chapter is a revised and expanded version of an earlier essay found in Michael Rogin, *Father and Children: Andrew Jackson and the Subjugation of the American Indian* (New York: Alfred A. Knopf, 1973), 3–15. My quotation, dependent on Rogin, is taken directly from the website of the American Presidency Project, http://www.presidency.ucsb.edu/ws/index.php?pid=29472.

11. Herman Melville, *The Confidence-Man: His Masquerade* in *Pierre, or the Ambiguities; Israel Potter, His Fifty Year of Exile; The Piazza Tales; The Confidence-Man, His Masquerade; Uncollected Prose; Billy Budd (An Inside Narrative)* (New York: Library of America, 1984). Subsequent page references to this work are provided in the text. On the significance of the position of the chapter, see Michael Rogin, *Subversive Genealogy: The Politics and Art of Herman Melville* (Berkeley: University of California Press, 1985), 245. At this point I wish to acknowledge a long-standing debt to the late Michael Rogin, beyond simply these meager citations.

12. James Hall, *Sketches of History, Life, and Manners, in the West* (Philadelphia: Harrison Hall, 1835), 456–461 in the Norton Critical Edition. All subsequent quotations can be found in those pages.

13. Laura Ingalls Wilder, *Little House on the Prairie,* illustrated by Garth Williams (New York: Harper Trophy, 1971), 2. This book was originally published in 1935; a revised edition, with illustrations by Garth Williams, was published in 1953. Subsequent page references to this work are provided in the text.

14. Nobert Elias, *The History of Manners,* vol. 1 of *The Civilizing Process,* trans. Edmund Jephcott (1939; New York: Pantheon Books, 1982), 101.

15. See, for instance, Robert (Bobby) Lake-Thum, Medicine Grizzly Bear, *Spirits of the Earth: A Guide to Native American Nature Symbols, Stories, and Ceremonies* (New York: Plume Books, 1997), 95.

16. Soldat du Chêne is the appellation that Laura Ingalls Wilder gives to the Indian, who also supposedly speaks French. However, it is quite likely that the name is a more general term for Indian chief. If there were Osage who spoke French, it is likely that they learned it from Louisiana Creoles. On the identity of the Indian in question, see Stephanie Vavra, *Who Really Saved Laura Ingalls? Soldat du Chêne or a soldat du chien?* (Morrison, IL: Quill Works, 2001).

17. For an extended discussion, see Thomas Dumm, *Loneliness as a Way of Life* (Cambridge, MA: Harvard University Press, 2008).

18. For the Ingallses to lose their appetite is indeed a signal of crisis. Those who are familiar with the series are aware of the enormous role that food—the hunting and slaughter of animals, the baking, the roasting, the boiling, the planting of crops, the gathering of nuts and fruits, in short, the emphasis on the American cornucopia of wild game and fertile lands—has in the lives of all involved. In fact, the entire narrative has to do with trying to find a suitable and sustainable life based on securing food.

19. For a recent, dramatic telling of the twentieth-century fate of the Osage tribe, see David Gramm, *Killers of the Flower Moon: The Osage Murders and the Birth of the FBI* (New York: Doubleday, 2017). My understanding of the nineteenth-century circumstances of the Osage is drawn from John Joseph Mathews, *The Osages: Children of the Middle Waters* (Norman: University of Oklahoma Press, 1981).

20. David Blight, *Race and Reunion: The Civil War in American Memory* (Cambridge, MA: Harvard University Press, 2002).

21. Tocqueville, *Democracy in America,* vol. 1, pt. 2, chap. 10, 302–396.

22. Tocqueville, 309–310.

23. William E. Connolly, *The Ethos of Pluralization* (Minneapolis: University of Minnesota Press, 1995), 168–169.

24. Fraser, *Prairie Fires,* 153–154.

25. Fraser, 154.

5. Emily Dickinson's House of Possibility

1. Jerome Charyn, *A Loaded Gun: Emily Dickinson for the 21st Century* (New York: Bellview Literary, 2016), 36.

2. Charyn, 20, citing Adrienne Rich, *On Lies, Secrets, and Silence: Selected Prose* (New York: W. W. Norton, 1995), 160.

3. Adrienne Rich, "Vesuvius at Home: The Power of Emily Dickinson," in *On Lies, Secrets, and Silence: Selected Prose, 1966–1978* (New York: W. W. Norton, 1979).

4. See, for example, Brenda Wineapple, *White Heat: The Friendship of Emily Dickinson and Thomas Wentworth Higginson* (New York: Alfred A. Knopf, 2008); and Polly Longsworth, *Austin and Mabel: The Amherst Affair and Love Letters of Austin Dickinson and Mabel Loomis Todd* (1984; Amherst: University of Massachusetts Press, 1999).

5. See Thomas Dumm, *My Father's House: On Will Barnet's Paintings* (Durham, NC: Duke University Press, 2014).

6. Will Barnet, drawings, Emily Dickinson, poems, introduction by Christopher Benfey, *World in a Frame* (New York: George Braziller, 1989), 80–81.

7. The numbering in *The Poems of Emily Dickinson, Reading Edition,* ed. R. W. Franklin (Cambridge, MA: Belknap Press of Harvard University Press, 1999) refers to the chronological order of the poem as determined by Franklin, who is responsible for the standard edition of her poems. I refer to those numbers throughout all subsequent citations of poems.

8. Henry David Thoreau, *Walden* (New York: Library of America, 2010), 74.

9. Helen Vendler, *Dickinson: Selected Poems and Commentaries* (Cambridge, MA: Belknap Press of Harvard University Press, 2010), 127.

10. Vendler, 126.

11. See Stanley Cavell, *"This New Yet Unapproachable America": Lectures after Wittgenstein after Emerson* (Albuquerque, NM: Living Batch, 1989).

12. Vendler, *Dickinson,* 222.

13. Thoreau, *Walden,* 195.

14. Vendler, *Dickinson,* 181–182.

15. Vendler, 400.

16. Vendler, 401.

6. Herman Wallace's Dream House

1. See Wilbert Rideau, *In Place of Justice* (New York: Alfred A. Knopf, 2010), for details of his life at Angola. This passage is from chapter 3, "Solitary," January 1972, https://www.npr.org/templates/story/story.php?storyId=126217412.

2. Giorgio Agamben, *Homo Sacer: Sovereign Power and Bare Life,* trans. David Heller-Roazen (Stanford, CA: Stanford University Press, 1998), 187.

3. Agamben, *Homo Sacer,* 166.

4. See especially Judith Butler, *Precarious Life: The Powers of Mourning and Violence* (New York: Verso, 2004); Butler, *Frames of War: When Is Life Grievable?* (New York: Verso, 2009); and Butler, *Toward a Performative Theory of Assembly* (Cambridge, MA: Harvard University Press, 2015).

5. I think here especially of Achille Mbembe, "Necropolitics," trans. Libby Meintjes, *Public Culture* 15, no. 1 (2003): 11–40; and Roberto Esposito, *Bios: Biopolitics and Philosophy,* trans. Timothy Campbell (Minneapolis: University of Minnesota Press, 2008), though the literature has become encyclopedic at this point.

6. For a more systematic argument about Foucault and freedom, see Thomas L. Dumm, *Michel Foucault and the Politics of Freedom,* 2nd ed. (Los Angeles: Rowman and Littlefield, 2002).

7. On arguments concerning the politics of becoming that have influenced my understanding of freedom, see William E. Connolly, *A World of Becoming* (Durham, NC: Duke University Press, 2011), and Connolly *The Fragility of Things* (Durham, NC: Duke University Press, 2013). This idea of becoming also resonates with Stanley Cavell's ideas concerning moral perfectionism. For an exemplary representation of his ideas concerning perfectionism, see especially Cavell, *Conditions Handsome and Unhandsome: The Constitution of Emersonian Perfectionism* (Chicago: University of Chicago Press, 1990).

8. Agamben, *Homo Sacer,* 174.

9. Primo Levi, *If This Be a Man,* in the *Complete Works of Primo Levi,* ed. Ann Goldstein, with an introduction by Toni Morrison (New York: Liveright, 2015), 87.

10. Interestingly enough, there has been no single book written about this affair. For basic information concerning the Angola Three, see the website for the organization Angola 3 (angola3.org). The organization was established to help free these prisoners and to publicize conditions at Angola. Some of the information concerning these cases has been gathered in a Wikipedia article, but that article is fragmented and incomplete. My information concerning Herman Wallace comes primarily from three sources. The first is Jackie Sumell and Herman Wallace, *The House That Herman Built,* ed. Jean-Baptiste Joly and Jackie Sumell (Stuttgart: merz&solitude, 2007), which is basically a gathering of primary documents concerning the Herman's House project. The second is *Herman's House,* a documentary film by Angad Singh Bhalla (Storyline Entertainment and Timeday Productions in association with Ford Foundation Just Films, 2012). I first came across this film as a *POV* presentation on PBS in 2012. All quotations from Summel and Wallace in the text are desig-

nated by the abbreviation HHB; those from Bhalla's film are designated by the abbreviation HH. Finally, the website hermanshouse.org serves as a source of information concerning the history of the exhibit, an advocacy site for the abolition of solitary confinement, and a source of information on Jackie Sumell.

11. Rideau, *In Place of Justice,* chap. 3.

12. For a discussion of solitary confinement and the origins of the American penitentiary, see Thomas L. Dumm, *Democracy and Punishment: Disciplinary Origins of the United States* (Madison: University of Wisconsin Press, 1987), esp. chaps. 3 and 4.

13. The classic statement on this fluidity remains Judith Butler, *Gender Trouble: Feminism and the Subversion of Identity* (New York: Routledge, 1990). Equally important is Butler, *Bodies That Matter* (New York: Routledge, 1993).

14. See Raja Parasuranam and Matthew Rizzo, *Neuroegonomics* (New York: Oxford University Press, 2008), 139.

15. For the classic treatment of the typographic element of this revolution, see Marshall McLuhan, *The Gutenberg Galaxy* (Toronto: University of Toronto Press, 1962).

16. See the American Friends Service Committee (AFSC) website: http://www .afsc.org/sites/afsc.civicactions.net/files/documents/QuakerAction_Fall2015 _HealingJustice_Infographic%20%281%29.pdf. These figures include those who are in local jails as well as state and federal prisons (which accounts for a discrepancy between the Federal Bureau of Prison Statistics figures and this report). The prison population overall has grown tenfold from 1980 to 2014. (It is perhaps a historical irony that AFSC is a leading advocate for ending solitary confinement, as the practice originated with Quakers in Pennsylvania; Dumm, *Democracy and Punishment,* "Friendly Persuasion.")

17. Michelle Alexander, *The New Jim Crow: Mass Incarceration in the Age of Colorblindness* (New York: New Press), 240. More generally, see her conclusion, "The Fire This Time."

18. Ta-Nehisi Coates, *Between the World and Me* (New York: Spiegel and Grau, 2015), 5.

19. Coates, *Between the World and Me,* 114.

20. See William E. Connolly, *Why I Am Not a Secularist* (Minneapolis: University of Minnesota Press, 2000).

21. Ralph Waldo Emerson, "Experience," in *Essays: Second Series,* in *Emerson: Essays and Lectures: Essays: Second Series,* ed. Joel Porte (New York: Library of America, 1981), 471.

Epilogue

1. Bruno Bettelheim, *The Uses of Enchantment: The Meaning and Importance of Fairy Tales* (New York: Viking, 1975), 5.

2. See Thomas Dumm, *Loneliness as a Way of Life* (Cambridge, MA: Harvard University Press, 2008), chap. 3, "Loving."

3. The study that opened the questioning of this era is by Betty Friedan, *The Feminine Mystique* (New York: W. W. Norton, 1963). There was a major class and racial dimension to this feminism that is well explored by Rosalind Rosenberg in her book *Jane Crow: The Life of Pauli Murray* (New York: Oxford University Press, 2017). See especially part 5, in which she discusses the struggle Murray had in trying to get Friedan and others to incorporate race into the issues of gender discrimination.

4. Michael Rogin, *Ronald Reagan, the Movie and Other Episodes in American Political Demonology* (Berkeley: University of California Press, 1987), 241.

5. This is one of the troubling dimensions of Hannah Arendt's argument against civil rights protests that involved children in *Crises of the Republic* (New York: Harcourt, Brace, Jovanovich, 1972), "Civil Disobedience."

6. Rosenberg, *Jane Crow*, 282, citing Daniel Patrick Moynihan, *The Negro Family: The Case for National Action*, Office of Policy Planning and Research, US Department of Labor, March 1965.

7. See Linda Gordon, *The Second Coming of the KKK: The Ku Klux Klan and the American Political Tradition* (New York: Liveright, 2017).

8. For a comprehensive study of this historical process, see Noel Ignatiev, *How the Irish Became White* (New York: Routledge, 2008). Ignatiev's study is of the Irish of the nineteenth century, but the dynamic continued to apply in the twentieth. On the dynamic process more generally, but also its application to Jewish immigrants, see Michael Rogin, *Black Face/White Noise: Jewish Immigrants in the Hollywood Melting Pot* (Berkeley: University of California Press, 1998).

9. Jacqueline Rose, *Mothers: An Essay on Love and Cruelty* (New York: Farrar, Straus and Giroux, 2018), 111–112, citing Bruno Bettelheim, in Elisabeth Badminter, *The Conflict: How Modern Motherhood Undermines the Status of Women*, trans. Adriana Hunter (New York: Metropolitan Books, 2012), 45.

10. Rose, *Mothers*, 113.

11. Rose, 113. Also see D. W. Winnicott, "Hate in the Counter-transference," *Journal of Psychotherapy Practice and Research* 3, no. 4 (Fall 1994): 350–356,

originally published in the *International Journal of Psycho-Analysis* 30 (1949): 69–74.

12. Winnicott, "Hate in the Counter-transference," 350.

13. Winnicott, 356.

14. Rose, *Mothers,* 116, citing Alison Bechdel, *Are You My Mother? A Comic Drama* (London: Jonathan Cape, 2012), 21.

15. Leslie Jamison, *The Empathy Exams: Essays* (Minneapolis: Graywolf Press, 2014), appendix, "Confession and Community."

16. Stanley Cavell, *Little Did I Know: Excerpts from Memory* (Stanford, CA: Stanford University Press, 2010), 4.

17. Dumm, *Loneliness as a Way of Life,* 125.

18. Cavell, *Little Did I Know,* 414–415.

19. Roberto Esposito, *Communitas: The Origin and Destiny of Community,* trans. Timothy Campbell (Stanford, CA: Stanford University Press, 2010), 3–6. Subsequent page references to this work are provided in the text; all emphases in the text are Esposito's.

20. Kaja Silverman, *Flesh of My Flesh* (Stanford, CA: Stanford University Press, 2009), 65.

Acknowledgments

The ten-year period of the gestation and completion of *Home in America* has been marked by losses—some predictable, some less so. Was it because of so many losses that my progress was so slow, or was I somehow meant to pause, to deliberate more deeply due to the circumstances of loss? I doubt I will ever know for sure one way or another. When we reflect on it, death is so much a part of the life of home as to be essential to it, so perhaps I have been fortunate in the losses I have experienced while thinking about home so obsessively over this past decade, even though it surely does not feel that way.

My first acknowledgments thus go to some of the friends I have lost to death while writing this book. I address or pray to them in the order in which I have lost them. William Blakesley of Oak Bluffs, Massachusetts, was a friend of mine for some ten years of the time I spent on Martha's Vineyard. Bill's art and his commitment to it were uncompromising. To take but one example, he once sketched my son, Jimmy, whom he found interesting as a subject, but at the same time refused to sketch my daughter,

Irene, whom he didn't. Our conversations over the years included but were not limited to the Great Depression, the Boston Red Sox—the day after Nomar Garciaparra was traded away to Los Angeles he informed me, "Little boys throughout New England cried themselves to sleep last night"—and, eventually, how to die. He passed in September of 2012 at the age of ninety-one.

Another artist friend passed that very same year, in November, at the age of one hundred and one. I had known Will Barnet for only a few years, having been introduced to him when he visited Amherst College in 2009, but our friendship became deep, quickly. His generosity to me was enormous, from inviting me to visit him in his apartment and studio at the National Art Club on Gramercy Park to sharing his insights into the twentieth-century history of the New York art scene, as well as his dark chocolates (which he claimed were responsible for his longevity). I ended up writing a book about some of his paintings—a distraction from completing this one—but his influence on this book should be clear, especially in the chapter on Emily Dickinson. He insisted that we need to address the presence of our family ghosts if we are to understand our homes at all.

In September 2015, I lost yet another friend, a political theorist from Johns Hopkins University, Richard Flathman, who died at the age of eighty-five. Dick was a constant presence in my intellectual life from the time another friend and mentor, Bill Connolly, first descended to Baltimore from Amherst in 1985 to fortify and reinforce what came to be called the Hopkins school of political theory. Dick and I disagreed about a lot of things, but he appreciated the idea that, as strange as it may have been, we were both liberal thinkers of an odd sort, he indebted to Wittgenstein, me to Foucault.

Later in the fall of 2015, a profound thinker and colleague died at the age of fifty, after a decades-long and courageous negotiation with illness. Nasser Hussain was an intellectual historian, a political theorist, a legal scholar, a human rights advocate, and a best friend, who left behind a legacy of thought and care. It was Nasser who mentored me through years of widower status and encouraged me to move from the town of Amherst to places beyond, to gain perspective on a place that too often lacks it. That

I have moved from Amherst to Vermont and then to Brooklyn over the course of writing a book about home would have both amused him and provided him with a validation of his deepest argument, that a small college gets smaller every year you remain there.

In February 2017, Theodore Lowi passed at the age of eighty-five. Ted served on my dissertation committee at Cornell in the early 1980s, but his influence on me exceeded the customary role of an advisor as an intellectual resource; he was a model of personal integrity. He loved the thinking life, was passionate about it, and ignored those who from their safe, bureaucratic perches would mock the idea that there ought to be passion at the heart of intellectual inquiry. The last time I visited him, Ted was thinking about compiling a book of prefaces he had written for other books (if I recall, there were about twenty of them). I asked him if he would consider me as the person who might write the preface to that book. He didn't commit, but he didn't refuse either. I remain available.

In 2018 Stanley Cavell died at the age of ninety-two. I hadn't spoken with Stanley for the last few years of his life, as his declining health didn't permit meaningful phone conversation, and I was unable to continue making the pilgrimage to Brookline, having set my romantic life in another geographical direction. But I continued to hold him close through his voluminous writings, through memories of the long conversations we had had at his home—a place crammed with books and music and love—and through memories of his public lectures in Amherst. In later years, he visited with and encouraged students in a class I taught that used his book, *Cities of Words,* as a central text. His work has been crucial to the shaping of mine, but more importantly, he modeled for me a way of thinking and being in the world that enables hope, even in these times.

These six old men, old in years, old in wisdom, remain in my company even as they don't. I can't believe that time passes as it does.

Among those who thankfully have not departed, my gratitude goes always to my friends and close interlocutors William Connolly and Jane Bennett. I feel that we've been on a long intellectual journey together, starting from when I descended upon them in Amherst in the summer of

1984 to participate in a National Endowment for the Humanities seminar with Bill. I have imagined us to have been constantly thinking together, or at least on parallel paths, ever since. The ongoing friendship and encouragement from Kathy Ferguson and Michael Shapiro of the University of Hawaii are also reasons for my gratitude. Among those of my generation of thinkers whose work has had such an impact on our common world, I especially want to express my gratitude to Cornel West and Judith Butler for their continued kindnesses and intellectual support. Being able to encounter such generous and thoughtful people is one of the major privileges I have had while living my life in the academy.

At Harvard University Press, Lindsay Waters has been a source of support and advice since he first suggested I work with him in the late 1990s. As with my last book with Harvard, *Loneliness as a Way of Life,* Lindsay has provided sage advice concerning the title of this book. His erudition and enthusiasm for the substance of my work and his own intellectual insights have always made working with him a pleasure. His patience with my slowness has always been a happy surprise to me. His friendship is as valuable to me as is his expertise.

More generally, the editorial team at Harvard has again been a pleasure to work with. Joy Deng especially deserves my thanks for her patience with my too often tardy responses to the many tasks required of authors when they submit their work to a press and my sometime impertinent questions concerning the production process. The entire editorial team there seems somehow to know how my work might appeal to audiences both within and beyond the bounds of the academy.

In recent years I've been fortunate to encounter a new generation of political theorists who, through their comments at panels, conversations at conferences, and even invitations to speak, have helped shape my thinking on the subject of home. In no particular order, James Martel, Libby Anker, Matt Scherer, Samantha Hill, Kaspar Villadsen, Steve Johnston, Kennan Ferguson, Davidé Panagia, and Jodi Dean—many of them associated with and carrying on the work of the journal *Theory & Event*—have all contributed to my thinking.

At key moments toward the completion of this manuscript, two colleagues of the Five College Consortium provided helpful readings of chapters. Monique Roelofs of Hampshire College's philosophy department carefully read a version of Chapter 2 and provided sage advice on how to clarify what I meant to say. Chris Benfey of Mt. Holyoke College, not only an important Emily Dickinson scholar but a prolific writer on all things concerning American culture, generously read a draft of my chapter on Dickinson and provided helpful advice.

At Amherst College Andrew Poe and Adam Sitze, denizens of what we have come to call "the theory corridor" in Clark House, have been constant intellectual companions. Adam provided detailed comments on the manuscript at an early stage, and Andrew has made valuable suggestions for further reading that helped profoundly. I am deeply grateful for our ongoing conversation. More generally, the Board of Trustees of Amherst College provided sabbatical support for the time I needed to write. Amherst College has an extraordinarily distinguished faculty. This is a result of the exceptional generosity of those who support our efforts.

My brother, John Dumm, of Charlottesville, Virginia, has read different chapters of this book and has been especially helpful in aiding my explorations of Monticello. He has my filial gratitude.

Not too long after I began work on this book, while in New York City to celebrate Will Barnet's one-hundredth birthday, I reunited with a former student, now a friend, in order to check on her pilgrim's progress through life. Little did I know that our reunion would lead to love and then marriage. This book is dedicated to Judith Piotrkowski. To the extent that I have a home, she is it.

Portions of Chapter 4 were first published as "The Metaphysics of Indian Hating Revisited" in *A Political Companion to Herman Melville,* ed. Jason Frank (Lexington: University Press of Kentucky, 2013). The Epilogue includes portions of text first published as "Misgivings: Stanley Cavell and the Politics of Autobiography," *Theory & Event* (February 2013). Chapter 5 builds on the second Will Barnet Annual Lecture, which I delivered at the Farnsworth Museum in Rockland, Maine, in October 2016.

Index

Accounting, Thoreau on, 136–139

Adam, 47

Adams, John, 93

Agamben, Giorgio, 268n19, 279nn2–3, 280n8; on *nomos* of camp, 216–220

Alexander, Michele, 270n6, 281n17

Altoona, Pennsylvania, 7–10, 15, 28, 243–245

Amherst, Massachusetts, 1, 192–193

Anderson, Benedict, 11, 265n1

Angola (country), 214

Angola (prison), 214–217; and *nomos* of camp, 217–218; and solitary confinement, 235

Angola Three (Robert King, Herman Wallace, Albert Woodfox), 220–222

Anthropocene, the, 24, 30, 32, 37–38, 40, 47, 219

Applegate, Marshall (Do), 38

Arendt, Hannah, 33, 39, 43–44, 266n6, 266n8, 268nn18–19, 274n2, 274n5, 282n5; compared with Foucault, 34–35, 43; on end of human life, 53, 59; and natality, 205–206; on technology, 35–37, 39, 43–44

Aries, Phillipe, 70, 270n43

Autobiography, 132, 133, 255–259; and Cavell, 255–256, 259–260; and Dickinson, 200; and Thoreau, 200

Bachelard, Gaston, 26, 266n10

Badminter, Elizabeth, 252–253

Baldwin, James, 22

Baptist, Edward E., 270n5

Barnet, Will, 194–195, 279n6; on Dickinson, 194–195; *My Father's House,* 195

Bechdel, Alison, 254, 283n14

291